UN-AMERICAN

UN-AMERICAN

A SOLDIER'S RECKONING OF OUR LONGEST WAR

ERIK EDSTROM

BLOOMSBURY PUBLISHING

NEW YORK · LONDON · OXFORD · NEW DELHI · SYDNEY

BLOOMSBURY PUBLISHING
Bloomsbury Publishing Inc.
1385 Broadway, New York, NY 10018, USA

BLOOMSBURY, BLOOMSBURY PUBLISHING, and the Diana logo are trademarks
of Bloomsbury Publishing Plc

First published in the United States 2020
Copyright © Erik Edstrom, 2020

Some names have been changed to protect the privacy of persons involved.
Conversations have been reproduced to the best of the author's ability;
some conversations may be paraphrased.

Bloomsbury Publishing Plc does not have any control over, or responsibility for, any third-party
websites referred to or in this book. All internet addresses given in this book were correct at the
time of going to press. The author and publisher regret any inconvenience caused if addresses
have changed or sites have ceased to exist, but can accept no responsibility for any such changes.

ISBN: HB: 978-1-63557-374-9; eBook: 978-1-63557-375-6

LIBRARY OF CONGRESS CATALOGING-IN-PUBLICATION DATA
Names: Edstrom, Erik, author.
Title: Un-American: a soldier's reckoning of our longest war / Erik Edstrom.
Other titles: Soldier's reckoning of our longest war
Description: New York: Bloomsbury Publishing, 2020.
Identifiers: LCCN 2019055362 (print) | LCCN 2019055363 (ebook) | ISBN 9781635573749
(hardcover) | ISBN 9781635573756 (ebook)
Subjects: LCSH: Edstrom, Erik. | Afghan War, 2001—Afghanistan—Kandahār (Province)—
Personal narratives. | Afghan War, 2001—Political aspects—United States. | United States.
Army—Officers—Conduct of life. | United States. Army. Infantry Division, 4th. Brigade, 4th. |
United States—Military policy. | War on Terrorism, 2001–2009—Moral and ethical aspects. |
Terrorism—Prevention—Evaluation. | United States. Army—Officers—Biography. |
United States Military Academy—Biography.
Classification: LCC DS371.413 .E37 2020 (print) | LCC DS371.413 (ebook) |
DDC 958.104/74092 [B]—dc23
LC record available at https://lccn.loc.gov/2019055362
LC ebook record available at https://lccn.loc.gov/2019055363

Typeset by Westchester Publishing Services
Printed and bound in the U.S.A. by Berryville Graphics Inc., Berryville, Virginia

To find out more about our authors and books visit www.bloomsbury.com and sign up
for our newsletters.

Bloomsbury books may be purchased for business or promotional use. For information on
bulk purchases please contact Macmillan Corporate and Premium Sales Department at
specialmarkets@macmillan.com.

This book is dedicated to the more than 312,000 civilians killed in America's War on Terror—more than one hundred 9/11s' worth of civilian death.

In American parlance, "Never Forget" is tacitly—and exclusively—reserved for Americans to serve in their role as righteous victims, never as aggressors. Instead, let us "Never Forget" the far larger costs of America's permanent war posture and realize that humanity's greatest problems will not be solved by the military. The future of humanity depends on our ability to grow our capacity for cooperation, not conflict.

CONTENTS

Three Visions

The difference between patriotism and nationalism is that the patriot is proud of his country for what it does, and the nationalist is proud of his country no matter what it does; the first attitude creates a feeling of responsibility, but the second a feeling of blind arrogance that leads to war.

—Sydney J. Harris

The decision to go to war should be accompanied by three visions: the vision of your own death in that war; the vision of experiencing the war from the other side; and the opportunity cost—what could have been *but was not*, because of the war. For the so-called Global War on Terrorism, these visions might look something like this:

First, your own death might feel hot, violent, and cruelly banal. Hear the "moon dirt" squeak and crunch beneath your suede-and-rubber-composite boots. Sense the sweat dripping from your lower back into the crack of your ass. Feel the weight of the helmet and body armor compressing your spine. You pause to rest. Just a moment's relief in the shade of a mud hut. In August, Kandahar hits 112 degrees Fahrenheit. Your hand, wrapped in a hard-knuckled, fire-retardant glove, rests upon one of your rectangular ammo pouches containing three thirty-round magazines of 5.56mm bullets; your trigger finger lies ready outside the trigger-well of your M4 assault rifle. You are always plagued by gnawing, low-grade anxiety, but today it's worse than usual. You cross a stream, up and over a makeshift bridge, and, turning the corner, your life ceases to exist. No glory, no romantic oil painting commemorating this awful little incident. Now rewind to the exact moment when you stepped on the IED. The moment it killed you. Your legs immediately ripped off in thick, unrecognizable hunks. The overpressure from the shock wave is like an invisible avalanche, hitting your body all at once; you never had a chance. The raw meat of your guts and arms flung into the overhanging orchard trees above. One of your buddies will have the grisly job of getting the pieces of you out of that tree. Now see the cold steel casket, flag held taut by rubber bands. The Honor Guard unloads your remains from the belly of C-5 or C-130 aircraft at Dover Air Force Base to the soundtrack of your family wailing uncontrollably. Now there is a sharp salute, tears, and a bugle playing "Taps." Your headstone in Section 60 of Arlington National Cemetery is there, next to the other freshly dug graves that do not yet contain their occupants. And in time, with more wars, these headstones become just like all the other headstones.

Second, envision that another country has violently occupied America in a preventive war to free you of America's current administration. The invasion is under the auspices of "fighting terrorism," and—not without lugubrious irony, seemingly lost on the invaders—they are systematically committing acts of "terrorism" under their own doctrinal definition of the word.[1] Your home is searched by anxious, heavily armed young men aching to kill a "terrorist American." They are covered in angular armor pads, eyes obscured by black Oakley sunglasses. Your home is no longer a home—it's been dehumanized, called a "compound," "cache," or "built-up area." Your nation has been relieved of its sovereignty. You are no longer a person but reduced to a slur, akin to *enemy, insurgent, terrorist, sand nigger, Haji, towel head, goat fucker, cocksucker,* or the all-inclusive, multipurpose, good-for-every-occasion *motherfucker.* Your liberators look at you hungrily, hoping to find the wafer-thin burden of proof needed to *shoot you in the motherfucking face*—to *get that CIB* (Combat Infantryman Badge)—to *pop their combat cherry.* After all, getting into direct combat earns them a coveted badge that helps with promotion. No one wants to face the shame of having not seen action. They use their "rules of engagement" to enforce a made-up curfew. They kill military-age males tending to their farm-land, claiming "suspicious activity." If there is an apology, it's hollow and melodramatic—"Any loss is too much"—but needless civilian death is not compelling enough to change their tactics. They stop traffic using heavily armored starship vehicles, force cars off the road, and throw water bottles filled with urine at children. They disrespect your religion. They kill anyone in your community who actively fights back in self-defense. Those who are accused of leading resistance forces are taken to black sites to be tortured. They tap your phones without warrant. Helicopters named after past victims of government-sanctioned genocides—Kiowa, Apache, Black Hawk—regularly hover above your community. Drones with names such as Predator or Reaper buzz your home—"to keep you safe," they say. You're afraid. Perhaps the greatest insult is their audacity to tell you they're "only here to help, to free the oppressed." You've never felt more oppressed in your life.

Third, envision the world as if the war had never happened. The American soldiers who had been killed are alive: learning, loving, and making dreams; the trillions in war debt spent on eye-watering military contracts and medical bills for facial reconstructions, hip disarticulations, "AK" (above-knee) amputation—an injury so common it gets its own shorthand jargon—never happened. The one in four post-9/11 veterans in the labor force who have a service-connected disability are perfectly healthy.[2]

On top of that, what if companies within the military-industrial complex didn't sell fear in the form of stupid high-tech equipment to their former subor-dinates in Department of Defense (DoD) procurement?

Honestly, it's hard to recall a time in American history when more was spent to accomplish less. Instead, imagine that politicians used the over $6.4 trillion of capital—the projected cost of the "War on Terror"—on long-term invest-ments that had a higher return on investment along with better social outcomes.

Could we live without white elephant weapon systems like the F-35 fighter, saving us over $1.5 trillion? With the money spent on this jet, America could have paid the bill on all student debt in the United States or hired Beyoncé for a private concert, every day, for the next thousand years. And once such an expensive project is complete, are we to believe that this new Ferrari weaponry will sit on an airfield to rust? *Of course not!* This is an anchor purchase guaranteeing our national addiction to war for decades to come.

But what if this had been invested elsewhere—perhaps renewable energy to stop the creeping genocide currently sponsored through willful ignorance and dithering political inaction? By failing to invest now, America is in effect investing in future wars—climate conflicts fought over water scarcity, crop failure, and internal displacement.

And if a clear and present danger like climate change feels too abstract, we could at least repair crumbling American infrastructure. Or invest in education, where "at 14% proficiency in math, Mississippi is on par with Bulgaria, Trinidad and Tobago, and Uruguay. At 8% math proficiency, DC is on par with Kazakhstan, Mexico and Thailand."[3] Imagine that America's reputation to the rest of the world, as measured by Gallup polls, didn't show America as the greatest threat to peace in the world.[4] And last, which I think is fitting, since they often receive no mention at all: the hundreds of thousands of noncombatants—the "unpeople" in that dusty, faraway land—are still alive, at home with their families too.[5]

The U.S. government sent me to Afghanistan at the age of twenty-three. I protected myself and three-quarters of the men in my platoon. I endangered and hurt many. I lived in mud shacks and trolled dirt roads for IEDs—either with my tires or, worse, my boots. We did dangerous, humdrum unilateral patrols without conducting any meaningful training with Afghan security forces. I accomplished nothing that one could consider "worth fighting for." I wasted *a lot* of taxpayer money. The Afghans I met either didn't want us there or wanted us to stay long enough to relieve us of our money—taxpayer dollars that the military was aching to spend on exorbitant military contracts, knowingly lining the pockets of warlords guilty of human rights abuses. On the ground, the war felt morally dubious, illegal in its scope, and unjust in terms of proportionality. Many of my friends died or became permanently handicapped. I personally buried one of my West Point classmates in Arlington National Cemetery, handing the folded American flag to his crying mother.

Another one of my soldiers killed himself after returning home. One of my soldiers is serving life in prison after murdering and dismembering the body of someone whom he never knew, in a bathtub in Oregon. With an accomplice, they rammed a crossbow bolt through the victim's ear while he was alive, trying to puncture his brain, and when this failed, they choked him to death with a chain.[6] After chopping up his body in a bathtub, they used his car to rob a bank. Divorce, alcohol, drugs, depression "zombie" medication—there is too much to capture here. I was very lucky: I compromised my morals and had the formative years of my life amputated by serving an unnecessary war.

My attitude toward the "Global War on Terrorism" has shifted radically. It's taken a long time to get to my present state of mind. In the beginning I did not think our wars were self-perpetuating, self-defeating, and immoral. Like most of the men and women I served with, I came of age in the wake of 9/11. I was swept up in the hysteria of the times. Everyone was.

Fear became currency. Terrorism threat ratings, like the weather forecast, became a consideration for daily life. A threat level of "orange" might compel us to change our plans. Then there were anthrax scares. Alleged weapons of mass destruction. We became trained to fear a lone backpack. In 2002, President George W. Bush appealed to fear: "We cannot wait for the final proof—the smoking gun—that could come in the form of a mushroom cloud."[7] It was intimated that we'd have another 9/11 on our hands if we didn't give the government a blank check to go on offense in the name of defense. I was a junior in high school when the towers came down, and I would soon need to make some decisions about my future. "Doing something about 9/11" was a consideration but not the only concern. I also had to contend with the reality of financial constraints. Two years of stocking shelves at the local grocery store didn't cover the first two months of tuition at university. Like many American parents, my parents looked at me with a vague sense of shame, perhaps to protect me from getting my hopes up for something that could never be financed, and forbade me from applying to private universities. I concluded that West Point was my best option. Despite having never visited the academy, I applied nowhere else.

> *The price of anything is the amount of life you exchange for it.*
>
> *—Henry David Thoreau*

At West Point, most of my classmates were motivated by similar altruistic desires: to be a force for good and provide security for people at home. We were the first class to apply to the academy after 9/11. We were proud of that. Our gold class rings—a "crass mass of brass and glass"[8]—were especially engraved with a fixed reminder: the Twin Towers, the Pentagon, and 9/11. Our motto, "Always Remember, Never Surrender," seemed prescient for the class destined to go headlong into America's longest war. At this point I believed in America's foreign policy. We put questions aside, focusing on what was needed to be leaders of soldiers in combat. The responsibility was not taken lightly, and we trained with vigilance. I was drilled, monkey-see, monkey-do, to pantomime a certain Army officer archetype. I felt some satisfaction from it. Hiking the ski slope in winter, on the weekend, with ninety pounds on your back to prepare for summer military training is a good way to make a great friend. Shared burdens bring people together. I felt deeply loyal to my classmates—to the Corps of Cadets. I felt like I was part of something bigger than myself.

Only after graduating from West Point did I begin to question things. I began to doubt the very underpinnings that originally attracted me to military service: the belief that what we did "over there" somehow kept the world safer. It was a spurious claim, soberly advanced by serious men with seriously short haircuts.

My deepest concerns were confirmed when I deployed to direct combat in Afghanistan. The people who were trying to kill me weren't international terrorists. They weren't attacking me because "they hate our freedoms" or some other bullshit Bush-era line.[9] They were angry farmers and teenagers with legitimate grievances. Their loved ones, breathing and laughing minutes before, had been transmuted before their eyes into something unrecognizable.[10] Like someone hit a piñata full of raw hamburger meat. They were now little more than stringy sinew and bloody mashed potatoes dressed up in tattered rags. That's what rockets fired from a pair of U.S. Kiowa helicopters do to civilians. It's always a mistake, always the result of extenuating circumstances, and always excused. The paperwork is easier if the corpses rest as "enemy" or "unknown."

I received cards from a class of American ten-year-olds. Tearing open a U.S. Postal Service parcel dropped in a remote part of Kandahar was always surreal. The desire to ship myself back to the box's point of origin was overwhelming. The kids thanked me for "keeping them safe at home" or "freeing Afghanistan." The cards had pictures of tanks and green Army men that were adorably ill-informed caricatures of reality in the same childish way as the letters themselves.

I knew I wasn't making them safer, but this was what they were being told. This sacred-cow belief is rooted in the national idea that by being part of the U.S. military, you are, ipso facto, making the world a better place. Nearly every American child is treated to these same fables.

With every deployment of U.S. soldiers year after year comes more ill will, stemming from a stew of atrocities: government-sanctioned torture[11] and black sites[12]; Guantánamo Bay and indefinite detention; the global drone assassination campaign; bombing Doctors Without Borders[13] and denying an international investigation; murderous rampages by rogue soldiers; extraordinary rendition; soldiers defiling corpses, keeping severed fingers for trophies,[14] burning Korans, night raids, and bulldozing property that poses a threat to Americans[15]; and propping up corrupt police and hated warlords despite prior knowledge of their history of human rights abuses. In my own Area of Operations (AO)—affectionately known as "the Heart of Darkness"—the U.S. National Guard machine-gunned a bus full of civilians; my platoon helped destroy the poppy crops of poor peasant farmers who live on approximately two dollars a day—their only asset—ruining their only hope of sustaining themselves that year.[16] By the end of deployment, I could just begin to empathize with the victims of our occupation. It's entirely inconsistent to dish out one hundred 9/11s' worth of noncombatant deaths during the GWOT and have the gall to maintain the pretense that it was, in that benignly imperial way, "for their own good." After all, the U.S. military is, according to George W. Bush, "the greatest force for human liberation the world has ever known."[17] The people of Iraq, Pakistan, Afghanistan, Yemen, Somalia, Vietnam, Cambodia, Laos, El Salvador, Nicaragua, Cuba, Chile, and a long, long list of others may argue otherwise. Once I crossed a moral threshold, I made a commitment to leave the armed forces and never support wars of aggression.

Writing has, at times, left me feeling empty and beleaguered. This topic is tender to the touch, and simply talking about this part of my life has been and continues to be hard. But beyond the personal discomfort, I have come to accept that everything I did was entirely unnecessary, despite the best efforts of well-intentioned people who try to convince me that my perception of my own lived experience is wrong.[18]

By writing this book I risk upsetting families with whom I have stood graveside, mourning the loss of extraordinary lives ended too soon; I risk upsetting soldiers who have given more of their lives—more tours of duty, more years of service—or are experiencing injuries, day in, day out, that I cannot begin to fathom. Perpetuating a comfortable lie, however, is a ghastly betrayal and far more harmful than confronting an inconvenient truth. The best way to protect troops' service is to ensure they are not sent to an unjust war. People need to announce, and loudly, when they believe we are in one. It's impossible to fix a problem if society refuses to acknowledge one exists.

The military is America's sacrosanct institution. Condemning America's use of political violence is viewed somewhere closer to treason than free speech. Part of this is the blinkered, either-you-are-with-us-or-you-are-with-the-terrorists false dichotomy of the post-9/11 era.[19] We have not outgrown it. Since it is comfortable to believe that U.S. foreign policy is always in support of "freedom" and "the peace process," it follows that anyone who opposes U.S. foreign policy opposes "freedom" and "the peace process." America is not morally infallible, and this war—the Global War on Terrorism—has been a deep stain on our nation's claim to be an upstanding force for good. However, I have encountered resentment when I shared my thoughts and opinions—thoughts and opinions based on firsthand experiences. One person, a member of my own family, caustically remarked, "It's only because of better men that you have the freedom to spew this anti-American garbage." I found this vitriol particularly rich, given that this person never served a day in uniform.

If I am not to give permission to express my opposition to the war in which I fought, who is? How "American"—how many metric "units of American"—do you need to be before you are able to condemn state actions?

The heated conversations I have had—with family, with friends, with strangers—has revealed the depth of the problem.

"American patriotism" is lobotomized patriotism.

The most "American" Americans are those who offer the most gratuitous forms of shallow praise to vets while thinking the least about what our military is actually being used for. This hurts everyone involved. The name of this book— Un-American—is tongue-in-cheek defiance to America's lobotomized patriots.

I am writing this book because the stakes are too high to remain silent. I feel called to challenge the notion that romantic militarism is a good thing. We are taught to unconsciously block out "unworthy facts," revising history to make it more palatable. We cherry-pick our favorite examples from the World War II highlight reel and conveniently exclude the times when America was less than upstanding: when our nation was responsible for the genocide of the Native Americans, carpet-bombed North Korea, and pulverized Vietnam, Laos, and Cambodia—including the prolific use of chemical weapons, which altogether killed millions. And America remains the only country to use a nuclear weapon against civilian targets. Twice.

Viewed from the present, the past seems loutish, primitive, and violent. It is laden with out-of-date, how-did-people-think-like-that prejudices and religious superstition masquerading as fact. If you are swayed by the evidence presented by Steven Pinker in *The Better Angels of Our Nature*—that the human condition is a good news story; that mankind is optimistically becoming more empathetic, less violent—then so, too, will today seem primitive in hindsight. Eventually there is an awakening.

Slavery became repugnant. Suffrage became an imperative. Business as usual became unthinkable. To debate the merits of such issues seems obscene by today's standards. Likewise, issues like wars of aggression, dithering on climate change, and battery-farmed animals will be viewed with similar contempt in the future. The post-9/11 era, symbolized by America's "weapons loose" foreign policy and denial—of extrajudicial assassinations, torture, never-ending occupations, and larger threats to organized human life—will be a palm-to-the-forehead moment for future generations. That is, if we choose to see.

I want to acknowledge the harm we are causing to the "unworthy victims"—the "unpeople." Our supreme international crimes of aggression are objectively responsible for far more human suffering than the terrorist horrors of 9/11.

Osama bin Laden was connected to the deaths of thousands of innocent civilians. George W. Bush and his administration, who manufactured the wars, and Presidents Obama and Trump, whose intrepid leadership has normalized this offensive grand strategy, are connected to the deaths of hundreds of thousands (at least one hundred 9/11s), not to speak of the unrecorded torments of millions. One can only argue that the invasions of Iraq and Afghanistan were less of a crime if Iraqi and Afghan noncombatants are counted as fractional human beings—if, that is, there is one set of rules for America and another, heavily enforced by the U.S. military, for the rest of the world. By any elementary appraisal, this should not comply with "American values."

Our political leadership has leveraged the future prosperity of America into trillions of dollars of debt, an intergenerational heist meant to give the appearance of being "tough on terror." To play a deadly game of Taliban Whack-A-Mole. That's a reality that should be unappealing to members of both political parties. For fiscally conservative Republicans keen on "small government," it bloats the budget and balloons the military bureaucracy; for Democrats, it diverts precious funding that might otherwise have gone into crucial social programs. Burdened by these debts, America has lost a chance to adequately deal with far larger threats, starting with the climate crisis and followed by other important issues, including technological surveillance and data rights, AI and vocational retraining, infrastructure, education, healthcare, and wealth inequality.

Like many Americans, I want to see our assets invested in projects that have long-term benefits. I want future generations to be armed with more than stylized facts so that they can see and understand the tradeoffs they will make by choosing to wear Army green over the freedom to wear anything else.

Young men and women looking to prove their worth to society should not be misled by the Disneyfication of military service. The bare minimum wager for joining the military includes your physical body, social relationships, psychological conscience, and emotional satisfaction. At the first sniff of adulthood—before being allowed to drink alcohol—the military bamboozles children into one of the largest life commitments ever conceived: to leave your life, be issued a new identity, and be sent across the world by an imagined order to inflict violence against people you don't know, for political reasons eighteen-year-olds are not meant to understand. At a time when I was too young to buy an R-rated ticket to see a movie depicting gory military combat, I was betting, without fully realizing it, that a stifling, nine-year military commitment during the formative years of life was going to be better than whatever opportunities or experiences existed elsewhere.

The consequence of my ill-informed decision is that I must carry Army-issued emotional duffel bags for the rest of my life. Had I known this would be the case, I would have made different life decisions. I would not have served the profession of political violence.

I am writing this because it is a hope that no more of my friends will have to die for this conflict. The darkest years are over—when friends were killed or maimed regularly. But others, on both sides, continue to die. However, it is now the next generation's turn; now the endless war is their problem. The war is not only a tragedy but a crime. But perhaps the greatest tragedy is that society lacks the conviction to say so.

If a millennium of the dead could speak: There is no betrayal more intimate than being sent to kill or die for nothing, by your own countrymen.

PART I

IMAGINE YOUR OWN DEATH

Would you personally die for this conflict? If not, don't encourage or support others to die for it either.

"During times of peace, the sons bury their fathers, but in war it is the fathers who send their sons to the grave."

—Croesus, quoted by Herodotus

American Boy

What a common soldier may lose is obvious enough. Without regarding the danger, however, young volunteers never enlist so readily as at the beginning of a new war; and though they have scarce any chance of preferment, they figure to themselves, in their youthful fancies, a thousand occasions of acquiring honour and distinction which never occur. These romantic hopes make the whole price of their blood. Their pay is less than that of common labourers, and in actual service their fatigues are much greater.

—*Adam Smith,* The Wealth of Nations *(1776)*

My curiosity about the military was given to me, standard issue, at a young age. It first came in the form of toys. Not more than five years of age, I had buckets of plastic, forest-green (American), gray ("Nazi"), and mustard ("Jap") figurines bedecked in World War II–era kit. Machine gunners, radio operators, leaders doing the heroic follow-me pose. All dutifully aligned along the soapy perimeter of the bathtub.

Then there were G.I. Joes: toy figurines, puzzles, board games, the TV show—whatever I could get my hands on. I watched *Top Gun* probably twenty times. I even had a few packs of Desert Storm collectible trading cards. I loved our ass-kicking political avatar: Captain America. At age twelve, I dressed in

Realtree camo and played paintball. Later, the military-entertainment complex got me hooked on their recruitment propaganda, thinly disguised as a free, first-person shooter game called *America's Army*. The tagline: "Empower yourself. Defend freedom." I was no more "American" or patriotic than anyone else. My own death certainly wasn't part of any of these games.

As a boy still aged in the single digits, I asked my dad to indulge me in a Las Vegas line of sorts. First, I contrived arbitrary matches between animals: *Who would win if a bear fought a cheetah? Or if a great white shark fought a crocodile?* Not long after, these wagers shifted from animals to real-life military conflict—America versus Russia, or America versus Germany—but in this exercise the winner was always the same: the United States.

It's unclear whether children from other countries would even pose such a question. Mexico doesn't make G.I. José action figures. There is no "Captain Italy." Only in America would military trading cards or public-funded, first-person shooter video games even exist. My Swedish relatives didn't measure their national self-worth in units of military might. But I learned early, in a uniquely American way, that we were militarily more powerful, which meant "better" than everyone else on the planet.

As elementary school students, we took turns raising the flag in the morning. At first a pair of us would be accompanied by a teacher. We learned that the flag was to be handled with deep respect, even reverence. We were taught to unfurl the banner from its neatly folded, isosceles-triangle shape to its full length. We would clip the eyelets to the fasteners on the rope and raise it to the tippity-top of the flagpole, being careful to not let it touch the ground. *Never let the flag touch the ground*, we were implored. We were taught to use basic sailor knots to secure the rope to the base of the flagpole. Over time, we didn't need oversight. This patriotic ritual became part of our default, day-to-day existence.

The flag is most intimately connected with military achievement, military memory. It represents the country not in its intensive life, but in its far-flung challenge to the world. The flag is primarily the banner of war; it is allied with patriotic anthem and holiday. It recalls old martial memories. A nation's patriotic history is solely the history of its wars, that is, of the State in its health and glorious functioning. So in responding to the appeal of the flag, we are responding to the appeal of the State, to the symbol of the herd organized as an offensive and defensive body, conscious of its prowess and its mystical herd strength.

—*Randolph Bourne,* The State *(1918)*

We were trained to recite the Pledge of Allegiance. To us, there was nothing strange about it. Nothing strange about public schools cajoling obedient, trustful children to stand every morning and, in blind repetition, swear an oath of loyalty to the state. It never entered my mind that a bunch of children chanting a commitment of obedience had some serious totalitarian vibes. More Pyongyang than Pittsburgh. No Western country institutes such covenants.

I joined the Cub Scouts and, later, the Boy Scouts. I enjoyed the hikes on the Appalachian Trail, the friendships, and the chili con carne around a campfire. Summer camp. Merit badges. A clear ascension of rank and authority—I was drawn to it. In many ways it was "the military, for kids." But I knew little of the origins of the modern Boy Scout movement. It derived its philosophy and mission from Lord Robert Baden-Powell, a British lieutenant general. Baden-Powell's ambition was to redress a perceived deterioration of chivalry and the preparedness for war. To this end, young boys would be trained in grand virtues and practical, quasi-military fieldcraft. It was straight from Marcus Aurelius and the philosophy of stoicism.

In his 1908 publication *Scouting for Boys*, Baden-Powell encourages Scouts: "*Be Prepared in Mind* by having disciplined yourself to be obedient to every order."[1] Within this preparation is the injunction to be willing "to die for your country . . . so that when the time comes you may charge home with confidence, not caring whether you are to be killed or not." In a section titled "Chivalry," Baden-Powell paints a romantic scene, prescriptively suggesting that "Just like Saint George of old, the Boy Scouts of today fight against everything evil and unclean."

Near the end of middle school my father remarried. Almost overnight I was incorporated into a new family. At the same time, my biological mother packed up my belongings and left them in garbage bags on my father's front lawn. She was done being a parent. She moved to the other side of the country and I haven't seen her since.

In the summer before my freshman year of high school, my dad, my stepmom, and I moved in with my now step-grandparents, in Canton, while my folks built a house in the neighboring town, Stoughton. They lived in a traditional two-story, two-car-garage suburban New England home at the end of a cul-de-sac worn from decades of heavy snowplows. I slept in a spare bedroom with pink wallpaper—the "music room." Here, Pa—my step-grandfather—kept his Casio keyboard, six-disc CD changer, opera CDs, and World War II Army uniform. Every day at four p.m., and with military punctuality, Pa came into this room to play the piano and sing.

After serving in World War II, Pa used his G.I. Bill benefits to attend the New England Conservatory in Boston, becoming a classically trained opera singer—"a tenor," he said, always eager to make the distinction. (Tenors are often the male spotlight role.) In the arena of singing, Pa embraced the spotlight. He regularly sang solos for the church choir and in his seventies even sang the National Anthem at Fenway Park before a Red Sox game.

No one spent time with Pa; rather, they "received his tutelage." He was a knowledgeable man and avid reader. I often asked him about his time in World War II.

"Those German bastards did a number on our boys in the hedgerows," he'd say. "They depressed those 88s [88mm antiaircraft cannon] and blew the hell out of them as they came through the hedge."

To most, he was not "Frank the insurance salesman" or "Frank the former opera singer." He was "Frank the World War II veteran." It seemed to be the thing others praised him for the most.

To be defined by one's military service—to exalt this singular identity above the others—is a uniquely American brand of nationalism. And this lionization of military service generated fertile grounds for George W. Bush's post-9/11 jingoism, which rested on the cultural memory and reverence for people like Frank, if not Frank himself.

The zeitgeist of the times granted unprecedented powers to the state, especially the military. These powers of surveillance and information collection, of access, of funding, helped to nudge me toward the military as a life choice.

After 9/11, you couldn't get away from America's military fetish. Multimillion-dollar war machines streak above college stadiums where amateur athletes tackle each other to control a brown leather ball. A flyover may cost more than $200,000 alone.[2] Then there is $500 million earmarked for Defense Department marching bands.[3] The sponsoring of the X Games and NASCAR; Black Hawk helicopter landings at schools.[4] The list goes on, and on.

In the post-9/11 era, the military and its servicemen became beneficiaries of a renewed wave of prestige, raising already exultant levels of institutional confidence to soaring new heights.[5] Social subsidies for the military expanded: military discounts, preferential hiring, veterans-only contracts, endless but shallow public praise. Veterans guilty of crimes often might even circumvent normal justice channels, receiving differentiated if not lighter punishment after the advent of "Veterans Courts."[6] A cult of military and veteran worship had swept across the United States. "Patriotic correctness," according to former Marine and National Book Award winner Phil Klay.[7]

> *A standing Army, however necessary it may be at some times, is always dangerous to the Liberties of the People. Soldiers are apt to consider themselves as a Body distinct from the rest of the Citizens . . . Such a Power should be watchd [sic] with a jealous Eye.*
>
> —*Samuel Adams in a letter to James Warren (1776)*

Although I didn't articulate it to myself at that age, I knew that veterans were a different class of people. They are entitled to services that provide a standard issue of dignity, whereas public transport drivers, teachers, retirement home caregivers, and the like are not. Serving in the military was more deserving, more special, than whatever everyone else was doing.

If the perishable social subsidies—military discounts, special attention, preferential hiring, etc.—given to America's military were to dry up, would the military be just like everything else—a plain old boring, tedious, frustrating job without any sparkle? No patriotic pixie dust. As an employer, the military traffics the story that military service equates to a higher sense of purpose, because "an individual might prefer working conditions in the civilian sector."[8] Without this belief, without hedonic uplift from society, the core aspects of the job—risks, culture, remuneration, living conditions, deprivation, regulations, and binding contracts—may make the military a less compelling career choice. Military service in other countries is not romanticized the same way. Soldiers from other countries seem far more aware of the risks and tradeoffs they are making when they sign the contract. As such, they are paid more fairly for the risks that they incur. For example, Australian soldiers who are deployed to combat in Afghanistan receive far more combat pay than do their American counterparts.[9] In essence, the perceived value of serving in the American military depresses salaries for American servicemen.

> *By an ingenious mixture of cajolery, agitation, intimidation, the herd is licked into shape, into an effective mechanical unity, if not into a spiritual whole. Men are told simultaneously that they will enter the military establishment of their own volition, as their splendid sacrifice for their country's welfare, and that if they do not enter they will be hunted down and punished with the most horrid penalties; and under a most indescribable confusion of democratic pride and personal fear they submit to the destruction of their livelihood if not their lives, in a way that would formerly have seemed to them so obnoxious as to be incredible.*
>
> —Randolph Bourne, The State *(1918)*

RECRUITMENT

In high school, I thought about what might come after I graduated. What was the purpose of twelve years of schooling? Where might I put myself to good use as an adult? It seemed like college was a good choice. My dad—a mathy computer software designer—recommended engineering. "The world will always need good engineers," he said. For him, life was about practicality. Meanwhile, for some of my friends, graduation was merely a shift from part-time at the pizza shop to full-time. One became a construction worker in Hawaii. Others promoted the idea of studying economics: "It's what you do if you want to get wicked rich, son." Without any meaningful concept of what day-in, day-out in any of these life paths actually entailed, it meant a major life decision was being made with very little information.

Yet, college in America has become increasingly unaffordable. The depth of the issue is denoted by what the *Financial Times* calls a "dangerous" $1.5 trillion U.S. college debt bubble.[10] Of the 44 million Americans who have student debt, 8 million of those borrowers are in default. If college remains both expensive and a form of mandatory certification for many desirable vocations, then it merely acts as a development tax for America's unlucky majority. Few higher education options save you from the debtor's shackles. However, one that is eager to trade college funding for the formative years of your life is the military. This is a perverse carrot to dangle: in the richest country on earth, you may literally have to kill for a decent education. On one hand, the Army obligation would be really long—longer than half of my life at the time. Army life, I was told, "is hard," and Army people would be gruff. I might need to deploy to a sandy place and fight in a dangerous war. On the other hand, it was a "free education." I was told that it would be a really good thing to do for the nation. I would get in better shape. I would "grow up" and "become a leader." I would be respected in the community and be bombarded with attractive career options later. *Skills developed from fighting wars are transferable and far more valuable in the private sector—whose day-to-day activities look nothing like war—than skills developed in the private sector, for the private sector—right?* I believed the rhetoric.

> *If I go there will be trouble*
> *And if I stay it will be double*
>
> —*The Clash, "Should I Stay or Should I Go"*

The military recruitment machine acquired additional inertia in January 2002, when George W. Bush signed into law the No Child Left Behind Act (NCLBA).[11] Despite the happy name, insidious provisions exist within. The voluminous 670 pages has a provision allowing military recruiters near-unimpeded access to the personal information of students, including minors.[12] On pain of forfeiture of federal funding, schools covered by the act are required to release to military recruiters students' names, grade point averages, ethnicity, addresses, and telephone numbers, among other details.[13] Children have their personal data collected and distributed to the military through a Department of Defense data mining program with the gobbledygook name "Joint Advertising Marketing Research & Studies"—or JAMRS for short.[14] Data collection informs military recruitment strategies, which is used to target those with the highest propensity to enlist. Coincidentally, high-propensity candidates are often the most socially, economically, and developmentally vulnerable. This is affectionately known as the "Poverty Draft." The Department of Defense acknowledges that enlistment propensity "declines with age . . . declines with increasing educational attainment . . . is highest among Hispanics" and among "unemployed youth."[15] Therefore, it is critical to get kids, especially kids from struggling backgrounds, hooked on military service before the age of consent, when they are psychologically more willing to take risks. This is not by accident but by design. Children start getting groomed for military service at an age when 10 percent of them are still wetting the bed.[16] Children as young as kindergarten age are being proselytized by Department of Defense career messaging under the auspices of STEM learning opportunities. These programs start young and continue until the student is eligible for military service. The U.S. Army Educational Outreach Program (AEOP) exists "to provide both students and teachers a collaborative, cohesive, portfolio of Army-sponsored STEM programs . . . and expose them to DoD STEM careers." *Yes, exposing six-year-olds to Department of Defense careers.*[17]

A worthy proposition for debate: education should be left to the Department of Education, not the Department of Defense.[18]

"The Department of Defense is the largest employer in the United States. The current size of the enlisted military force is 1.2 million and approximately 200,000 new recruits are needed each year to maintain this level."[19] Bottom line: recruiters need kids to sign binding contracts. Careers are made or shattered based on recruiters' ability to meet quotas. No other public service vocations—firefighters, police officers, paramedics, social workers—were given or had the budget for such expansive recruiting efforts. And only the military was entitled to roam hallways and nudge children—a distinct bias. High school was, in effect, a de facto recruiting station.[20] The U.S. military receives the privilege of penetrating schools at the "right" moment—targeting under-informed children just when they must transition to adulthood—with the "right" message—*We offer transcendent purpose, leadership, honor, and, by the way, money for college*—at the "right" touch point—school—which offers perhaps the largest catchment area. Perfect for trawling.

Schools are intended to be safe, wholesome institutions, free of physical violence. They are meant to educate without bias or dogma. The military, hosted at schools, gets to wear the same halo by affiliation and partnership. However, the U.S. military, as it is currently used, is not a wholesome institution: it escalates violence around the world, devastating lives under the false banner of "national security."

The hype and mysticism surrounding military service in America is generously bolstered by hundreds of millions of dollars spent on Defense Department advertising.[21] More than enough money to manufacture consent among a relatively uninformed audience. Guaranteeing children a sense of "transcendent purpose" without "informed consent" is the single most pervasive cliché in the military recruitment process.

Recruiters engage schools as the military might engage a counterinsurgency. Upon arrival, recruiters *build rapport* with *local power brokers* to create a *permissive environment*. According to doctrine, recruiters are taught to butter up administrators with gifts, presumably hoping it buys goodwill and greater access to children. *The School Recruiting Program Handbook*[22] provides a friendly reminder on this: "Don't forget the administrative staff . . . Have something to give them (pen, calendar, cup, donuts, etc.) and always remember secretary's [*sic*] week, with a card or flowers . . . Deliver donuts and coffee for the faculty once a month. This will help in scheduling classroom presentations . . ."[23] After rubbing shoulders with teachers and secretaries at the tactical level, recruiters must generate goodwill at a more strategic level: "You must convince them [administrators] that you have their students' best interests in mind." *Convince* is the operative word, because enlistment targets are a direct conflict of interest with students' "best interests."[24] Needless to say, students' interests will always be subordinate to the interests of the military and the recruiters. Recruiters are instructed to target popular kids to get access to other, more susceptible children: "Some influential students such as the student president or the captain of the football team may not enlist; however, they can and will provide you with referrals who will enlist."

In my high school, military recruiters in dress uniforms regularly perched themselves in the lunchroom to "prospect." The ones I interacted with were nice enough. Not cartoon villains by any means, even if they were intimidating—both as uniformed authority figures and in sheer physical stature. As a kid with my upbringing, it would feel wrong—almost illegal—not to listen to a man in uniform, especially when the request to speak came from someone who *hunted people* in Afghanistan for a living. *Barrel-chested freedom fighters* as they are sometimes described. Ten percent of their career, it seemed, was spent in the barber's chair, 40 percent in the weight room. And they were everywhere around school. At school awards nights. At our sports games—in all seasons, even in the bitter winter. They enticed kids for ice-breaker conversations with stickers, pens, and toys. As friendly as they were trying to be, they had an agenda.

I stepped up to the recruitment tables and took the glossy pamphlets, devouring the promises of adventure: excitement, fun, prestige, progress, purpose. You could have sworn that you were going to be issued a "humanitarian aid rifle" that would fire apples and warm blankets to the needy. There was no mention of risk. No discussion about combat, suicide, PTSD, killing, injuries. There was no discussion about the ongoing war we were embroiled in, who the enemy actually was, or why we are at war at all. The conversation menu did not adequately inform prospective recruits. Military recruitment focuses on the *proximate outcomes*—stuff like the skills and fitness you will develop—but not on the *ultimate outcomes*—like how war equates to peace or how you will feel when you're done with your service. The device of omission was deception by design.[25] The truth: from birth to basic training, most Americans are raised on a diet of brain-addling military mythologies.[26] In some countries cigarette packs are sold with pictures of cancerous lungs and necrotic feet—the effects of smoking. Perhaps the government should require images of gunshot wounds and amputations to be displayed on the front pages of all recruitment propaganda and shown regularly during training. Common law theory should incentivize this, although I'm sure the military escapes minor matters, such as the responsibility to create an environment of informed consent. Military ads could include photos of the wedding parties that were obliterated by drones after they were mistaken for Taliban gatherings, or the families shot to death by automatic weapons at a checkpoint because the soldier thought the car was riding low on the axle, indicating that it might be carrying a bomb.

It's fascinating that schools would never permit children to display graphic images of dead American soldiers in the classroom, but those same children can be recruited in broad daylight, at school, to sign up to become those dead bodies without fully knowing it. It seems as though kids in America are mature enough to die deluded but not mature enough to live well-informed. War is needless suffering. Ignorance to the evils of war seems ever more needless still.

The sum of all of these conditions was enough for me to decide to serve in the military. The service academies seemed appealing. I began having discussions with West Point alumni, dotingly referred to as "Old Grads."

The "Old Grads" seemed impressive. Most had left the military and had jobs that required a suit and tie. Their class rings—golden, bulbous orbs—looked like a clear signal that they had "made it." Most Old Grads seemed to have a comfortable existence, and though far from their fighting weight, one could sense a keen fighting spirit. They presented as warm, respectable family men. I did not get the opportunity to meet any female Old Grads.

Over stilted meetings in Marriott hotel lobbies or local coffee shops, I realized that I didn't have the faintest idea what I should talk about. *What should I ask them? What questions are appropriate? What questions matter? What questions show that I've done my homework?*

They repeatedly asked me why I wanted to be an officer in the United States Army. "I want to serve my country. I want to become a leader that others can count on," I responded. They seemed satisfied with that.

The more effort I expended, the further I progressed with the application—and the further I progressed, the more my desire to attend West Point grew.

If only I knew that I was signing up to risk my life, and the lives of the men in my platoon, babysitting a highway.

If America knew what that death felt like—deep down to our bone marrow—would we still encourage young people looking for direction to join the armed forces? Or would you trade places with a soldier if the stirring phrase *go to war* was arithmetic, equaling some young person from your hometown—barely more than a kid—having both his legs blown off? Would you commit to war with the same resolve if you, like one of my former soldiers, became two feet shorter after horrifically gruesome amputations? Would you commit yourself to war if it meant dying of a fungal infection from those amputations in Walter Reed hospital? How far does blind nationalism go? Do thousands of deaths like this, in similarly dreadful ways, quench our country's misguided thirst for revenge or pride? If you are not ready to die for the conflict, don't sign up to the armed forces. Don't encourage anyone else to either.

But I did not have this information when I was faced with the decision to attend West Point.[27] I did not know that nationalism is a mind-altering drug that puts pressure on well-intentioned people to make choices—sometimes terrible, delusional choices—often at vulnerable and critical junctures in life.

> *Let me be clear: the war in Afghanistan is unnecessary, unwinnable, and wasteful. For sixteen years we have thrown lives and money into a quagmire. While Americans here at home struggle to afford healthcare and our infrastructure crumbles, our government has spent trillions of dollars trying to turn Afghanistan into a western style democracy— something it never has been and never will be . . .*

> *I am a veteran. This Veterans Day I don't want you to buy me a beer. I don't care if you stand or if you kneel for the national anthem. I don't want you to shake my hand. I don't want you to thank me for my service. What I want is for you to get involved. I want my fellow Americans to talk to each other and discuss the pros and cons of our military's actions around the world. I want us all to engage with our elected representatives and let them know that we expect them to debate the merits of our wars . . .*

> *America's troops don't need to be thanked; they [sic] need to know that they are being used wisely and judiciously. Sixteen straight years of war is anything but wise.*

> *—Dan Berschinski, a West Point classmate; "Veterans' Day Special: An Afghan War Casualty Looks Back and Wonders Why"*

THE CALL

My step-aunt was cutting my hair in her basement when I got "the call": the West Point letter had arrived. I put on two pairs of socks, donned a beanie, and jammed my feet into well-worn running shoes, and started running home through the winter chill.

The streets were sprinkled with Styrofoam Dunkin' Donuts coffee cups and flimsy, selfish, one-use plastic grocery bags on the side of the road, like flotsam washed up on shore after a shipwreck. Gray, decaying snow melted on the sidewalk next to used-car lots and the newspapered-over glass windows of boarded-up shops in the center of town.

Stoughton, Massachusetts, is an easy-to-overlook satellite suburb on the outskirts of Boston, best known for Ikea; Alex's, a seedy strip club; and Town Spa, my favorite greasy pizza joint where locals sit in burnt-orange vinyl booths and order "linguiça pizzah with honey mustahd dippin' sauce." It's hardly the Kibera slums of Nairobi, but there is a sense of economic struggle. Most people seemed to be swimming to shore with enough to sustain them, but few, it seemed, reached solid ground. To Stoughton High School students, they referred to Stoughton as "Toughtown." In the working class, commuter suburbs south of Boston, people were acutely aware of their socioeconomic status.

Brockton, the next town over, was tougher—then, as it is now. Brockton was ranked in the top 100 most dangerous cities in the United States based on number of violent crimes relative to population size.[28] Meanwhile, in the other direction, if you have money to live closer to the city, is Milton, home of the private high school, Milton Academy—where boarding tuition is $59,560 per year, per rich kid.[29]

When I was a teenager, Stoughton was the fulcrum in the middle of this seesaw. A fifteen-minute drive one way or the other would lead you to an entirely different existence. For a kid from here, an offer to West Point felt akin to winning the lottery.

My nerves made me feel like I was going to barf as I jogged to my step-grandparents' house. In tribal fashion, the family had assembled. My stepmom, the steward of all things, handed me the padded envelope. It would have been a letdown if it was rejection, but with an older sister they'd done this before; thick envelopes were a good sign. And besides, looking at the flap on the envelope, it appeared that someone had already tampered with the contents.

I extracted a green folder. A gilded U.S. Army crest was on the cover. On the inside: a welcome letter with images of a ceremonial tar bucket hat, sabers, and all the other West Point accoutrements. Success! I had been accepted. A cheer. Pizza and a cake. I was told that it had been over a decade since the last person from my public high school had been accepted to a service academy. I felt so lucky. Everyone seemed so happy for me.

Pa cupped me on the shoulder firmly. "You've made this old sergeant proud," he said. "I will be honored to salute you when you are a lieutenant."

Life, it felt, was starting to go somewhere.

The next day I obediently rode in the back seat of my parents' brown Mercury station wagon, daydreaming about my all-but-certain future: *the returning war hero who just did soldier stuff, wearing badass combat boots and riding a Ducati motorcycle with a hot chick who whispers the sexiest things in my ear while Fourth of July fireworks explode in the night sky . . .*

And then the porno in my mind was over. I returned to reality: the back seat of my parents' station wagon and the sound of early-riser Republican news talk shows.

America was determined to invade Iraq. Our country—the richest country on earth, with a military larger than the next nine countries combined—was training 320 million people to be terrified of a country whose military we had obliterated a decade earlier,[30] with a population of 25 million people, whose GDP per capita was roughly $2,000. Afghanistan, the other country we had already invaded, had a GDP per capita of $120; it was one of the poorest countries on earth. Many Afghans suffered from food insecurity and few were familiar with the comforting *click* of an electric light switch.[31] Somehow, these were our enemies.

"What do you think about this Iraq invasion stuff?" I asked.

"It'll be over before you graduate," my stepmom said with an air of certainty—both about the war and the guarantee that I would accept my offer from West Point.

My father was silent. He was always silent. A spectator as I became argument roadkill.

My stepmom, a Catholic school teacher, continued, "Saddam is a bad man. The Taliban, those 'Afghanis'[32] [*sic*], are bad people who harbor terrorists. Do you know what those Muslims do to women? To gay people? They stone them! It's unbelievable!"[33]

Without knowing better, I nodded along.

"Even if we don't find nukes, we're going to free those poor Iraqi people. You should be proud of that. About what you're going to do. You'll be a leader in the greatest military—of the greatest country—in history."

I hoped she would claim an easy victory, allowing me to return to daydreaming.

"How can you not do something when these countries harbor terrorists?"

"I'm not saying we shouldn't do *something*. I don't . . . I'm just not sure what to think about this. Didn't we already do 'sanctions' or whatever they're called? A teacher in school said America was responsible for killing, like, half a million people in Iraq 'cause of economic sanctions."[34]

"We would never do that," my stepmom retorted. "America is a Christian country, based on Christian values . . ."

A moment passed before she flip-flopped, covering all bases. "And if we did do that, they're obviously not getting the message, are they? They shouldn't be building weapons of mass destruction."

"Yeah, but what about the pope?"

"Yes, Erik—*what about the pope?*"—heading off whatever sacrilege I was destined to poke at.

"The pope doesn't support invading Iraq—or war in general. He's openly against it."[35]

"I certainly can't argue with the pope, but he doesn't have a background in military strategy, does he?"

"And President Bush does?"

"Shut up, Erik! America wouldn't be doing this unless it was a good idea. There are a lot of smart people in the military—lots of secret information none of us here know about—and maybe if you listen—listen to those who are older and know more than you, since you seem to know everything already—you could be one of them someday. Bottom line: we have a duty to show them what freedom looks like."

That was that. Settled.

And so I accepted my West Point offer, without my post-Army knowledge but knowing full well that I was likely to deploy to war—that I might kill bad people, accidentally kill innocent people, or maybe even be killed—but I made that decision not knowing what that *truly* meant, at an age when I was a virgin, had never drunk alcohol, had an eleven p.m. curfew, couldn't tell you three facts about Iraq or Afghanistan, and briefly thought about getting a tattoo, in Japanese, saying "Death Before Dishonor." I knew nothing—and yet I was willing to sacrifice everything.

Families are complicated. Fortunately, I am on far better terms with my parents today.

At awards night, just before high school graduation, as the senior class treasurer, I was assigned to lead an auditorium filled with several hundred people—students, family, and friends—in the Pledge of Allegiance. Despite having reflexively repeated this oath of loyalty thousands of times as a kid, I went home and practiced. I wanted to put some gravitas behind it. I wanted to establish a good pace and take a dramatic pause or two, saying it with a bit of a flourish. The flag, our country—West Point—demanded that it be done well. Soon, at least in some tangential way, I would be a representative of the flag, and the flag would represent me. It was important that I didn't screw it up.

Somewhere in the middle of awards night, the principal announced that I had accepted my offer to go to West Point and would one day serve as an Army officer to protect our country. I received a thunderous standing ovation.

It was a strange thing, a standing ovation. The applause was coming from people who I had never met. And yet, I hadn't even done anything. It was almost instinctive, a culturally trained reaction like saying "Bless you" to someone who sneezed. *See soldiers; thank them for their service.* Joining the military was automatically wonderful.

One thing was for certain: this was more recognition than many of my classmates were getting. Perhaps undeservedly. Plenty were smarter, several harder working than me. I wasn't any more special than they were. But on this night, it sure felt like it.

I had, in this moment, crossed a liminal threshold. I was now someone else.

The whole thing makes you wonder: What responsibility do citizens have—what expectation of basic foreign policy competence is required—to send soldiers to war or go to war yourself? Looking at evidence, it appears the answer is: none. "Going to war" does not even require citizens to know where on the map we are sending our soldiers or whether the country we are invading is even loosely connected with the crime we seek to avenge. The *Washington Post* reported that roughly 70 percent of Americans wrongly believed that Iraq was responsible for 9/11.[36] Meanwhile, *National Geographic* revealed the extent of America's geographic illiteracy: "Only 17 percent of young adults in the United States could find Afghanistan on a map . . ."[37] But these were strange times. War is peace. Occupation is freedom. Torture is justice. Bombing is saving. Speculation is guilt. Terrorism is counterterrorism.[38]

To contemplate war is to think about the most horrible of human experiences . . . As this nation stands at the brink of battle, every American on some level must be contemplating the horrors of war . . .

Yet, this chamber is, for the most part, ominously, ominously, dreadfully silent . . . There is no debate, there's no discussion, there's no attempt to lay out for the nation the pros and cons of this particular war. There's nothing.

—Senator Robert Byrd

West Point

*There is a kind of quiet radiance associated in my mind with the name
West Point—because you have preserved the spirit of those original
founding principles and you are their symbol. There were contradictions
and omissions in those principles, and there may be in yours—
but I am speaking of the essentials.*

*. . . The army of a free country has a great responsibility: the right to use
force, but not as an instrument of compulsion and brute conquest—as
the armies of other countries have done in their histories—only as an
instrument of a free nation's self-defense, which means: the defense of a
man's individual rights. The principle of using force only in retaliation
against those who initiate its use is the principle of subordinating might to
right. The highest integrity and sense of honor are required for such
a task. No other army in the world has achieved it. You have.*

—Ayn Rand in an address to the
West Point graduating class of 1974

Four columns abreast, a platoon of cadets marched around the inside of the
cadet area. A centipede of dour skinheads.

"*Smirk off, new cadets!*" snapped the cadre. Smiles denoted insubordination.
There were none. The most fearsome members of the cadre wielded their voices

like an auditory whip. When they singled you out and "got in that ass," it felt like an electric convulsion, or that squirmy feeling when the dentist drills a nerve. The first few times I was targeted, I merely tried to maintain sphincter control.

It was a cheerless place.

This was my first summer at West Point, known as "Beast Barracks"—"Beast" for short. It marked the beginning of our military indoctrination. For me, "Beast" took place in the summer of 2003. I was seventeen years old. My first year at West Point, as for most of my classmates, was characterized by fear, intimidation, rote memorization, exhaustion, and infantilizing rituals.

Early on we were sent to Robinson Auditorium—"Rob Aud" in cadet vernacular—for a "motivational spirit briefing." On the way, our cadet platoon sergeant—two years older than us—marched us to cadence:

> *Left right, left right, left right KILL!*
> *Left right, left right, you know I will;*
> *I went to the mosque, where all the terrorists pray,*
> *I set up my claymore, AND BLEW 'EM ALL AWAY!*

> *Left right, left right, left right KILL!*
> *Left right, left right, you know I will.*
> *I went to the store where all the women shop,*
> *Pulled out my machete, AND I BEGAN TO CHOP!*

> *Left right, left right, left right KILL!*
> *Left right, left right, you know I will . . .*
> *I went to the playground where all the kiddies play,*
> *I pulled out my Uzi, AND I BEGAN TO SPRAY!*

I didn't know what to make of it. Was it badass? Was I some kinda tough guy now? Across the path of tilty stone pavers, we reached Thayer Hall, a peculiar, near-windowless building once used for equestrian practice, when *cavalry* meant horses, not helicopters and armored vehicles. We were led inside and took seats in the auditorium.

Severe-looking officers took turns mounting the stage, addressing us in kind. We didn't know who they were or what they did, but they carried gravity. An authoritative presence. I wanted that.

"All of you who graduate from here will almost certainly be sent to war in Iraq or Afghanistan," said a lieutenant colonel, doing what appeared to be a rendition of the famous opening scene in *Patton*—the scene when Patton galvanizes his troops with a speech about going through "the Hun" like "shit through a goose."[1] The lieutenant colonel continued, "I want you to look within and ask yourself if you are willing to lead men and women in combat. It's not for everyone and if you want to quit, do everyone a favor—just stand up and walk out of this auditorium right now."

No one budged.

"Your class, the West Point Class of 2007, has the auspicious honor of being the first class to apply to West Point after 9/11. That moment was a call to action. You, the men and women sitting in this auditorium, answered that call."

Hoots and *Hooah*s from the new cadets.

"That is true patriotism—the essence of what it is to be American. Now it's time to share a motivational video so you can see what some of our forward-deployed troops are doing to win this war. Are you *motivated*?"

To this we responded with our summer camp chant:

"M-ma-ma-ma-mo-motivated."

"New cadets, are you *dedicated*?"

"D-de-de-de-de-dedicated."

The lights dimmed. We heard the recognizable opening chords of "Bodies" by Drowning Pool—basically the theme song for the "War on Terror."

> *Let the bodies hit the floor,*
> *let the bodies hit the floor*

The auditorium went wild. Ravenous screams. My skin turned to gooseflesh. The hairs on my arms stood erect. The anticipation and adrenaline were amplified: this was what we had come here for. The video began.

A highlight reel of death and destruction. Supernova nighttime explosions in an Iraqi city. M1 Abrams tanks rolling through Baghdad—the infamous "Thunder Run." Dismounted infantrymen patrolling dusty, rubble-strewn streets, communicating with hand and arm signals.

An AC-130 Spectre gunship flew a large orbit around its objective: a couple of sedans and a beat-up pickup. A small assemblage of people was jaw-jacking around the sides. So *killable*. Unbeknownst to them, they were seconds from death. The crosshairs were on them, center mass. The Bofors 40mm antiaircraft gun began pounding them. Literally to pieces. Through the white-hot thermal lens, a yard sale of body parts; the heat signature from the thermal camera showed streaks of white—splashes of blood and chunks of still-warm flesh scattered around the engagement area.

We cheered, practically frothing at the mouth.

A man escaped. A squirter.[1] He started running. The gunner switched to the 25mm Gatling gun and hosed him down. A snail trail of blood. A video game, but not.[2] The camera panned out, revealing a Jackson Pollock painting made of gore. Where was the popcorn? We were loving it. Finish him!

Different scene. First-person shooter. A .50-cal machine gunner cranked hot, salt-shaker-sized shells at a building. TOW missiles exploded. Now the screen was pixelated and green. Night vision goggles. Soldiers on a night raid. They stacked on the side of a mud shanty. Flashbang grenades were tossed inside. Bright lights and deafening sounds. The soldiers flowed through the "fatal funnel" into a room, surprising what appeared to be a family. Their faces revealed what might only be called *a pants-shitting expression*.

My classmates and I reached a fever pitch of feral screams. Hoots. Applause. Glee. Was this—all this delighted cheering and fist-pumping—the response that West Point wanted us to give, expected us to give, to this video?

At a place like West Point, you couldn't help but get excited at the prospect of shooting, bombing, and invading. It was presented as a borderline pornographic affair. And if it were pornography, the genre would be autoerotic, masturbatory, and self-indulgent, seeking climax at the thought of one's own greatness. Maybe we cheered because everyone was doing it. Maybe because we didn't want to be seen as "unmotivated"—a term slung around with the intensity of a slur. Or maybe we had already developed a taste for it.

Whatever sorcery drove us to mania, we accepted it. We embraced it. After all, this was West Point, the world's most celebrated military academy. It's hard to find an institution more iconically "American" than West Point, and it's hard to find Americans "more American" than West Point cadets. Actually, a book written by *Rolling Stone* correspondent David Lipsky about West Point cadets is titled *Absolutely American*. We certainly didn't want to be anything less than absolute in our ideological devotion to the cause.

Whatever was happening in this auditorium was as "American" as it could get. You're welcome, Middle East. Tell us, how would you like your freedom: large, extra large, or super-size?

> *Power is in tearing human minds to pieces and putting them together again in new shapes of your own choosing.*
>
> —*George Orwell*, Nineteen Eighty-four

LIFE AT CASTLE GRAY SKULL

> *Pay attention to when the cart is getting before the horse. Notice when a painful initiation leads to irrational devotion, or when unsatisfying jobs start to seem worthwhile. Remind yourself pledges and promises have power, as do uniforms and parades. Remember in the absence of extrinsic rewards you will seek out or create intrinsic ones. Take into account [that] the higher the price you pay for your decisions the more you value them. See that ambivalence becomes certainty with time. Realize that lukewarm feelings become stronger once you commit to a group, club, or product. Be wary of the roles you play and the acts you put on, because you tend to fulfill the labels you accept. Above all, remember the more harm you cause, the more hate you feel. The more kindness you express, the more you come to love those you help.*
>
> —*David McRaney*, You Can Beat Your Brain

And this is where I spent the next four years of my life. The formative years of my late teens and early twenties.

At West Point, if you were allowed to look around—a rare occurrence—you could catch some captivating scenery. From the ground, the road leading to the academy features precipitous cliff faces, highways occasionally closed by falling rocks, and, in winter, twenty-meter-high ice flow waterfalls. From the air, the twisting, switchbacking roads look like asphalt spaghetti overturned on a map of tight cartographic contour lines. The careening, plunging cliffs near Storm King Mountain and the surrounding Catskill Escarpment make for a memorable drive.

West Point and its system of historic redoubts stand proudly at attention at the midpoint of an S-bend curve in the Hudson River. The original fortifications were built in the late 1770s during the American Revolution as a means of defending the Hudson Valley waterways. The narrow turn at this point in the river made West Point strategically valuable. A ship slowly navigating the almost oxbow slalom would become a juicy target. Multiple fighting positions could greet the enemy ship with salvos of pelting cannon fire. There was also the "Great Chain"—a heavy iron chain that traversed the Hudson. This deterred captains from attempting passage for fear they might damage their ships' hulls. The fortifications were successful: no British ships attempted to run the chain.

Arriving at the academy, it's easy to feel what might be described as a King Arthur–esque vibe. America's Camelot. Later, with more time, and once the fear and intimidation wore off, it seemed more like the Imperial Death Star from *Star Wars* after a public relations makeover. Or hard-core S&M without the sex.

It's not a "college" and definitely not a "campus." It is a military base, an agglomeration of training grounds, a cadet area, and a barracks. When one envisions an elite university, delete the colorful, friendly images: laughter spilling in the air, liberal irreverence, disheveled cyclists riding to class, a nutty-chocolate scent wafting from a hipster café, or the din from a passionate debate taking place in the corner of a verdant quad. There are no bright-colored flyers stapled thirty-deep to a phone pole, advertising things like group Pilates, upcoming concerts, climate change awareness marches, tattoo parlors, and Turkish food festivals. No kebab trucks or pizza vans. No protests. No nightlife. No date nights. No romance. No drugs.[3] No bouncy, free spirits.

West Point is a harsh, masculine, unwelcoming place of order, deprivation, and restraint. A place constantly at war with the serenity of its natural surroundings. Here, there is little time or space for contemplation. Everyone is rushing around and sweaty. The hallways vigilantly maintain the dank musk of moist wool uniforms, a faint wet-dog odor. Officers' homes are decorated in almost cookie-cutter mid-century American country style; walls are adorned with patriotic prints of old battle scenes, often depicting Old Glory held proudly by a standard-bearer.

And in this severe and peculiar place, many of America's greatest military leaders were educated and trained. The transition from civilian to military officer is indeed a bold metamorphosis and worth a closer look.

————

INDIVIDUAL GROUP MEMBER indoctrination starts abruptly Plebe year but changes both in tone and style year on year, as cadets assume greater responsibilities and advance in rank.

Plebe (freshman) year is one of deindividuation and fear. Conformity. Subservience. Intimidation.

Yuk (sophomore) year is one of cynicism and doubt. Rebellion. Sarcasm. Questions.

Cow (junior) year is one of commitment and responsibility. Binding contracts. Control. Hazing.

Firstie (senior) year is one of anticipation and magnanimity. Swagger. Decisions. Ownership. Pride. And finally graduation.

The cadet company is the nucleus of all things. Most friendships are forged here. Each company consists of roughly 30 cadets from each of the four year groups, making a tribal group of about 120 cadets. You eat, sleep, study, march, haze, train, and play sports as a company. It is your "home," and your company mates are your de facto "family."

The company area is your block of assigned living space within the barracks. The barracks come in various shapes and sizes, usually with an imposing stone facade. I felt a twinge of jealousy knowing Pershing barracks had gargoyles and huge windows. All barracks were named after West Point generals: Eisenhower, MacArthur, Bradley, Pershing, Sherman, Lee, Grant, to name a few.

My barracks had arrow-straight corridors, seemingly one hundred meters long. The interiors were dated and drab, painted in a shade of *blehhh*—a government cream-white. The halls were harshly, fluorescently lit. In summer, industrial-sized hallway fans thrummed away all day, providing a white-noise backdrop, partially offsetting the upperclassmen yelling.

To personalize these spaces, artsy cadets painted wall murals, often featuring the company mascot or phrases thought to be motivational. Our company, Company E-2, known as "Easy Deuce," had the motto "Easy Come, Easy Go," and featured a Saint Bernard wearing an American flag neckerchief. Another common feature in the company area is a memorial. Still embroiled in America's longest war, plaques and memorials were set up, honoring alumni killed in combat. It was one of many acknowledgments that something other than glory might follow graduation.[4]

Aside from cadet murals, the only other color comes from the "suicide wall." One wall in each two- or three-man shared room is painted a subtly different color. A robin's-egg blue, *café con leche* brown, or milky tangerine. Cadet lore has it that the "suicide wall" statistically decreases the likelihood that you will "off" yourself.

Cadets plaster the company area with lighthearted flyers or announcements. Perhaps the 1972 *Cosmopolitan* centerfold of Burt Reynolds, naked, sprawled on a bearskin rug, face Photoshopped out and substituted with a cadet's, might offer the reminder "Don't be naughty, clean the trunk room before Thanksgiving leave."

The physical development officer puts reminders to work out. THE TALIBAN DIDN'T SKIP LEG DAY, HOW ABOUT YOU? Coincidentally, Michael Nguyen, the savvy cadet who did a lot of the daily announcements during my Plebe year, later "entered guilty pleas to theft and money-laundering charges" for stealing nearly $700,000 of hard "U.S. currency entrusted to him as the battalion project purchasing officer in Muqdadiyah, Iraq," according to the *Seattle Times*.[5] The coverage was damning.[6] I didn't see that coming.

TWO HUNDRED YEARS OF TIMELESS INDOCTRINATION

Patriotism is the willingness to kill and be killed for trivial reasons.

—Bertrand Russell

We arrived young, most of us still teenagers. Like clean paper, we were ready to receive whatsoever the military would like to imprint upon us. The question: How does the academy get these all-American swimmers, pious altar boys, cauliflower-eared wrestlers, nerdy class treasurers, and Eagle Scouts to, in four years' time, be fired up about "shooting some motherfucking Hajjis in the face"?

This transition requires industrial-strength brainwashing. The Army's old slogan—"Be all that *you can be*"—may more aptly be, as I've heard it put—"Be all that *they want you to be*."

Military indoctrination is the voluntary surrender of one's own identity to join a profession that often takes away the human dignity of others by force. Through repetition, servicemen have their values, behaviors, and identity recalibrated with the ultimate aim of making them willing to kill or be killed in political violence without thinking about it too much. It is the construction of blind faith in the state and the deconstruction of any critical thinking that could stand in opposition to the state's aims.[7] It began by stripping us of our civilian, at-home identity. Civilian clothes were locked away in the *trunk room*. Relics of individuality were snuffed out. We were no longer *back on the block*, as we were reminded. *"Hey! What are you doing, walking around like that? You think you're back on the block? Move out!"*

We were anonymized. Fitted to a mold. One of the earliest stations is the barbershop. The old me was shorn from my head and scattered on the barber's floor like mousy cremated ashes and unceremoniously swept into a dustpan with the clumps of other discarded souls. The group of us were led around like cattle: meat bags, all penned up and nervous. I received my Geneva Convention identification card with chip, bar code, and Social Security number. I was one square unit of soldier. I was on my way to becoming a *fourth-class cadet*.

The bathroom was *the latrine*. The bed was *the rack*. The standard-issue green blanket was my *green girl*. It wasn't a hat, it was a *cover*. Shoes were now *low quarters*. If language was any indicator, it was clear we were in a different dimension. Everything on the inside of the gates, *on post*, was taxonomically different than the civilian world, *off post*.

I was issued with new beliefs, new goals, new morals, and new dreams—the whole lot. By the end, it was unclear whose beliefs were in operation—or if I controlled them at all. It was a bit like the paradox of Grandfather's ax: If the ax handle breaks and you replace it, is it still Grandfather's ax? What about if you replace both the handle and the ax-head at the same time? For better or worse, the margin between who I truly was and who I was becoming grew by the day.

I felt a rousing patriotic pride in uniform, in formation, but I also felt a sense of dissonance. The uniform felt like a costume that, when worn, altered my personality and behavior. Over time, with enough method acting, this borrowed personality became "me."

"Army me" was different—rigid, hyper-masculine, hawkish, naively trusting, loud, extroverted. I tacitly knew that if I extricated myself from that world, I would think, act, and perceive my surroundings in radically different ways.

Indoctrination would be a vastly different experience if it was part-time and spread out over a longer duration. Indoctrination demands a closed shock-and-awe system. We were isolated, separated from families and support networks. External contact during initial indoctrination is decidedly limited, sheltering us from anything that could temper or make us question the military dogma. It is a hermetically sealed world, tightly policed.

We developed new tribal clusters with similar people who held—or were taught to hold—similar beliefs and who, in time, would have similar roles, in similar places, in similar conditions. We kept each other in line to reach this preordained destiny. "Cooperate to graduate" was the saying. And with this sense of mutual reliance came a sense of belonging.

To unify a group of hungry achievement seekers, place a yoke on their shoulders. Tell them that only "America's best and brightest" (a self-adulating expression used by West Pointers and the academy website to refer to themselves[8]) can pull it. And tell them they must pull together or else fail their countrymen. This helped to establish a herd mentality.

Deviating from the herd brought social shame and the eviscerating notion that one was incapable of adapting. The fear of becoming a "shit bag" was a powerful motivator. Part of "fitting in" was not showing fear. To cower from an opponent in the boxing ring was pathetic. Likewise, to hesitate at the edge of the eighty-foot-high "slide for life"—a zip line that traverses Lake Popolopen—was embarrassing. But pushing through fear and anxiety is one thing; feeling it was another. That was inevitable and pervasive.

FEAR WAS MANUFACTURED to coerce and control behavior. Fear of being locked up or hazed by upperclassmen. Fear of group rejection for being "ate up." Fear of falling behind if you weren't constantly outworking your peers. Fear of the penalties and shame that came with academic, military, or physical failure. Fear of failing your future soldiers. Fear that no one would want to be led by you.

Fear of getting others killed. *Meta-fear*: fear of showing fear, especially in combat. And, of course, fear of the enemy.

This enemy needed to be developed, appearing both plausibly threatening and unapologetically evil. Images of beardy, under-washed Muslims carrying AKs or RPGs, doing the universal check-out-my-sweet-gun pose, did the trick. These deindividualized, homogeneous, caricature villains had their barbarous credentials sensationalized, justifying the sweat and sacrifices required to subdue them. The enemy needed to be *killable*.

I tried to keep my fear front of mind and used my insecurities of underperforming or disappointing others as a mechanism to train harder. In my shared room, I kept a motivational quote sticky-tacked to my faux-wood bookshelf. It was entitled "True Believer":

> *Somewhere a true believer is training to kill you. He is training with minimum food and water, in austere conditions, day and night. The only thing clean on him is his weapon. He doesn't worry about what workout to do—his rucksack weighs what it weighs, and he runs until the enemy stops chasing him. The true believer doesn't care how hard it is; he knows that he either wins or dies. He doesn't go home at 1700; he is home. He only knows the cause. Now. Who wants to quit?*

And to think I once thought that being a "true believer"[9] was a good thing. One of the chief preoccupations of the military is to create unfailing fanaticism for "the cause." To get people to give away ever more of themselves, as if in a competition. I was becoming a fanatic. But the quote—I believed it. In a short time, I was going to fight desperate people. They would make us, the U.S.-led occupation, leave their country or die trying. I had to be so well trained, so motivated, that I could subdue an uncooperative population fueled by the type of relentless resistance that can only arise from deep legitimate grievances. I needed the fear.

When we were meant to give more of ourselves over to the cause, the insurgents were characterized as competent, scheming, formidable, and hardworking opponents. Officers, NCOs, and other cadets constantly reminded us that "at this very moment, terrorists are training to kill your family and destroy the American way of life." Whipped by illusions of terror, we designed our training to be more extreme than the extremists. We needed to be more disciplined. Move faster. Push harder. This required us to drown out doubt and execute on command. We needed to become protocol followers.

PROTOCOL FOLLOWERSHIP AND THE WAR ON ENTROPY

We have gained reality and lost dream. No more lounging under a tree and peering at the sky between one's big and second toes; there's work to be done. To be efficient, one cannot be hungry and dreamy but must eat steak and keep moving. It is exactly as though the old, inefficient breed of humanity had fallen asleep on an anthill and found, when the new breed awoke, that the ants had crept into its bloodstream, making it move frantically ever since, unable to shake off that rotten feeling of antlike industry.

—*Robert Musil,* The Man Without Qualities

In a training environment where the military cannot replicate the danger of combat, combat stress is replicated by other means. It seemed that the stupidest things were treated with life-and-death importance; meanwhile, actual life and death was treated with flippancy. This is both one of the great paradoxes of military indoctrination and one of its critical linchpins.

In this universe, superiors spew spittle, gesticulating wildly about the importance of "folding your socks so they smile." They are deadly serious: "Don't you want your socks to be happy!?" Such trivialities routinely provoke heart-quaking indignation.

Meaningless tasks are a "feature," not a "bug." The more meaningless, the better. If the academy could get us to willingly submit ourselves to sleep deprivation to tape never-to-be-worn, tighty-whitey underwear, folded into near-perfect squares, to the inside of our dresser drawer on a Friday night, they have won. At this point they successfully beat the why out of us. If we wouldn't question this nonsense, what *would* we question?

This process instills a sense of unexamined vigilance. A devotion to high fixed-cost rituals. The laundry list of tasks assigned to us were not done for the inherent value of the tasks themselves—not because they made us better officers or more technically proficient—but rather for their indirect benefit, to engender a remarkable degree of subservience. We were being indoctrinated to become auto-followers, so that on other days, with equally stupid tasks, in far more dangerous situations, we wouldn't think twice. Possibly not even once.

From R-Day (Reception Day) until the end of Plebe year, even the act of eating in the mess hall felt thoroughly unpleasant. The stress of class, up to three fitness sessions per day,[10] and being hazed left a wolverine in my stomach—a hypoglycemic, angry wolverine. I sat straight-backed on the edge of my chair, two fist distances away from the back of the chair, one fist distance away from the tablecloth—eyes submissively cast downward, fixated upon the little West Point crest on the top of the plate. Saliva pooled in my mouth. As Plebes, we performed "table duties"—a choreographed set of phrases and actions during mealtime. Meanwhile, upperclassmen took turns knocking over condiments, getting us to arrange them in height order, and timed us. When upperclassmen were having a bad day, meals were miserable. Each mouthful of food was scrutinized. We were not allowed to chew our food more than five to seven times before swallowing. If we subjugated ourselves adequately, we sometimes got the "privilege" of "big bites," meaning our mouthfuls would not be hawkishly monitored. Any transgression would invite a fist slamming into the table, shaking the silverware, followed by a drawn-out chastisement for whatever the perceived infraction was. The whole escapade was a waste of time and talent.

When upperclassmen were in a playful mood, there were games straight out of a delinquent all-boys boarding school. For their enjoyment, I was made to play "cupcake roulette," where I was made to eat cupcakes filled with mayo, steak sauce, and Texas Pete hot sauce—and then we were made to eat the "Beat Navy Bread," the grease-soaked toast whose sole purpose in life was to sop up the lard beneath dripping mess hall sausages. Plebes diverted time from studies to memorize jokes or skits as required by the upperclassmen at a particular table. Plebes also did the "gallon challenge"—drinking a gallon of milk in one meal; those who failed spewed vomit into the mess hall water pitchers. After a time, this was stopped because the mess hall staff had to throw away too many pitchers due to hygiene concerns. I didn't think of it then, but it seems cringeworthy now that the upperclassmen who presided over these things would, in short order, be leaders in combat.

Military discipline is merely a willingness to do the basics right. A standard was given and there was an expectation that you would do it. This involved a heavy use of what I refer to as "prescriptive discipline": following a checklist.

Prescriptive discipline is middle-management thinking and it does not guarantee that you are solving the right problem. It requires you to show up and follow instructions. Nearly absent was a sense of what I'll call "innovative discipline," in which no one tells you what to do. Instead, you must independently determine the real problem you want to solve, prioritize what's important, and then summon the discipline to ignore everything else. In my experience, the military is heavy on the former and light on the latter. In fact, the latter is often punished.

In many instances, appearance was prioritized over performance. There was a disproportionate focus on things that made us *look* competent, thieving time from things that actually *made us* competent. Like the parable of the drunk man looking for his keys only where there is a streetlight, not where the keys are most likely to be, focus was on easy-to-identify problems, not the problems that mattered. The wearing of a reflective belt, a rogue hand in a pocket, a clean toothbrush holder, and uniformity of tent flaps or room shades—whether opened or closed—were of utmost importance. New cadets penned a little ditty capturing these dutiful amputations of time (sung to the theme of *The Flintstones*):

> *Right pocket, now your left pocket, it's the ever-changing SOP [standard operating procedures];*
> *Covers [hats] on, now your covers off, oh, fuck it, throw it in the tree.*

Later, I saw that all of these games fit into the larger picture. To kill, allegedly in the name of global beneficence, you must look the part. If you and your instruments of death are brighter and shinier and more space-age than the other side, it means you are more legitimate. When comparing U.S. weapons to the rusty AK-47s of the insurgents, it's like going to court with a battalion of lawyers in three-piece suits to prosecute a group of people with tribal face tattoos. It doesn't mean we have a case, but it sure looks it. The *sameish* Velcro patches, the dress-right-dress equipment, the haircuts, the *shmick* body armor—these are the stage props that lend an air of officialdom to murder. It was our duty to preserve the illusion.

*The West won the world not by the superiority of its ideas or values or
religion [. . .] but rather by its superiority in applying organized violence.
Westerners often forget this fact; non-Westerners never do.*

—*Samuel P. Huntington,* The Clash of Civilizations and
the Remaking of World Order

What we were being given was an education in deontology in which morality and the very concept of good and bad hinges on obeying the rules. It is "the science of duty." A *shit bag* or *shammer* is one who fails to meet—or intentionally skirts—*the standards.* Meanwhile those who are *high-speed* or *squared away* are dutiful protocol followers. If you play the game and follow the rules, you get the food pellets of positive reinforcement from the academy. Punishment comes swiftly to those who resist.

We learned to tolerate anything. Even if it was dehumanizing or demeaning. In the early days of West Point, the cadre formed us up and marched us to stand on "the Apron"—a colossal wraparound concrete walkway that faced the rear end of an oxidized green statue of George Washington riding a horse.[11] We were ordered to drink water from our olive drab two-quart canteens. Standing at parade rest, we committed ourselves to rote memorization[12] from our "knowledge books." During one of these "knowledge sessions," I requested to use the bathroom. I was denied. Another command: "Drink water, new cadets." I followed orders and held my position. A few minutes later I asked again—pleading my case with greater urgency. I was denied again. I squirmed, clenching my fists and curling my toes. And then I broke. Still in formation, I peed my pants, letting the warm urine slowly trickle and seep into my black wool boot socks.

IN-GROUPS AND OUT-GROUPS

Social standing was like a totem pole. Firsties on top, Plebes on the bottom. However, social groups were defined in other ways.

Good officers, it was implied, had some spiritual bedrock. When it came to religion at the academy, belief in a "spooky father figure," as the late comedian George Carlin described it, was strongly encouraged.[13] During Beast (cadet basic training), cadets were sorted by religion. The cadre put us in new formations.

"Catholics form up over here, Protestants over here. No denomination over here." Non-Christian religions seemed to have little representation.

Joining the atheists, sometimes referred to as the "heathens," felt deviant, shameful. Either you publicly self-identified with some denomination and went to church with most everyone, or you were marched back to your room, alone, presumably to align your hats or something. Religion was baked into academy culture as the "default setting."

Mandatory events featured religious exercises. Formal dinners came with prayer, invocations, and benedictions offered up to "our heavenly father" by an Army chaplain. You didn't have to participate in prayers, but there certainly was a feeling that you *should*, and you were mandated, at the minimum, to be exposed to their messaging. One could not leave events featuring religious overtures. Why it wasn't possible for the military to keep religion for personal time? Who knows. Separation of church and state was—to be generous—blurry. Some instructors carried their dogma to work, proclaiming the U.S. was a "Christian nation." I recall one U.S. Army captain saying, "We need to fight the war in Afghanistan because the insurgency is a threat to Christianity."

I went to church groups for the first year despite not being religious. The Christian fellowship was warm, welcoming, and filled with nice people. I gave it a shot. I tried to pray the logic away. Furthermore, the academy gave special passes to religious groups, which, when shackled to the academy grounds, was a powerful incentive to magically find your long-lost faith. The academy would never allow me to celebrate atheism by giving me a weekend pass to go mountain biking or to go to a local college party. I just couldn't fake it forever.

Social strata were sliced a second way: athletes and nonathletes.

The demarcation between "slug" and "corps squadder" was defined by participation in varsity sports. Slugs didn't play varsity sports. Instead, they were stereotyped as parochial, shoe-shining, pizza-eating rule enforcers who weren't talented or hardworking enough to compete at higher-level athletics and, as a result, focused their time on haircuts or something equally arbitrary. Slugs didn't play sports; they played stupid games—poorly.

Corps squadders, on the other hand were stereotyped as "ghosts" and "shammers." They were entitled prima donnas who ran away to the shelter of their sports teams to avoid responsibility. They were given special privileges: exemption from necessary duties, like delivering laundry, and low-value military training like marching up and down the square; they received extra food allowances, paid-for sports camps, and premium wash-and-fold laundry services, but ultimately it was the sexy kit from Nike that separated the athletic class. Meanwhile the rest of us peasants wore bog-standard Army fitness uniforms that fit and felt remarkably like kitchen garbage bags with sleeves.

I started out as a slug, doing "Sandhurst"—a daylong military endurance competition against the British Royal Military Academy. Gas mask runs. Rowing a zodiac boat across a lake. Rappelling off cliff faces. Shooting targets. River crossings. Moving stretchers and equipment. Scaling a ten-foot wall as a team. I liked it. Through training, I met teammates like Adam Snyder, a Firstie who became a mentor of mine Plebe year. Tough, thoughtful, but also a joker, Snyder was likable and respected. He trained me well. A rakish-looking Captain America doppelgänger, Snyder branched infantry and was posted to the storied 101st Airborne Division, the "Screaming Eagles." I looked up to him and the decisions he made. He inspired me to branch infantry.

But I wanted to actually feel like an athlete again. I looked for sports where I had a chance of making the team. I found crew. Crew was a club sport. Club teams were a hybrid, bastard child between varsity and company sports. We spent just as much time training as the varsity—twice a day during the week, racing on the weekends—and although exempt from drill and ceremony, there were fewer perks: no budget, no professional coaches, no coherent training plan to make our team a powerhouse. For an entire season we had no coach at all. The oarsmen made up their own training. It was the blind leading the blind.

Nonetheless, rowing became my religious experience. It is lactic acid ballet. It is max-pressure meditation. It is a triadic catharsis: mental, emotional, and physical, all at once. Water demands patience. You cannot flog water and expect to have your way with it. You have to respect its density. You have to connect with it.

To move a boat—that is, if you want to move it with the intention of winning—you cannot pull the oar through the water, tearing the surface; rather, you have to attach oar to water and lever the boat past the oar. And when timing, force, and flow are achieved, oh, how the boat sings.

The willowy sway of the hands away
And the water boiling aft

—*Steve Fairbairn,* "The Oarsman's Song"

I still think fondly of rowing in the predawn darkness of the Hudson River with the self-proclaimed "fastest eight in Army crew history." Here, golden light would stream across the hilltops and saddles of the Hudson River Valley, dispelling stubborn pockets of shade as our team shouldered the boat at the end of a hard morning practice, panting, exhausted. It felt like we were beating the day before it ever had the chance to start.

Our team spent racing season in threadbare Econovans, driving up and down the Eastern Seaboard, along Highway I-95: Pennsylvania, Massachusetts, Virginia, Delaware, with spring training often in Florida. In time, we memorized which gas stations had which fast-food restaurants. We became connoisseurs of truck stop cuisine, quick to embrace McDonald's, maybe Taco Bell, slow to stop at Popeyes.

Amid bloodied, bandaged hands and Nutella-and-banana sandwiches, and bound together by the common pursuit of "better," I fostered friendships with teammates, older and younger alike. A remarkable sense of brotherhood was built in these unremarkable places.

I first met Andy Byers when I was a Yuk and he was a Plebe. At practice we were one team, and peers on equal footing. On the water, there was no rank, no supplication, no suppression. But as soon as we left practice, he and all other Plebes had to assume their submissive, subjugated role. Without an upperclassman around, they were voiceless, not permitted to speak. I took pride in shielding younger teammates from the torment and molestation that accompanied a simple walk across the cadet area.

I also met Sam. He was a year older than me and the stroke of the varsity eight. He was one of the leaders of the team. He was patient, thoughtful, principled. And together, Sam, Andy, myself, and the rest of the squad cobbled together a couple fine seasons for our big-hearted, slim-walleted, slightly dysfunctional team.

Rowing shifted from hobby to devotion, and devotion grew into bonfire obsession. I brought a condemned rowing machine home with me to train over

Christmas. In December in Massachusetts, I trained in my parents' garage wearing a fleece hat and spandex unisuit from Penn AC.[14] It was night, the door was ajar, and through the driveway floodlights I watched the snow flurries. Listening to my iPod, I had one care governing every decision in the day: *Will it make the boat go faster?* The academy taught us to honor the work. To "embrace the suck." Most alumni anecdotally describe a positive-growth story during their four-year struggle. I transitioned from self-doubt to self-confidence; from insecurity and mediocrity to grit and conviction.

Acquiring this grittiness, however, comes at an eye-watering cost. Joining the military is one of the most extreme decisions you can make with your life. Indoctrination was taken to a new level.

WAR LUST

You'll never have a quiet world till you knock the patriotism out of the human race.

—*George Bernard Shaw,* O'Flaherty V.C.

The military, as a tribe, communicates in symbols, badges, and technobabble jargon. With our handy "knowledge book," we decoded the cryptographic meanings. We memorized the unit patches of the ten active Army divisions, their mottos, and where they were stationed. In almost no time I could differentiate between the rank of a staff sergeant and sergeant first class. Not long after that, I could look at the curriculum vitae on someone's chest and make sense of the flair. Later, I'd be able to perform this evaluation at ten paces.

With time, I hung judgments on the universe around me. Which is a "better unit": 1st Ranger Battalion or 1st Infantry Division? Are these actions worthy of an Army Achievement Medal or an Army Commendation Medal? What is a "better" military school to go to: Airborne or Sapper? But without actual experience, my beliefs were merely the recycled beliefs of others—trusted mentors. Day in, day out, their experience taught us how to see the world.

Extreme cultures generate extreme beliefs. Cultural context tells us what is important, where we should apply our time and effort. Military indoctrination shifts this context. Shortly, I found myself measuring my self-esteem and self-worth differently from the way I had just months earlier.

Success or failure was measured in push-ups, in obstacle course times, in golden wreath pins, in Velcro tabs worn on the left shoulder. I began to want things—things that the mystical forces around West Point conditioned me to want. Six months before starting West Point, I didn't know shit about the infantry, Ranger School, the Reconnaissance and Surveillance Leaders Course (RSLC), or Special Forces Assessment and Selection (SFAS), and now, with the greatest conviction, I rearranged all of my bodily energy to follow this path. The academy successfully manufactured desire.

The first decision led to the next, often more extreme one, almost effortlessly. *Why go to West Point unless you wanted to do hard-core military stuff? You can push paper elsewhere, for better pay.* The logic continued along the same vector. *If you're going to go infantry, why not go to the Rangers—work with better trained troops?* Knowing there was something "better" was seduction enough to pursue it. In that moment, it made sense.

It didn't take me long to seek roles that would ultimately put me in close proximity to death—even if death remained a romantically tempered abstraction. This was how respect was earned and measured, it seemed: by likelihood of dying for the flag. "Dick measuring" happened across several dimensions: who had the most deployments, the hardest deployments, who passed the toughest military schools, had more airborne jumps, the fastest two-mile run, or who belonged to the most special units with the blackest ops. As a young type-A achievement seeker, the accumulation of military merit badges was an easy MacGuffin to chase, despite being a never-ending and primitive endeavor.

A soldier will fight long and hard for a bit of coloured ribbon.

—Napoleon

This was buttressed by the social value of these awards on display daily. The prior service combat veterans in our class were treated differently. They had more respect. No upperclassmen dared to fuck with them. A Combat Infantryman Badge and Ranger Tab seemed to be the sine qua non.

To not participate in political violence[15] was not just a shame but shameful. In the "big Army" those who hadn't been to war are derided as "slick sleeve" or "cherry." The route to respect, it seemed, went directly through a war zone. Non-combat roles were seen, with few exceptions (e.g., aviation and medical service), as inferior, unsexy, and perhaps even cowardly. Selecting certain combat support branches was almost a sign of shirking one's duty to the nation. It could symbolize a fear of death in combat, and there is no scarlet letter worse than refusing to confront a threat to America head-on. It's tough to find a military action movie that would cast a finance, ordnance, or air defense artillery soldier as the protagonist. Within the military, you were either combat arms or in the shadow of combat arms.

Running cadences illustrated this hierarchy:

> *I wanna be an Airborne Ranger,*
> *Live the life of guts and danger.*
> *Airborne Ranger,*
> *Life of danger.*

> *I wanna be a PowerPoint Ranger*
> *Live the life of paper-cut danger . . .*
> *PowerPoint Ranger,*
> *Paper-cut danger.*

With so much training and emphasis placed on combat, my hope—to participate in war versus live in peace—was always in open tension.

Unsurprisingly, the military perennially claims peaceful motives.

> *Why we serve*
> *As Soldiers, we are committed to do our duty to contribute to the "common defense"; we share a love of our country and of our Army Family . . . we serve "not to promote war, but to preserve peace."*

—The Soldier's Blue Book: The Guide for Initial Entry Training Soldiers (*U.S. Army Training and Doctrine Command*)

> *"Peace Is Our Profession"—so proclaimed the Strategic Air Command, the Cold War–era nuclear strike force that stood ready at a moment's notice to turn large cities into rubble while incinerating millions.*

—*Andrew J. Bacevich,* America's War for the Greater Middle East: A Military History

Young soldiers want—or are taught to want—to "see action." There is an eagerness to stop playing Army games in the woods—to quit jousting—and get to combat. War lust comes in many forms, even the clothing that many troops—especially young enlisted troops—wear.

Veteran-owned clothing companies celebrate war, violence, and xenophobia, making walking caricatures of the junior enlisted soldiers who buy the stuff, and pay tribute to one of America's most well-defined features: a famine of cultural self-awareness. Unfortunately, the T-shirts are not worn as satire. They accurately depict the anti-intellectual, ignorant-and-proud, "Team America" philosophy that pervades military units. Spartan helmets cloaked in red, white, and blue. References to Valhalla or Vikings. "Back to Back World War Champs" T-shirts. Some might be cutesy: Abraham Lincoln dressed in a plate carrier, carrying an assault rifle. But all are tributes to war lust.

Privates are often seen walking into the on-post mini-mall to buy Monster energy drinks and cigarettes—vices that the Spartans they so sanctify would never have indulged in—wearing loutish hoodies that say, "Sticks and stones may break my bones but hollow points expand on impact." Another T-shirt displays the phrase "Ask not who your country can kill for you but who you can kill for your country." Likewise, you can buy patches designed for wear on tactical equipment that says, "Freedom has a nice ring to it and a bit of recoil."

All of it supports the deeply damaging "Durka durka!" American belief that "freedom" is best transferred by bullets to some brown person's face. *America, fuck yeah!"—am I right?* Unfortunately, the joke is on all of us, because this *'Murrica* culture perpetuates the war that gets these same soldiers killed.

And during wartime, those who have never deployed or are not permitted to deploy for whatever reason often feel a tremendous amount of shame and guilt.

After our tour to Afghanistan, a former soldier of mine was listed as non-deployable for mental health reasons. He committed suicide as his unit deployed again without him. When war provides meaning for one's career, not going to war makes one feel meaningless.

Furthermore, in the absence of war, you'd still be fighting, but against a different enemy: boredom. You'd be, in essence, a firefighter who never left the firehouse. It would be a career of inspections, formations, push-ups, fried chicken, and lonely masturbation. Asking generals if they want a war to fight is like asking Tom Brady what he wants to do on Sunday, according to one veteran's 9/11 anniversary article in the *New York Times*.[16] Sometimes I wonder if it's not about the war but about the cultural cohesion and unification of purpose we seem to get—as an army, as a nation—from going to war. I, for one, was hoping for a particular experience, an uncomplicated war.

I didn't want to go to a miserable or dangerous war. I wanted combat to feel like *Call of Duty* on "easy" mode. I wanted to pulverize lobotomized baddies, machine-gunning evil incarnate troglodytes in the chest without much physical risk. My own death was a non-consideration. At the end of this twinkle-in-the-eye patriotic fantasy, I'd return home, proud, to a nation even prouder. In America, being a veteran, regardless of what else one does after, seems enough. It is the ticket to lifelong personal validation. A powerful incentive.

The thing America seems afraid of losing is not the wars we fight (we've lost plenty)—it's the part of our pride, national identity, and sense of courage that wars awaken. Without a forever war—without armed occupations, targeted killings, torture, and prison camps—are we still American? Violent conflict and military excursions have become normalized. It is the default position.[17] They hardly register in our collective consciousness. To most Americans, war is elevator music.

Since we were joining the profession of political violence, violence itself had to be viewed as the solution to some of the world's most intractable problems, not the problem itself. As such, cadets grow an affinity for violence. But we lacked a place to put it. It was a bucket of testosterone inside a pressure cooker.

With few outlets outside of *mandatory fun*, cadets become desperate. Forms of violence become a substitute for entertainment. Cadets rip off their harnesses and muzzles, and occasionally, just occasionally, in a "just-this-once" matriarchal style, the academy looks away. It's all part of well-worn "tradition," I guess. The moral: if you smother young, piss-and-vinegar people hard enough and long enough, a bit of anarchy eventually squeezes out the sides.

Consider the annual Plebe pillow fight.

Plebes clad in Kevlar helmets, hard-knuckle gloves, knee pads, and elbow pads run down the stairs into Central Area carrying a weaponized pillowcase. Many pillowcases contained items far more damaging than a pillow. Books. Soap. Padlocks. The entire metal lock box itself.

We were encouraged to fight valiantly and beat up the rival companies' Plebes. It wasn't about being concerned about injury to self or others, it was about not acting like a coward. That was an important lesson.

Looking down into Central Area, hundreds of Plebes bludgeoned each other in a medieval melee. The result: many returned bruised or bloody. Broken noses. Broken ribs. One year the *New York Times* covered the scrum. The correspondent reported that one cadet had his leg shattered—pretty hard to do to a teenage athlete. In 2015 thirty cadets were injured. Twenty-four had concussions.[18] This was our "fun." Or, at least, the closest thing we had to it.

We also threw "birthday parties." A birthday party is when a mob of Plebes mug an upperclassman—usually a haze—and violate and disgrace him on his birthday.[19] We ripped off one male Firstie's shirt and forcibly held him down. Meanwhile another cadet opened a bottle of black "edge dressing"—normally used to stain the sides of your dress shoes. We stained his pale pink nipples completely black. With the edge dressing we drew the standard repertoire of meathead phrases down his arms and back. "I love cock"—a classic. In haste, and with the "birthday boy" bucking everywhere like a live fish at the bottom of a boat, we *splish-splashed* and dribbled dye all over him. He looked like a Rorschach test—with welts. Then we hog-tied him with zip ties. While bound, we grabbed hair clippers and shaved a skin-tight landing strip down the center of his head, requiring him to shave the rest before morning formation. Finally, we covered him in lunch table condiments[20] and sour milk, leaving him by himself, on his stomach, under an icy shower. He bellowed pathetically. We took pleasure in his comeuppance.

The culture carried on like this recursively. The academy begrudgingly concedes the need for *some outlet* and shrugs off these pranks until they can't any longer. When they have devolved into a public relations fiasco. Only public embarrassment, it seems, provides a powerful enough shove to *do something*. In typical knee-jerk reaction, new policy is written to treat the symptoms, but rarely does it address the underlying problem of a hyper-masculine, hyper-domineering culture.

In my third year as a cadet, I was given the opportunity to train with 10th Special Forces Group in Germany. For nearly two months, I signed out weapons from the arms room to hone my skills. With coaching from a cadet from the Combat Weapons Team, I practiced rifle-to-pistol transitions, weapons malfunctions, room clearing, and draws from sling or retention holster.

I learned the meaning of "hearts and minds": two bullets in the heart, one in the mind.

In my barracks room I shot "Abdullah." Abdullah[21] was a paper target hung from the wall. I used him for blank rifle and pistol drills using plastic "dummy" rounds. He was a mean Arab-looking man with a checkered scarf.

I imagined shooting Abdullah before he could shoot me.

For the first two years of West Point, I had full confidence that America was morally upstanding and that this war was a good thing to do. I strove to model myself as America's "True Believer." In the discombobulation of youth, it felt nice to trust that my mission was worthy. Later events injected doubt.

One day—maybe the day I started shooting Abdullah—I crossed a line. I was now capable of hunting people. Not only that, I was looking forward to it. I imagined the adrenaline. Aiming my ACOG (advanced combat optical gunsight) optic center mass, squeezing the trigger, and watching the "terrorist"— read: angry farmer—in shock when he realizes he's been hit. See him slump or fall in a heap. Shoot half a dozen. Full dozen. Didn't matter. Soon I started demeaning Middle Easterners in the same way, with the same intensity, as I heard others do: "Haj," "terrorists," "goat fuckers." I painted these people with a single brush, a thousand miles wide.

When I became capable of killing, I killed a part of my former self. I was absolutely and irreversibly changed. Indoctrination is a double declaration—of what is gained and lost, simultaneously. I gained an identity, military skills, and personal confidence. I was losing my future and my moral self.

It's quite fun to shoot them, you know. It's a hell of a hoot. It's fun to shoot some people.

—*Jim Mattis, former U.S. secretary of defense,*
former Marine Corps general

PARTITIONING MORALITY

With a heavy dose of fear and violence, and a lot of money for projects,
I think we can convince these people that we are here to help them.

—*LTC Nathan Sassaman*

Beyond conditioning a basic mechanical reaction—to raise a weapon and take aim at a person you know absolutely nothing about, and feverishly pull the trigger until their life has rivered from the holes you just created—comes a second form of conditioning. Moral conditioning.

I have found the phrase *partitioning morality* to be an effective descriptor for what I experienced. It is the act of manufacturing a series of beliefs in such a way that, before and after violence, you are encouraged to feel a sense of moral righteousness. As if by killing this person you were doing him and the rest of the world some divine favor. We were taught to obsess over how to kill these people, not question *Why kill these people?*

People, unlike weapon systems designed by Lockheed Martin, Raytheon, and the rest of the military-industrial complex, have a substantial glitch: they often come with a conscience. Since not every act of political violence is legal or justifiable, soldiers must have aspects of their conscience compartmentalized or beaten out of them, so no matter how dubious the justification, they commit the supreme international crime of aggression not only willingly, but with relish, whenever the state orders it.

Ultimately, the academy's job is to deliver a product: high-quality junior officers, willing to wholeheartedly give their character and capabilities to the mission, *no matter the mission.* Cadets must be kept enthusiastic about their military career, especially before they have committed to a binding contract.

The academy generally doesn't teach those facts that would cause cadets to feel embarrassed by or skeptical of the state. Instead, I was trained to believe that I should be concerned only with things I could immediately influence: the conduct of myself and those around me. Soldiers are made to win wars, not think about them.[22] I was taught to think about *how to win my small part of the war*, not *whether we should be at war.* Being sure that the enemy is the enemy is an imperative of combat, so it's essential that no one thinks about this topic too much or too deeply. Leave that to the politicians, I was told. What requires your cognitive investment is your Area of Operations and whatever can be seen through your rifle scope. "Stay in your lane" is a popular Army aphorism.

Less than 20 percent of the faculty are civilians. The vast majority of instructors are Army officers, and a great proportion of these are West Point graduates. When the majority of instructors are informed by a remarkably similar set of life experiences, it results in much less variation of beliefs, which are more tightly held.

Cadets, who are trained to accept the word of superiors, act like stenographers, dutifully transcribing the gospel presented to them by the thirty-two-year-old military officer at the front of the classroom, ink still drying on his or her master's diploma.[23] These military instructors have done, in many cases, the exact same things that cadets are preparing to embark on; we might as well be taught by an older, more experienced version of ourselves. The West Point method of education can be codified as *ontological incest*: passed down from West Point senior leadership to instructors to cadets who, in time, move up the ladder, becoming West Point instructors themselves who cascade a near-identical view of the world, round and round, in perpetuity.

At West Point, I never met military instructors who strongly advanced antiwar views. Perhaps such renegade thoughts were not permitted, or perhaps we were trained well enough never to have them in the first place.

They taught us instead that, a few bad apples aside, throughout its history the United States has always been "the good guy," never the perpetrator. Some operations may have been "flawed," maybe "ill-conceived," but the U.S. military does not admit liability for immoral wars. U.S. war crimes and atrocities are denied, euphemistically recategorized, mitigated, or otherwise excused.

For example, America's use of chemical warfare in Vietnam—indiscriminately dumping Agent Orange across the civilian populace—has never collectively registered in the nation's consciousness as a war crime. Vietnam estimates that up to 3 million of its 84 million people have birth defects or other health problems related to dioxin.[24] At West Point, military historians might acknowledge it happened but find ample excuses to diminish its conclusion. Whatever happened in Vietnam probably wasn't great, but it wasn't morally reprehensible. Definitely not illegal.

America's greatest fear is that someone will do to us what our military already does to so many other countries. What matters to us is 9/11: *9/11 this, terrorism that.* We will do whatever it takes to provide an illusion of greater national security for our people, even if that means ignoring larger threats and waging a preventive war, devastating far more people somewhere else. A reprehensible crime that killed several thousand American people in New York overshadows America's wholesale devastation of entire countries—far larger atrocities, committed far more frequently—with little concern for the people on the receiving end of "freedom." Americans are worthy victims; *they* are *unworthy* victims. Americans are people; *they* are *unpeople*. "All men are created equal." Right.

Sure, Agent Orange killed essential livestock, poisoned water catchments and soil for generations, put toxic chemicals into the food chain, and caused grotesque health problems and birth defects—all part of a larger war of aggression that killed roughly two million Vietnamese noncombatant civilians— hundreds of 9/11s worth of civilian deaths.[25] We destroyed the social fabric of multiple countries, but ultimately none of that matters. Unworthy victims like the peasant population of Laos was pulverized by the United States, which now, thanks to us, holds the title of being the most heavily bombed nation in history.[26] Or like one U.S. commander once said of a village in Vietnam: "We had to destroy it in order to save it."[27]

Some cadets and faculty had the gall to excuse our use of Agent Orange on the basis that it "affected both sides."[28] Yes, true. Soldiers had incidental exposure . . . when they were deliberately and indiscriminately dumping poison all over huge swaths of a peasant country. It's not just misleading and morally short-sighted; it is willfully ignorant. But I was no historian and trusted the knowledge and believability of the culture above my own. At this time, I had few doubts and went with the flow. I didn't want to attract negative attention for thoughts that weren't fully formed.

Dangerously, the academy's culture of indifference toward the morality of past political violence entrenches a feeling of indifference toward the justifications for current and future wars. The institution prefers to cast a glow of romance and nostalgia around military action, even if that action is the product of decisions that were dreadfully wrong.[29] Men at war need to forge for themselves a special moral world in which, unlike in the civilian world, killing is a virtue, not something prohibited.

Although I couldn't articulate it at the time, I thought of morality and political violence as a matter of choice. A matter of free will. Soldiers who fought according to the guidelines—rules of engagement, Geneva Conventions, et cetera—were offering an "honorable sacrifice" independent and irrespective of the war in which they fought.

And if soldiers chose not to follow the rules of land warfare—a fractional minority—they should be held accountable for their "repugnant war crimes." My naive assumption: all U.S.-led violence automatically had a moral stamp of approval. I slept soundly knowing, no matter the war, it would be *the right thing to do*. After serving in Afghanistan, my views changed drastically.

Acknowledging that illegal and immoral wars exist and that America is not immune from perpetrating them, the prickly question becomes: Is it even possible to serve—and kill—honorably in a war in which "doing your duty" constitutes killing people with legitimate grievances; who are merely *defending themselves from you*; who see your presence as an "occupation"; and who, under other circumstances—had their country not been bombed, invaded, and occupied—would not be seeking to harm Americans (the same response we would have if someone invaded and occupied the national territory of the United States)?

My views evolved. Military service is not an absolute good, but only as good as the purpose for which it is being used. The morality of one's service is deeply intertwined and dependent on the nature of the war itself.

> *War is essentially an evil thing. Its consequences are not confined to the belligerent states alone, but affect the whole world. To initiate a war of aggression, therefore, is not only an international crime; it is the supreme international crime differing only from other war crimes in that it contains within itself the accumulated evil of the whole.*
>
> —*Nuremberg Trials, September 30, 1946*

Due to an overriding obligation to the state and a purely subordinate obligation to the truth, West Point is structurally incapable of adhering to its own values in practice.[30] In this conflict of interest, when facts collide with state objectives—making them decidedly annoying and inconvenient—the military prefers to mislead its people rather than publicly admit that the war they are being sent to die for is both morally dubious and completely unnecessary. In times of unjustifiable war, telling the truth is a treasonous act. Acknowledging all the emotive connotations that come with the word, one could still credibly call this practice "brainwashing."

Even today at West Point, it's still possible to believe that we are fighting in the interests of the Afghan people when, for eighteen years, a coalition of the most powerful armies on earth led by the United States—supposedly with the support of most Afghans—hasn't been able to get rid of a few thousand ragtag Taliban fighters. Why is it that, at the academy, the contradictoriness of such claims never leads to an inconvenient but possibly more reasonable explanation: that we've failed because enough of them oppose us; that we're part of the problem, not the solution? In his final address to the Afghan parliament in 2014, President Hamid Karzai suggested as much, claiming that the last twelve years of war had been "imposed" on Afghanistan.

The very act of misleading a generation of people, making them willing participants (and I include myself in this) in our nation's supreme international crime, should qualify as a tragedy. At West Point, convincing cadets of George W. Bush and Dick Cheney's widely discredited, false narrative is also a lie by West Point's own doctrinal definition of the word. The academy's honor code defines lying as "an untruth or . . . the telling of a partial truth and the vague or ambiguous use of information or language with the intent to deceive or mislead."[31] To fool young people into believing that wars of aggression are justifiable and necessary is indeed—to not mince words—a moral obscenity.

Could our military fill its ranks if angry farmers weren't "terrorists"? How much more would the military need to pay soldiers if they knew they would be "killing during an unauthorized invasion" rather than "killing in honorable warfare"? How would the military attract quality leaders if suffering in combat—and possibly experiencing a lifetime of depression afterward—would never equate to greater protection for Americans at home?

For the last eighteen years of war, the remedy seems to be a cocktail of comfortable fables and distorted truths—to overemphasize agreeable facts and marginalize disagreeable facts, always ensuring that cadets' beliefs stay within tolerance to fit the state's insatiable need for military adventurism.

The cosmic question is: "How come I didn't notice? How come doubts did not emerge?" I would maintain that much of the reason is psychological. People hate to endure pointless torment but will go to great lengths and endure much hardship if it's driven by meaning.

Unless you are radically open-minded, questioning tightly held beliefs is deeply uncomfortable. Especially questioning beliefs that underpin your decision to commit to one of the most extreme decisions out there: signing a binding contract to join a military at war. The suffering—the funerals, the divorces, the years spent in a sweaty vinyl and plywood tent—*it must have deeper meaning*. In a closed-minded, amygdala-type reaction, it's easy to withdraw. To dismiss. To feel irritable. It's easier to excuse our unjust wars or retrofit them with value than admit they have none.

To admit that our nation's decision to go to war was immoral, illegal, or unjustifiable—whatever you want to call it—is to acknowledge and accept that the cause you committed your life to was a small part in a large tragedy. This is a large psychological blow.

With considerable success, I repressed my doubts. If I had a coping mechanism, it was to trust the institution above myself. There must be good reasons, even if I can't fully see them.

A "YUK" STATE OF MIND

If you can't get them to salute when they should salute and wear the clothes you tell them to wear, how are you going to get them to die for their country?

—*George S. Patton*

Initially, the academy takes away your humanity, and sometimes your human dignity, but then they give it back to you sparingly, in smaller parcels, rebranding it a "privilege"—something they can take back again at a moment's notice. For such a prudish institution, there is an uncanny similarity to BDSM (bondage and discipline, dominance and submission, sadism and masochism): you stand erect, restrained in a rigid position of obsequious fealty, speak when spoken to, and if you work to earn it—*if you work really hard*—they might release you on a "pass" to see the world briefly (although restrictions apply).

Some of our new "privileges" included the ability to speak with one another outside our barracks rooms, to stroll rather than racewalk, and we no longer needed to spout off greetings to every upperclassman like talking parrots coked to the eyeballs. The most welcome "privilege" was to "look around." For the entire first year you had to keep "head and eyes straight ahead" as if wearing an invisible neck brace.

The prophecy had not come true. No snarling Ducati motorcycle, sculpted physique, or beautiful women at Fourth of July parties. Alas, there was much to be desired. But I found my footing and was headed in the right direction. The worst of the mindlessness seemed behind me; however small, there was advancement in rank; and we were getting a taste of basic human freedoms.

With all this "freedom," upperclassmen, usually Yuks, make unwelcome observations about the world they inhabit. Observations that the lowest rung—Plebes—would never dare. For sharing observations that are products of logical dissonance, Yuks are known as the "cynics."

I found a clear distinction. "Cynics" are aware of their surroundings and acknowledge when they are subordinating themselves for an unworthy purpose. "Leaders" subordinate themselves willingly and without question to the interests of the institution.

You can get an aspiring group of people to do almost anything if you first affix the lofty word *leadership* to the cause, which contributes a sudden and inflated sense of worth and authority to whatever it is you are being told to do.

We started to question the guiding principles—in little bits at first, then all at once.

It made me wonder: If we are a product of our practice, what, then, does the daily allocation of time in the military say about the organization's priorities? And with so many priorities, could we claim to have any priorities at all? If some of these Sisyphean, entropy-fighting activities were removed, a gift of a couple hours would magically reappear. Perhaps it could be reinvested in more compelling development opportunities elsewhere? By a quick back-of-the-envelope calc, two hours per day of military pomp equated to an extra sixty-two forty-hour workweeks—more than a full year—over the course of our four-year stint at the academy. In short: to upkeep your prescribed identity as a cadet or serviceman requires a tremendous amount of busywork and emotional energy.

Raising questions or identifying better ways of doing things did not come with an invitation. A careful review of what we were doing—merely asking "Why?" and "Prove it"—basic scientific, evidence-based questions—was the sign of a *bad attitude*, not *good strategic thinking*. The notion of an "idea meritocracy,"[32] in which the best idea won the day, did not exist. By and large, time in grade, not insight, drove decisions. Even though we were becoming "leaders"—a word in such wide circulation that it has lost all meaning—we had very little agency. The result: a deep feeling of impotence and disillusionment. I feared becoming a rigid caretaker, protocol automaton, process checklist weenie, or status quo enforcer.

By the time another year passed—when I was a Cow—I felt like I was starting to master my new self.

At nineteen years old, I had tried out for, trained for, and successfully passed Special Forces Assessment and Selection (SFAS), the crucible used to select future Green Berets, who are known by the sobriquet "snake eaters." It was comforting to know that, despite having finished only two years at the academy, I was outperforming commissioned infantry officers who had already led units in direct combat, had five or six more years in uniform, and were specially picked to attend this course. As draconian as the West Point system was, it did its job. Although my own military record was hardly illustrious, this was a transformational milestone in my life. With newfound self-esteem and smugness, I thought, *Maybe I was born for this.* But the truth is, the underlying DNA of most cadets—grittiness, desire to serve a higher purpose, and hunger for excellence—could be applied almost anywhere else with favorable results; I was not born for the military; I was heavily configured for it.

Despite the abject seriousness of our profession, we were still immature kids. Child soldiers. We were hunting for our fugitive youth. I was too young to know what I was doing, what I was actually training for, but old enough to know that I was missing out on the basics. Missing out on "thrillz," romance, and chasing dreams too idealistic to hold a place in reality.

Many of us—my roommate and I included—fantasized about quitting.

Roughly one in five of the people who showed up on R-Day didn't make it to graduation. Those who chose to leave the academy of their own accord[33]—the "quitters"—were quickly cast away. I never maintained friendships with quitters. They'd go off and attend "normal college"—a phrase that was packed with as much envy and disdain as possible. Allowing friendships to shrivel on the vine may have been a subconscious defense mechanism; it saved me from reassessing my own decision to stay. Not an unreasonable hypothesis, given that almost all service academies—West Point, Annapolis, and the Coast Guard Academy—rank in the top dozen of the *Princeton Review* for the "Least Happy Students" superlative.[34]

Knowing what I know now, I would want to tell cadets that places exist where you will be accepted for who you are, and finding a place that cares about your interests and thoughts isn't "weakness," a "crutch," or a "handout." I want them to know that you can become a "leader of character" without serving in the military—that the military does not have a monopoly or special trademark on "leadership." And despite the Army's inexhaustible usage of the word, not all make for good leaders. Although society might be willing to accept the false causation that *military* is code for *great leadership skills*—military leaders are not by default "better" than civilian leaders.

Andrew, my swarthy, six-foot-four-inch Floridian roommate with an uncanny four-season tan, had reached his breaking point. With his signature deadpan delivery, he looked to me and said it:

"Fuck it. I'm quitting."

"*Hah*, if you will, I will."

"I'm serious. I hate this fucking place."[35]

"You know the University of Florida is calling your name."

Andrew, a University of Florida fan, was anchored to the illusion that Gainesville was some swampy Shangri-La-la land. UF was always trying to seduce him away. The longer we were inside the walls, the more enticing the outside became.

When it came to quitting, we were always longing, never daring. Despite our protestations, both of us stayed. At the time of publication of this book, Andrew is still serving.

Meanwhile, I remained a frustrated virgin, my proverbial bedpost notchless. I didn't know love. I knew fierce competition and aggression. Boxing. Combatives. *Birthday parties.* Shooting. And not knowing intimacy or love made me feel more irksome still. I wanted to know what it would be like to press the palm of my hand against another, tangle our fingers in communion—as if a lover's prayer—and be warm together as one, wrapped in fresh cotton, asleep in each other's arms. Our repeatedly suppressed human desires felt unbearable.

The military made all male-female interactions awkward, especially in the barracks. The academy infantilizes cadets, fostering separatism between the sexes. Male and female cadets cannot occupy the same room alone unless the door is open at 90 degrees.

Male and female cadets are not permitted to share the same "horizontal surface"—sofa, bed, desk, et cetera. Even the term *horizontal surface* sounds clinical and icky. These restrictions, along with many others, served to isolate and alienate the sexes, creating emotional, social, and physical distance.

Instead, I received intimate instructions on how to kill people. "It's better to aim short than long," I was told. "Walk the rounds into their face. This way you have a chance of hitting them off the ricochet, and from the enemy's perspective the sight of bullets impacting toward you is far more disrupting—so they can't shoot you—than if the bullets went over their heads." Or how to sneak up behind a sentry and slit his throat with a knife, followed by putting him down on the ground in such a way that you knock the wind out of him so he can't scream to alert others.

"I'll print the application checklist."

"I'd rather gargle broken glass than be here."

"I'll one up you. I'd drop a kettle bell on my nutsack to join a Cornell frat."

> *West Point is a "free" $250,000 education . . . shoved up your ass one nickel at a time.*
>
> —*Cadet maxim*

No matter how much cadets may have wanted to leave, we had been hard-wired never to quit. Neither of us could follow through. We were marionettes. We couldn't surmount the belief that "quitting"—euphemistically "choosing a new life path"—would be the greatest shame of our lives. The point: once you start down the path, throwing it in reverse felt like suicide.[36]

My memories capture the banality of our social lives. Entertainment was a car full of cadets heading down Highway 293 toward Woodbury Commons—an outlet mall—in Central Valley, New York, to eat at Applebee's. The highlight of a long week.

It felt so good: windows down, stars out, cold wind flicking our seat belts, the headlights mining a tunnel through the night. The Killers' *Hot Fuss* was blasting on the speakers. Tone-deaf, we belted out "Mr. Brightside":

> *I'm coming out of my cage*
> *And I've been doing just fine*
> *Gotta gotta be down*
> *Because I want it all*

The lyrics, the emotions—it made sense to us. An anthem for the jilted. The Killers had written lyrics that were symbolic of the cadet condition. When it came to professional ambitions, our plans diverged; but when it came to stories of attraction, lust, and love, the plot was mostly the same: thrills, then disappointment, frustration, and loneliness.[37] By association, living at the academy was a vow of near celibacy. A romantic desert. We had to cope. Brasso and shoe polish had to substitute for human intimacy. The academy took a particularly dim view of affection. "Ca-dating" was precarious. Two cadets holding hands in secret felt like a brazen affair. No one kissed each other goodbye—at least, not in the open. And despite the obvious internal supply-and-demand issues generated by an 85/15 male-female split, love rarely got past the gate guards. West Point has a famed "Two-Percent Club"—allegedly only 2 percent of relationships predating admission survive four years of academy life. The whole thing is just savage on the libido. For most cadets, dating stories look like this:

There once was that rare time at a "normal college" when I met this girl I liked. We kissed. There was a connection.

But with too few opportunities, too much desire and expectation were unfairly lumped on one night. After a few texts and phone calls, the distance, the restricted visitation, would cause her, this great shining hope, to move on—with somebody else. The photographic evidence on social media made you feel sick, as if you'd gone to a convenience store cash register, reached in the till, grabbed a handful of loose change, and swallowed it. Tethered to West Point, *what could have been* felt like it would never be.

None of this dampened our enthusiasm. For we. Were alone. Together. We finished the verse, a five-beer serenade.[38] A shoulder-slapping pep talk, Novocain smiles, a couple margaritas, and a chain-restaurant chicken fried steak later, and you'd be back on the rails in no time. We had all been there. Sometimes the small freedom—a movie, a visit to "normal college," a day trip to New York City—was worst of all, for it cast true freedom into painful relief.

I started getting trickle truths of the world I was entering year on year, as my older cadet friends graduated and shipped off to various Army bases around the United States. I started getting calls that implied that the sexual tourniquet does not loosen much after getting to the "real" Army. Relationship opportunities and options remain severely limited in these "target-poor environments."

Upon graduation, you go from one sexually repressive environment to another: various military towns, most of which are not known for being well cultured, diverse, or aspirational places to find love. No one says, "I'm going to Fort Polk, Louisiana, for the dating scene." Take your pick: Fort Bragg, Benning, Drum, Hood, and others; they are all sprawling, post-apocalyptic, one-star towns where dreams have died long ago, and fast-food restaurants, payday loan shops, tattoo parlors, budget strip clubs, and boarded-up watering holes are the carrion vultures that feed on the entrails of hope.

Men not yet forty years old palliate themselves on liquor and Bud Light in sticky-floored bars where advertisements for bail bonds hang above the fermenting, piss-drenched urinals. Cigarette butts are stamped out in ashtrays, their nubs jutting in all directions like tombstones in a post-earthquake graveyard. Big trucks with pendulous metal "truck nuts" (a set of metal testicles hanging beneath the rear bumper), dirty babies, overdue bills, restraining orders, glow-in-the-dark tongue piercings, and half-filled "spitters" from Copenhagen chewing tobacco supply the imagery; for many military towns, the struggle and lack of opportunities is palpable.

You can't say that military towns are entirely uncultured, because that creates its own problematic assertions, such as "What is culture?" and "Who gets to determine what is good and what is bad?"—fine points for a sophomore-year liberal arts paper. The point is that whatever ones thinks about chrome rims; fried pickles; mega-churches and highway billboards with pictures of zombies condemning you to hell if you don't repent; public schools that rival Cambodia's; guns; shrimp po'boys; and progress-resistant strains of racism, this will be your destiny. And there is little you can do aside from using your freedom not to take a job that contractually owns you.

Given the low exposure to high-quality partners, many people in the Army (including West Point alumni) commit themselves, often prematurely, to yet another long-lasting, high-stakes commitment—marriage—without truly knowing or having the means to know what is out there for them in an open market of their peers had they decided to choose a less repressive lifestyle. It's subjective optimization, pure and simple: whatever you have seems better than that which you can no longer obtain.[39]

Sure, I wanted more and different, but in these moments, singing along in the car with friends, I was happy—or sheltered enough to not know the true meaning of the word. In retrospect, I should have cherished the simple things more, because things could be—and would be—worse once we got to our ultimate destination: war. And between seventeen and twenty-one, when I graduated, it was sometimes too hard to focus on actual death; weekend passes and broken hearts felt like life-and-death already. Sometimes the twenty-one-year-old part of us had the power to overtake the Army part of us. No institution, not even West Point, could fully tame youth.

Beyond my abhorrence for the repressive lifestyle, I started to question the mission: what I would ultimately serve upon graduation. Little calmed my anxiety about the type of war we were perpetrating, especially after reading about Abu Ghraib, Guantánamo Bay, and a host of other atrocities in the *New York Times*, delivered every morning to our door by the Plebes. Was I going to be joining a "good" war? It certainly didn't feel as clean or as principled as West Point was trying to make us believe.

Training for war, especially *this* war, seemed like a costly exchange. Was it a good deal in a utilitarian sense to bypass my youth—late teens until late twenties, minimum—to have the privilege of going headlong into the Iraq and Afghanistan meat grinder? My answer to this oscillated from "Absolutely yes" to "Definitely not"—and everything between. This internal discord roiled just beneath the surface.

> *Education ought to foster the wish for truth, not the conviction that some particular creed is the truth. But it is creeds that hold men together in fighting organizations: Churches, States, political parties. It is intensity of belief in a creed that produces efficiency in fighting: victory comes to those who feel the strongest certainty about matters on which doubt is the only rational attitude.*
>
> —*Bertrand Russell,* Why Men Fight: A Method of Abolishing the International Duel *(1917)*

In some ways, we relished our own pigheadedness. We were willing to give up personal comfort for an abstract cause. We were willing to resist temptation with monk-like devotion. The private sector may evaluate a colleague by the

"airport test": Can you tolerate him or her for a few hours during a long layover? At West Point, we evaluated our peers by the more venerable "foxhole test": Would you go to war with this person in an austere environment when hostile forces are actively trying to kill you?

Passing the foxhole test required a certain—and, in our humble opinion, superior—temperament. You needed to find happiness in misery; "play well with others"; grow closer as things got worse; be good on your word; have a cool head; continuously strive to beat your average; share when others were in need; and carry more when others were hurting. In short, it felt like a higher standard was required to earn friendship and trust here. I was proud of that. And being surrounded by such people, whether such sacrifices were needed or not, was a compelling reason to stay.

And after being around people who had been trained to have a high tolerance for misery and self-flagellation, it seemed intolerable to be around anyone who didn't.

NATIONALISM'S PHONY SYMPHONY

The most curious thing about our four defeats in Fourth Generation War—Lebanon, Somalia, Iraq, and Afghanistan—is the utter silence in the American officer corps. Defeat in Vietnam bred a generation of military reformers . . . Today, the landscape is barren. Not a military voice is heard calling for thoughtful, substantive change. Just more money, please.

—*William S. Lind,* American Conservative

As we came closer—closer to the end of the runway, closer to leaving the hermetically sealed cadet bubble—the future felt increasingly foreboding. My older friends, recent academy graduates, had proceeded farther down the Army's conveyor belt. Some had been thrust into war; the rest followed close order behind them.

Unvarnished stories trickled into our consciousness. Emails and phone calls offered sobering accounts of training and deployment. These stories subverted the romantic hype ascribed to the "profession of arms."

Accounts revealed a grimy reality not spoken of in newspapers. Some of my buddies faced serious kinetic combat: RPGs, outposts overrun by break-of-dawn Taliban raids, raking machine-gun fire, IEDs, mortars, "S-vests" (suicide vests), and recoilless rifles. But most described deployment in themes less august: criminal wastage of American treasure on stupid projects; a string of snafus that got soldiers killed; ham-handed foreign policy; bungling, solipsistic field-grade officers; corrupt local contractors; extremely corrupt local police; and insufferable local nationals who couldn't get out of their own way, literally, if their lives depended on it.

Bloody boot prints, amputated limbs, gunshot wounds, grotesque infections, ribbons of raw flesh, and mutilated internal organs were coming for us, the graduating class. The only question was who. Who was going to lose in war's game of musical chairs? Who was going to be caught out, dying for a war that, according to Andrew J. Bacevich, West Point graduate, historian, and author of *America's War for the Greater Middle East*, had "no plan"? This messaging was consistently applied to Iraq also: "In June 2004, when General George C. Casey, Jr., arrived in Baghdad . . . he made an astonishing discovery: There was no plan . . . What was the ultimate objective? What interim steps would move coalition forces toward that objective? No document providing answers to these questions existed."[40]

Despite rumblings of the war going off the rails in the Middle East, I stayed in my lane with ever greater devotion. As an upperclassman responsible for *shaping* and *inculcating* Plebes to be future officers capable of leading soldiers in combat—a case of the blind leading the blind—I began mimicking the same "leadership" style that I had been exposed to. I acted like a dick.

With time, I, too, became the upperclassman I used to hate so much. I threw condiments. I learned to yell, to have unhinged, adult temper tantrums. I learned how to pound my tightened fist on the dining hall table like a gavel, shaking the silverware. I mocked kids for being physically and emotionally weak. I singled them out. I tormented them. I didn't care if I made them cry. I enjoyed exposing their weakness for all to see. And even on the other side of torment, it did not make either of us better people; it probably made us worse. I didn't even have to fake my outrage at Plebes failing to "pop off" and greet me as I walked to class: West Point conditioned my blood to boil.

Despite being completely incompetent when it came to death or wounds from combat, it did not stop me from chastising younger cadets at haircut inspection, in the mess hall, on the street, with the tired proclamation: "You just killed your whole platoon."

The United States Corps of Cadets (USCC) marches, four thousand strong, into the mess hall every day for lunch. A minute passes as everyone gets settled at their assigned tables. A Firstie approaches the "poop deck"—a balcony located in the central stone colonnade. I could never see the actual person—the man behind the curtain, like the Wizard of Oz; I could only hear the announcements. "Attention to orders!" says a stentorian male voice. In unison, the corps moves to an apathetic position of attention.

The disembodied voice often made banal announcements about sports, uniforms, mandatory briefings. "Congratulate Army Rugby for beating Navy yesterday afternoon." Cheers. A drumroll of fists on tables, tinkling the silverware.

But with increasing regularity lunch announcements became more somber.

More and more, we had a moment of silence for members of "the Long Gray Line" who lost their lives in the War on Terror. In 2006, at the beginning of my Firstie year, we lost our former cadet brigade sergeant major. She had been a star performer and was killed by an IED in Iraq. She was twenty-three. And she was cut down not much more than a year after graduation. There was no information about how she had died, only that she died.

Although I didn't personally know her, I knew *of* her. She was a *someone*—a real person—someone I saw, who I knew existed. She was more than a number, a name, a rank, or a percentage. And now she was dead. Now she was in the ground. The future felt both menacing and inevitable.

After a respectful twenty-second silence in the mess hall, the disembodied voice ordered us to "take seats." It was done with none of the regular pomp and vigor. More mournful. The usual mess hall din was tempered to reverent whispers. For a minute. But ultimately the show must go on. It always does. We ate our "chicken crispitos"—faux Mexican deep-fried chicken cigars—and "congo bars"—quasi-cookie cakes—before returning to engineering lectures. Preparation for war doesn't stop just because people, sometimes friends, die. The American war machine must keep turning down the dirt road to nowhere.

I was not the only one who seemed sucker-punched by the War on Terror. One article from the *Chicago Tribune* captured the emotions of the cadets who knew "the fallen":

> *"The fact that she's died—it makes what's going on in the Middle [East] . . . so much more real. I mean, here at West Point, it's kind of like Camelot, you know—everything just seems to work," Sylvia Amegashie, 21, of Woodbridge, Va., co-captain of West Point's track team, said as she stood on the cemetery grass, holding back tears. "What happened to her, being out there in Iraq, it's real. Her death really makes everything seem more like it's going to happen."[41]*

Not to be deterred from committing our lives to a war we hardly knew, the academy did a remarkably good job of keeping us at arm's length from the suffering aspect of war, which is to say they actively hid from us the open-casket truth.

Serving in direct combat requires one to confront death. West Point, but also the military at large, dealt with death, especially death of fellow U.S. soldiers, like training a mortuary affairs specialist without ever letting him or her see a dead body. Uncensored photos of U.S. soldiers in pieces are not displayed. Nor are videos of a U.S. soldier drowning in his own blood from a sucking chest wound; nor do they show documentaries of a twenty-two-year-old medic hacking into his buddy's throat to do a backwoods tracheotomy—the first time he performed the procedure.

Is it disrespectful to show the gruesome truth of what happens to our countrymen when they're sent to war? I don't know. On the other hand, is it wildly irresponsible to not show recruits and servicemen the truth about what they are signing up for, providing at least a hint of informed consent?

We had near-zero exposure to those who suffered the heaviest costs of war. We had no concept of how they coped. We never saw depleted veterans returning home, ejected into society like empty shell casings.[42] We never saw coffee tables topped with half-empty pill bottles adjacent to half-empty liquor bottles. Nor did we bear witness to a tearful night when a devastated veteran wraps his shaky hand around a loaded Springfield XD 9mm pistol. We certainly didn't speak to Iraqis or Afghans maimed by U.S. forces. Never did we hear from internally displaced people driven from their homes. We gave them, "the unpeople," no audience or voice. Ever. Without gratuitous realism, how would we know what we were in for? Or know what we would unwittingly do to others, perhaps by accident? In short, we never experienced how victims of war felt.

*   *   *

Although business-as-usual tasks demanded hyper-vigilance, I felt it was important to take the war's pulse regularly, if only for ten minutes per day. Each morning I glanced at the newspaper.

News about America's wars, especially in the mid-2000s, was like an industrial-scale shit-to-fan conveyor belt. I was particularly transfixed by pictures and articles on Abu Ghraib. The most jarring photos were often just south of the masthead. The infamous mock execution, crucifixion-pose, "bag over head" guy stood upon an MRE box, wires dangling from his hands. Other photos showed U.S. soldiers clearly getting off on America's systematic use of torture. But, seeing this, I barely felt anything. I was morally numb. All was clear so long as my eyes were shut, imagining a better truth. We were trained this way.

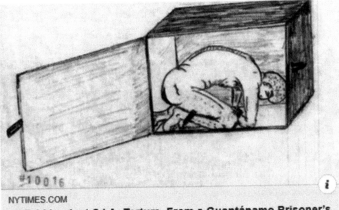

NYTIMES.COM
A Vivid Look at C.I.A. Torture, From a Guantánamo Prisoner's Sketches

You are brutalizing them in chains, O cruel one,
That's why the poor are sighing in their chains.

You built the hateful prison in Cuba,
Giving electric shocks to the detainees in chains there.
If you brutalize them today in chains, the turn for us,
the poor, will come too;
You will remember this in chains later on . . .

—Maftoun, *"Letter in Chains," in* Poetry of the Taliban

War is like one of those gestalt images. Famously, there is the duck-rabbit where depending on how you look at the image, you see either a duck or a rabbit. If you look at it one way, you see one image; if you are able to look at the other side, you see a different image. When it came to war, I was trained to see only the rightness of the War on Terror, and ignore how it tessellated with an overwhelming and inverse wrongness.

At the time, Abu Ghraib was, in my mind, an unfortunate little mishap: a few soldiers doing the wrong thing. They got carried away and abused their (uniquely American) privileges (to bomb, invade, detain, and torture people with little evidence, contemptuously disavowing international law). That's not good. Punish them. Ensure we don't do it again. And let's move on. We shouldn't make a big deal of this lest it distract from the main effort.

We talked about these unforced errors—in class, in barracks rooms, and in little parable-ish case studies affectionately called "vignettes." By and large the moral of the story was tamped down—bad, but no matter how frequent or brazen, these acts were never seen as representative of the war, or representative of Army values, or representative of the American soldier—*Time* magazine's 2003 person of the year. They were discrete, disconnected events that we assumed provided no rationale or footing for the invaded to hold grievances against us, the invaders.

Any *Whoopsies!* war crimes were excused as part of the "No True Scotsman" Fallacy—no true American soldier would act this way, therefore soldiers responsible for heinous acts aren't true American soldiers; they are excluded from the collective group, redrawing the boundary lines so that the military apparatus remains forever untarnished, no matter what it does.

I, too, had a gut reaction to defend the institution—the institution I belonged to. In a way, I was defending myself. "Sure, mistakes were made," using the passive voice to avoid all personal accountability, "but that's war."

My family didn't put much credence in disparaging reports either. To them it was sensationalist, un-American, liberal tripe. And although Pa read the *Boston Globe* every morning (not known to be wildly right wing), he said the flagship newspapers—the *New York Times*, the *Washington Post*, et cetera—were "left of *Pravda*," a Russian communist newspaper left over from the Soviet era whose name translates to "truth." Likewise, CNN was the "Clinton News Network." Even the *Economist*, which gave its endorsement to George W. Bush in 2000 and switched to John Kerry in 2004, was accused of being lefty whenever it published something disparaging about America's wars. Other members of my family were not only skeptical of certain news outlets, they were contemptuous of irrefutable facts. Academic research and investigative reporting—if it didn't align—couldn't be trusted. Anything that was critical of America was un-American, and anything that was un-American couldn't be true because it did not fit the image we had crafted for ourselves. Inconvenient truths equated to hating the troops, hating America. I never understood why.

We swallow greedily any lie that flatters us, but we sip only little by little at a truth we find bitter.

—Denis Diderot

By and large, I was happy to be a Firstie. We were on top of the pecking order and we were nearly done with our four-year internment at Castle Gray Skull. As we reached the pinnacle, praise was heaped upon us. We were told over and over again that we were ready to fight and win America's wars. I was twenty-one.

The first time I put on my West Point class ring, I felt like I had "made it." Gold, granite, and two emerald specks—my little ring of power. A symbol of grit and character for the warrior-scholar, I thought. It was the same type of ring I had seen years before, when I was applying. I had made it. I was part of "the Long Gray Line."

In the aftermath of graduation, my classmates started getting married. Most got hitched young, several by the age of twenty-four. In many cases it represented their first adult relationship. Everyone seemed so eager to trade in the youth they didn't have for rumpus rooms and baby strollers. We were neither too young nor too old to waste any time.

Weddings and funerals would take on special significance. Like bookends, the group would reunite for one wedding and shortly thereafter someone from the wedding party would be killed in combat, and we'd all reunite again—this time at the funeral.

Early on at weddings, we, the freshly minted officers, had shamefully naked uniforms. No bling. No accoutrements. Meanwhile, our older friends looked more weathered, more like real officers. Airborne wings. Ranger Tab. Combat Infantryman Badge. Unit commendation medals. Combat patch. Colored cords on the shoulder. All sorts of flair. Going to a military wedding felt like being thirteen years old and walking into a Gold's Gym. Just trying to put on my big-boy pants. In hardly any other vocation do people wear their CVs on their torsos and receive respect based on the stories the little bits of cloth and metal tell.

At one of these weddings, I met up with Sam, my former rowing teammate. His uniform looked baggy. His eyes were lugging purple baggage. However, he had made it. He proudly wore the half-moon, black-and-gold Ranger Tab.

Over loose-pour, open-bar rum and Cokes, Sam laid out the tea leaves for what my future was going to hold. It sounded grim. The U.S. Army describes Ranger School as "one of the toughest training courses for which a Soldier can volunteer . . . For more than two months, Ranger students train to exhaustion, pushing the limits of their minds and bodies . . . The Rangers' primary mission is to engage in close combat and direct-fire battles."[43] To strip away the niceties, Ranger School trains you to endure more than your enemy so you can stumble through swamps, set up an ambush line, and shoot motherfuckers in the face, at night, in a rainstorm—like a boss.

Ranger School is spoken of in tones of hushed respect for those who haven't been; dread for those who have yet to go; hatred for those stuck in the middle of it; and chest-beating pride for those who've finished. Sam was a different man now. People would treat him with respect.

At that moment, I was eager to be in Sam's position—to fast-forward through the drudgery of yet another rubber-stamping exercise. Fort Benning promised incompetence and lots of standing around; Ranger School promised shivering, hunger, and chronic sleep deprivation. And finishing it all, Sam had emerged from a five-year funnel of training.

Though visibly exhausted, Sam still looked eager and determined, spurred on by a series of "firsts." He was going to his first unit, to lead his first platoon, during his first deployment. The thought of leading soldiers in political violence trumped all concerns about what that meant. We were "dying to fight," even if that literally meant dying.

In addition to the cheer and love and celebration that normally accompanies ordinary weddings, military weddings sometime seem plagued by a foreboding, ephemeral unease. We were all going to war—it was inevitable—but for some of us we didn't know where, or when we would be *getting our fight on.*

I stabbed at the ice cubes in my drink with a cocktail stirrer as I received wisdom from other, older officers. Captains and majors who, also several drinks in, were happy to share war stories and advice, knowing the well-trodden path we were about to embark on. I listened to them intently, swirled my drink, downed it, and ordered more, hoping that I looked more like them—the real officers—than the twenty-one-year-old kid that I was. With half a dozen or more cocktails, the room spun with the same intensity as if it, too, had been stirred with a cocktail straw. The black bow ties came undone; the "Blues" jackets were tossed over the backs of chairs (unthinkable just one day earlier).

And when all of the dignified, serious officers were sufficiently wasted, the herd of in-shape, almost exclusively white dudes, sporting cookie-cutter haircuts, moved to the dance floor. And there we "danced," Bambi-like, with all the grace of newborn calves. We would grind and thrust and bro-out, American-style, in a way that betrayed the fact that none of us knew what to do with a body that was suddenly asked to express itself freely.

The songs by Journey had been played, and then came "Closing Time" by Semisonic, and just like that, the wedding reception was over. We were asked to leave.

Military guys embrace heartily—more so than most civilians I know. We're all huggers. With unironic seriousness, we wished each other safe travels—and meant it.

My last year of training before deployment was everything Sam said it would be. Officer training at Fort Benning was a "goat rope"—disorganized, wasteful, and uninspiring. Later, during deployment, I would reflect back on how hollow, how un-nutritious this training was—how little those courses actually prepared me for combat. For every day of poor or nonexistent training, the Army was, in effect, gambling with our lives, the lives of our soldiers, and the lives of the Afghan civilians who would inevitably endure the brunt of our decisions.

I wished that we were given much greater depth in practical stuff like how to recognize an IED, or how to use the mine-resistant vehicles that we would eventually be given in combat. Learning about those things would have saved lives. Instead, we pulled staff duty shifts, stood around, and because the captain running the office told us that we needed "to earn our pay," we spent an afternoon picking up paint chips, flake by flake, and putting them into plastic pails because no other worthy training had been arranged.

Ranger School was a different matter. It was two months of starvation, sleep deprivation, and complete physical exhaustion that took me to the brink of my physical and mental limits. Combatives included a Ranger instructor who placed a Taser between two Ranger students and offered simple instructions: "First one to electrocute the other wins." Then there was the dreaded "walk until daylight," during which we would walk the unimproved trails until four-something a.m. Artillery simulators exploding in our patrol base disrupted sleep night after night, causing us to hallucinate. Even the fittest amongst us were reduced to gasping, whimpering invalids.

Ranger School taught me that I could endure misery and persevere. I would need this, and more, to be ready for Afghanistan.

By the time I made it to Ranger School graduation, I was a shadow of my former self. My stepsister, Andrea, and her husband, Dave, newly wed, travelled more than 1,000 miles to pin my Ranger Tab and witness me eat myself into oblivion.

I was, and remain to this day, close with my new family, blurring the distinction between two inconsistent truths: that objectively, we are not related by blood—that she is, my "stepsister"—but that we also share a brother-sister closeness indistinguishable from those who grew up together.

I had missed their wedding. The Ranger instructors didn't even permit me five minutes to call Andrea on her wedding day. I felt awful about it, but no one in the family held it over my head. Needs of the Army always outranked needs of the family, it seemed.

A couple months later—after Airborne school and out-processing—I was at Fort Carson, in Colorado Springs, where I joined my first unit.

They were licking their wounds from having had a really rough deployment to Ramadi, Iraq. From the time I arrived, I immediately started getting a sense of the severity of the psychological toll that had been inflicted on them.

One night, while serving as the staff duty officer, overwatching the barracks, I got a call. Private First Class Timothy Ryan Alderman had slit his wrists with a razor blade.

His mutilated arms looked like a map of bloody grid squares. Lines going both vertically and horizontally, six inches up his wrist. He had not cut himself deep enough to end his life. When the military medics arrived, they expressed what I could only describe as mild irritation for getting the call. "Come on, why would you play tic-tac-toe on your wrists with a razor?" The medics seemed like they had dealt with this sort of thing before.

Afterward, the Army briefly put the troubled soldier in an inpatient mental health ward. Private Alderman was given meds that made him seem "dangerously stoned."[44] Eventually he was sent back to the unit. Missing from formation one morning, he was found dead in his barracks room. He had overdosed on a massive concoction of prescription drugs the Army gave him, plus a couple of his own. Before his death, and according to Alderman's friend, "the first sergeant 'blew [Alderman] off' and said, 'Everybody sees what you saw' in Iraq. At one point, alleged the friend, another sergeant told Alderman, 'I wish you would just go ahead and kill yourself. It would save us a lot of paperwork.'"[45] It was apparent that soon I would be going to war with soldiers suffering from severe psychological and emotional traumas.[46]

Meanwhile, I tried to keep in touch with Sam and learned that my unit would be relieving his unit—in the same remote part of Kandahar, Afghanistan. We were literally going to be able to high-five each other as I went in and he went out. I looked forward to that moment.

But after Sam deployed, news came less frequently. The next information that I got about Sam—and only a couple months into his tour—wasn't from him but rather came in a phone call from his mother.

As I normally did, I woke up at 5:00 a.m. and turned off my alarm. But this time I saw a voice mail notification. It was from Sam's mom.

Without providing much detail, she sounded distraught. "Sam was wounded yesterday," she said. "He is coming back to the United States for treatment. Sam had a list of friends for me to call in case he was injured—you were on it. Sam needs our prayers. Thank you and God bless."

I packed my bags and the following weekend I flew out to visit him in the hospital.

WATCHING SAM BURN

There is no glory in war—only good men dying terrible deaths.

—*Lieutenant Larry Gwin, quoted in Lieutenant General Harold G. Moore and Joseph L. Galloway,* We Are Soldiers Still: A Journey Back to the Battlefields of Vietnam

You can never prepare yourself for visiting a friend in the intensive care burn unit. Seeing a burn victim writhe in invisible, inextinguishable flames felt vile, dirty, almost voyeuristic. And as for the stench of burnt but still living human flesh—my vocabulary fails me. But this wasn't just *someone* to me; this was the odor of *my friend's burnt flesh*. He was so exposed and suffering so completely.

Sam, the man lying in bed, was an old friend from the West Point crew team; but now his lithe, six-foot-four-inch frame was mummified in gauze; only the necessary portions of his body were exposed, making room for intravenous tubes. He was nearly unrecognizable. His defining facial features had been melted away like a green plastic Army man dropped into a crackling, cast-iron skillet. Parts of his flesh were raw and marbled, as if a psychopath had flayed him with a cheese slicer and then worked him over with a blowtorch. His ears and nose were charred black, and a stiff breeze would've made them crumble to dust like burnt toast. His lips were split, oozing a putrid brownish wax. He was covered in greasy ointment. Although his hands were bandaged like oven mitts, I noticed a missing finger. His resting heart rate was in the 130s—a constant jog just to survive. Sam was a living revenant.

Sam's mother tenderly rubbed his feet and ankles—one of the few parts that weren't burned. She cooed to him reassuringly. What else could a mother do? I couldn't imagine what she was feeling, looking at her son—the one she had raised from birth—charred alive, in a hospital bed beside her. She seemed unexpectedly resilient.

Foolishly, I had packed up my Xbox 360 and games, hoping they'd provide Sam with a bit of entertainment and distraction during what I assumed would be a dull recovery process. In my mind he'd be on a sofa somewhere, sipping milkshakes and being chastised for pushing the limits of his rehab, complaining that his run times were slipping. I felt like an idiot when it dawned on me that I had brought a video game console for a man who had fingers literally burnt off and lacked the strength to speak. Seeing Sam in that bed, I felt like I had not lived a day in my life.

Only when I got to the hospital did I collect pieces of the story. Sam's vehicle hit an antitank mine. The explosion killed his soldier sitting in the back seat instantly, and it was powerful enough to ignite the fuel tank, engulfing Sam in a ball of fire inside the vehicle. Once Sam got the door open, he rolled on the ground, grabbing fistfuls of dirt to extinguish his flaming face. "I've got you," said one of his men, rushing over to help his burning lieutenant. Sam blacked out and was placed in a medically induced coma. And here he was, one week later, on the other side of the world, in incomprehensible pain, teetering on the verge of life and death. It had happened so quickly.

It was impossible not to connect the dots: in a few months I would be in his boots. My infantry battalion was preparing to relieve his exact unit. I would literally be driving the same roads and walking the same dirt paths as Sam when he was injured. Seeing Sam was a foreshadowing, a premonition of what death in this war could be. With deployment comes death, maybe worse.

Sam made a noise. A couple garbled words. I looked to his mother. She gave me the universal facial expression for "I don't know." I held my ear closer, inches from his mouth.

Again a couple pained words. Again I couldn't understand. I was embarrassed. "Sorry, buddy, I couldn't quite make out what you were saying."

He nudged my forearm with what was his less-burned hand.

I found a part of his body that was not burned and placed my hand on him in a brotherly fashion for just a moment, trying to return the sentiment as carefully as possible.

We were gently told that visiting hours were over. Sam needed to rest. We said our goodbyes and departed the sterile room for an antechamber. We removed the sterilized smocks and booties and changed back into our civilian attire.

Sam's mother and I crossed the well-polished floors to the elevator. Inside, and as soon as the doors clicked shut, I fell apart. I began to sniffle, then let out a sob, then cry outright. Then Sam's mom began to cry. I couldn't remember the last time I had cried before this.

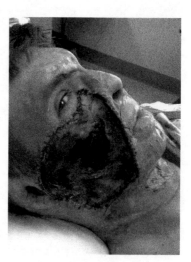

"It's a lot to see," she said. "It might seem hard to recognize him at first glance, but as soon as you see those big, beautiful brown eyes, you know it's Sam."

Yes, you could see those eyes. You could see those eyes.

DYING YOUNG AND TALENTED

I was there, and I know what was happening in my part of the war. For me that war was an experience that shaped the whole course of my thought, it was the deepest personal shock that I have ever had, the worst and most intimate tragedy of my life. It destroyed my patriotism, it changed

my ideals, it made me question the whole notion of duty, and it horrified
me and made me sad.

—*Louis de Bernières,* Captain Correlli's Mandolin

After Sam, my education in grief continued, picking up velocity as the duo of ill-fated "small wars" devolved further, throughout the mid- and late 2000s. Now my mentors and peers were leading units in direct combat as lieutenants and junior captains—many of them in the infantry. They were the proverbial "pointy end of the spear." A small subset of a subset of a subset who faced the most concentrated combat hazards. Fodder for small-arms fire and IEDs.

Major General Robert H. Scales noted this disproportionate risk: "Historically, the infantry made up around 80 per cent of US combat deaths, even though they accounted for just 4 per cent of the total force."[47]

Next, there was Adam. I heard the Army gossip. Adam Snyder, my Plebe year role model and "Sandhurst" teammate (three years ahead of me at West Point), died in a hospital in Balad, Iraq, after his vehicle was struck by an improvised explosive device.

Adam's death marked a new era. It was a time when I received regular notifications about friends gruesomely injured or killed in war. During those dark years, I spent a lot of time googling articles about my now-dead friends.

If there was any reporting on their deaths, it was often superficial. Their deaths rarely registered as more than a blip in the news: name, rank, date, location, and method of termination. Death notifications read like a ledger for parking violations, not human beings who died fighting for some abstract cause. The human dimension was missing.

Quite frequently I'd have to get news about my dead friends from some Podunk hometown gazette or town crier. But these articles usually captured the sentimental details about the wife or kids they left behind, their love of basketball or cars, or maybe a vanilla description about being a good member of the community or whatnot. Such reporting could provoke sadness but never outrage. You never heard about *how* they died. How futile and stupid the mission was. How gory and awful it was to be blown to smithereens. How it was entirely unnecessary and avoidable. Outrage was what America needed— incessant, excruciating stories about ineptitude, suffering, and pointlessness, with vivid details about U.S. soldiers' suffering and deaths. Only this sort of reporting would galvanize resistance to war. But the reporting that supplied outrage never seemed to register in America's collective consciousness.

Adam's death, however, was covered more broadly and with a tone of futility that the Global War on Terrorism deserves. The *New York Times* mentioned Snyder's death in an article dishearteningly titled "Veterans Watch as Gains Their Friends Died for Are Erased by Insurgents." Snyder "idealized the Middle East [according to his fellow platoon leader] . . . In Hawija, though, the idealism 'fell apart for him, the reality of trying to effect change through force.' By the time they had deployed to Baiji, 'he had become disillusioned over the whole thing.' "[48] Adam was twenty-six, tall, blond, and handsome when he died. To hear that he was disillusioned with the war at the hour of his death only exacerbated my disillusionment.

In the decade following graduation, I had more soldiers and friends injured or killed than I had fingers to count them. Some were shot to death. Others were blown up. One died in a helicopter crash. A couple committed suicide. Many more were maimed and horrifically disfigured. Nearly all of us harbored internal demons.

Most combat deaths are sudden; all are arresting. This certainly was the case with Dan.

Dan was a superstar, one of the four regimental commanders at West Point, which made him responsible for one thousand cadets at the age of twenty-one.

Ranked high in our class, Dan selected Hawaii as his first duty station. However, he didn't have much time to enjoy it before he was given orders to deploy to Iraq. Once in Iraq, it wasn't long before he was hit by a grenade that penetrated the roof of his vehicle. Not long after that, he went back home to California—in a government-issue coffin. It happened so quickly. I heard the news roughly one month before I was deploying to Kandahar, Afghanistan.

This was not just the first funeral I attended for someone who died in combat; it was the first funeral I attended for someone I personally knew.

On the weekend of Dan's funeral, West Point alumni flocked to Modesto, California, like migratory birds, guided by a deep respect for the man being interred. I was unaccustomed to suits and I fiddled with my tie knot, then stuffed a wad of tissues in my jacket pocket.

The funeral procession was flanked by a cordon of patriotic townspeople waving American flags as we went to the graveyard. Everyone seemed happy to "support the troops," but it never seemed to inspire critical thinking. Did Dan's death, or thousands like it, contribute to a worthy goal? The more I read—in books, in newspapers—the more uncertainty I felt.

> *U.S. and British soldiers are in effect dying in Afghanistan in order to make the world more dangerous for American and British peoples.*
>
> —*Anatol Lieven,* "A Mutiny Grows in Punjab"

At that moment, the glowing romance of war and serving one's country died for me. My puerile expectations of combat were transfigured into dread when Dan's flag-draped casket was placed next to a tidy grave. There was nothing abstract about what we were doing anymore. The eulogies, the smell of funeral parlor candles and incense, the tear-jerking childhood stories, and a playlist of somber piano solos capped by Puff Daddy's "I'll Be Missing You"—all of this was real. Very real.

Numbers, names, and percentages don't go in the graveyard. People do.

PART II

IMAGINE THE OTHER SIDE

What if the birth lottery allocated you to Iraq or Afghanistan? Would you have legitimate grievances against America's occupation of your homeland?

I heard such bad news today that
Trembling came on my heart.

For the inhabitants of some village,
Today red flames rose up to the blue sky.
From the poetic atmosphere of that wedding,
My God, sounds like crying came.
Their pleasant songs were red with blood,
Roofs came down on every window
. . .
The young bride was killed here,
The groom and his wishes were martyred here.
The hearts full of hopes were looted here,
Not just those two but the whole group is martyred.
The children were murdered,
The story full of love is martyred here.
. . .
But the news brings press releases from Bagram,
Saying that "we have killed the terrorists."

—*"The Young Bride Was Killed Here," August 18, 2008,*
from Poetry of the Taliban

A US air strike killed 47 civilians, including 39 women and children,
as they were travelling to a wedding in Afghanistan, an official
inquiry found today. The bride was among the dead . . .
The US military initially denied any civilians had been killed.

—The Guardian, *July 11, 2008*

First Contact

Even before our first experience with combat, the newness of the place was stimulant enough. There was too much to absorb and everything felt starch fresh. For the first couple days it wasn't so bad.

We relieved our dull-eyed, haggard-looking Army brothers. Sending them home to their families created an intense feeling of camaraderie—*soldiers looking out for soldiers*. Their broken expressions reminded me of despairing, overdosed street addicts. We were sending them back home—to rehab. But this sense of brotherhood was dampened when, upon signing for the vehicles, I saw on their sun-scorched faces not only relief but apology in their eyes. They knew what would befall us, but they wouldn't spill a bitter truth: some of us who made it possible for them to go home would not go home ourselves.

Irrespective of the spooky vibes we got from the outgoing unit, everything was as we might have expected. Sure, patrols were tiring. But the long days in the heat made us feel like we had earned our supper. We remained cautious but unafraid.

I tried to push the worries out of my mind so I could focus on the newness of it all.

I heard my first "call to prayer"; I saw dusty mountains that resembled cremation urns spilling their sandstorm ashes, marmalade sunrises, new flora, and a *Galeodes arabs* (camel spider). I witnessed the spectacle of "jingle trucks." These were Soviet-era, long-haul shipping trucks converted into art cars, painted in a palette of vibrant colors as broad as one's imagination. On the sides were murals: waterfalls, watchful eyes, or the *Mashallah* symbol, translated as "as God has willed."

If you turned away from the anachronisms posed by phones, cars, and automatic weapons, it felt like you were living a History Channel flashback, thrust two hundred years back in time. I was consciously aware that I was "living an experience."

I became a caricature of a military officer—hunched over maps and charts, squinting at topographical features, matching streams and bends in the road to the geography around me.

A whole world lay outside the gates of our compound. Farmers, truck drivers, families, local provincial leaders, elders—and I was curious about how they saw us. Would we be liberators? Dollar signs? Dickheads? War criminals? Did they want us around? Unfortunately, the sad truth is that no one asks poor people if they want war. And if they did, their answer wouldn't count.

The question remained: How could I build good relationships with the locals?

I knew virtually nothing about what it meant to be an Afghan. My thoughts betrayed my ignorance.

What did they believe in?

What did they love?

How would an Afghan define good living?

Would we look at the world the same way if we had grown up under similar circumstances?

Unfortunately, the military's official—and unofficial—cultural training left something to be desired.

Our unit had been given *cultural sensitivity training*, from which the best take-away was "Don't show the soles of your bare feet when seated; it's considered rude." We did not spend any meaningful amount of time with actual Afghan people.

To "validate" our preparedness to deploy, our unit had been sent to the joint readiness training center (JRTC) at Fort Polk, Louisiana, a place where you train for offense-only wars in the name of defense. The main training area, known as "the Box," was a badly rendered, fabricated place that tried to panto-mime the culture and values of some Iraq-Afghanistan hybrid country.

Curiously, there never seemed to be any training areas there, or anywhere in the military, that prepared American soldiers for the defense of their own national territory. No mock defense of Washington, D.C., or San Diego. It was all offense, all the time.

> *The U.S. military nearly always trains (and fights) in someone else's neighborhood, usually many thousands of miles away from our Atlantic or Pacific shores . . . Isn't it remarkable, America's military posture, that is? Always outward, always forward, always assuming it has interests and passage rights anywhere on the globe . . .*
>
> —Major Danny Sjursen, "Department of Offense"

Within the area meant to replicate Afghanistan, you'd find shipping containers or splintered shoot houses with squiggly, faux Arabic-looking symbols, garbage strewn about, and "No infidels" or "Deth to America" hastily spray-painted on the walls.

There were some real, flesh-and-blood Afghans hired as theatrical props, but what stuck with me was a corpulent sergeant, an Iraq vet, who, like a talking parrot, repeated the phrase *"Durka, Durka, Muhammad Jihad"*—a line from *Team America*. He wore a *thawb* (traditional Arabic long tunic), which soldiers—including me—were taught to refer to as a "man dress."

After the exercise, I received some advice: "All these people from Muslim countries—all they understand is force. You haven't been there yet, sir, but you'll see. Stubborn motherfuckers are too stupid for anything else," he'd say. "You can't treat 'em like people 'cause they're not."

It was a curious thing to experience this and compare it to the expectations set out by the Army's *FM (Field Manual) 3-24: Insurgencies and Countering*

Insurgencies. It seemed unrealistic that a soldier like this would be considered well-equipped to "decipher cultural narratives," as the field manual advised.

We may have been physically fit and capable of reading maps, but when it came to human and cultural terrain, we were totally hosed.

Even though the memory of Sam's burnt body was still fresh in my mind, there was still a part of me that wished this would be fantasyland—a *Lawrence of Arabia*–type fiction filled with horses and camels and *pulwars*.[1] We'd drink black tea with too much sugar, making it treacly sweet; we'd sit cross-legged on octagonal patterned, hand-knotted Daulatabad rugs of claret red and tobacco. And we would outwit the black-clad Taliban in an uneventful skirmish. The schools would be reopened and the villages would sing our praises. We would return home dusty, tan, and more interesting—a rough-and-tumble life ornament that we could place upon the mantel as part of a well-rounded, adventure-filled life. That naive sentiment dissolved rapidly. It took less than a week before my platoon started getting ripped apart.

THE FIELD MANUAL defines a platoon as having forty-two soldiers separated into four squads of nine—three rifle squads, one weapons squad. Add in a head-quarters element[2] and you've got the ingredients. But a platoon is not merely roles organized into subordinate units, any more than a home is concrete, boards, drywall, and shingles stuck together. Every platoon is different in its own way. We started out as a miscellaneous group of socially incompatible strangers, age eighteen to nearly twice that, with an equally wide spectrum of capabilities and tics, collected from every corner of society and cobbled together by the workings of fate and an imagined order.

My crooked and wobbly assemblage of lovable misfits and Marlboro Men would never have naturally sought one another out, let alone formed a group. Hard-core military history buffs next to conspiracy theorists; painters and banjo players next to bow-hunting enthusiasts and professional video gamers; racists, avid readers, atheists, and rodeo cowboys sandwiched in bunks between white rappers, family men, gym rats, homophobes, hustlers, investors, peacetime alcoholics, and Bible thumpers. For better or worse, in the Army, there is little choice about who you work and spend time with.

To serve in the military is to realize that there is no monolithic America. No singular descriptor, no singular narrative. Everyone had a story and every story

was incredibly different from the last. But if we were going to survive combat together, we needed more than diversity and solo efforts: we needed inclusion and teamwork.

We fell in line beneath our assigned remit and adopted the personality that the ranks on our chests told us we could afford. Not all of my soldiers liked one another, but with time we loved each other like a dysfunctional family. A hypermacho, belligerent kibbutz.

In relatively short order, something uniting happened to us—the collective us. The most extreme prejudices were tucked out of sight as an olive branch in the name of mutual survival.

For the first part of deployment, my platoon was given the task of route clearance. We were meant to keep a forty-kilometer strip of Highway 1 in Maywand District "trafficable" and free of roadside bombs. The concept is pretty simple: drive down the road at three miles per hour until you find a bomb—either with your tires, in which case your vehicle is blown to pieces, or preferably from a distance, with your eyes. Once we found a roadside bomb, the only move I had was to cordon the area, call the explosive ordnance disposal team, and wait. If you don't get blown up, the road "might be clear"—for twenty minutes.

However simple in concept, our training had been close to nil. I didn't really know what I was looking for—wires and suspicious garbage, I guess. Or a conspicuous artillery shell just sitting in the open. I had never even set foot inside the vehicles we used until I was on the ground in Afghanistan. Instead we did drills using things like a cardboard MRE box and 550 cord (550-pound test strength parachute cord that is thin, OD-green, and Army-issue) as a make-believe bomb, and we maneuvered around the box on foot, driving imaginary vehicles and covering our sectors using imaginary guns, which we shot by saying *"Bang."* It was the military equivalent of finger painting.

Our preparedness in other areas was lacking as well. I successfully went for an entire calendar year without firing a live round from my rifle—from the end of the Infantry Basic Officer Leader Course (IBOLC) through the first several months at Fort Carson with 4th Infantry Division. Training was always canceled. There was always an excuse.

The botched training proved costly, however. We only made it through four days of patrols before my first four soldiers were injured.

There was no romantic daybreak assault on our position. No action-packed shoot-out. Instead, we drove down a dusty road in Maywand District when my squad leader's vehicle hit an antipersonnel mine linked to 250 pounds of homemade explosives. We evacuated our four injured friends, not fully knowing the extent of their injuries or whether they would be permanently handicapped. Then we collected the wreckage and towed away the catastrophically destroyed vehicle hull. The end.

The attack was devastating, but the act itself was eerily . . . well, anticlimactic. We didn't even see the "enemy." A meaningless act of violence inside another, larger, meaningless act of violence.

The sad irony of it all was that I got a badge for it. The Combat Infantryman Badge (CIB) is an award given to soldiers who, while assigned to infantry, Ranger, or Special Forces units, engage or *are engaged by* hostile enemy forces. It's the piece of bling that infantry soldiers hope to get from combat.

After my battalion commander blood-pinned me, punching the spikes of the medal into my chest, he said the most unexpected thing: "Congratulations, Lieutenant."

Congratulations? For getting blown up?

It was an assembly-line operation: everyone who had their CIB punched everyone who was only just receiving it. Each time the spikes were extracted from my now openly bleeding chest. A new spot was found. The metal spikes were punched back inside me. Fresh blood flowed anew. Then the line shifted to the next station and a new soldier took his mark in front of me to do it all over again.

Now, when someone asked me that loaded question about what I did in Afghanistan, I had an answer: "Yes, I saw action."

ON THAT AUSPICIOUS fourth day of my deployment, after my injured soldiers had been shipped to higher-level medical care, I called my family from the phone tent. I heard the voices of my dad and stepmom. They sensed my anguish. They knew something was terribly wrong.

Some soldiers opt for honesty, whereas others choose avoidance, half-truths, or full-blown lies, thinking the truth doesn't help; it only creates worry without a cure.

When the booming explosions from a Canadian M777 howitzer quaked the phone tent, the soldier may respond, "Oh, those sounds—that's nothing, baby girl. It was just . . . just a movie in the background—a soldier getting his ass chewed by the *platoon sarn't*, ya know."

I chose shovel-to-the-face honesty.

I explained to my parents how one of my platoon's vehicles had been catastrophically destroyed. How I called in an air medevac helicopter. How I checked on my now barely conscious soldiers, some so doped up on morphine or ketamine that one was curled up in the fetal position, talking like a baby; another thought he was in Iraq.

I admitted that I lied to one of my injured soldiers, reassuring him that he was "going to be OK"—when truthfully I didn't know.

And what did *OK* in battlefield injury–speak even mean? Did *OK* mean quadruple amputee with a pulse? Did *OK* mean years of horrific facial reconstruction surgeries? Or the loss of only one eye? Paralyzed from just waist down? Or maybe *OK* meant being really lucky—a traumatic brain injury or a single leg amputation, below the knee, which is what my wounded friends from Walter Reed hospital called a "paper cut."

I told them about the blood. How the bright-red blood caked with the brown of the dirt, creating a clotted crimson paste that flowed, cracked and dribbled in rivulets down my soldier's lips and chin like cooling lava.

I told them about the words that AJ, a black eighteen-year-old automatic rifleman, said over and over again: "I want to come back. I want to come back to the platoon."

For all four of these injured soldiers, this would be one second, felt for life.

Sitting on that gray metal folding chair in the phone tent, I gulped, hoping I could send the sadness back down inside of me. It refused. It returned, this time as a sniffle. I tried once more, clenching my jaw, nearly cracking my molars, attempting to stay composed, but I couldn't. I cried, wiping the tears on my shirtsleeve, hoping no one else saw me, the officer, lose his shit.

I felt so delicate, so tender-hearted.

My parents were crying too. They've never admitted to it, but maybe at that moment they regretted pressuring me to join the military.

Four days down, only 361 to go. If we had kept up that pace—if we averaged one casualty per day for much longer—we'd be wiped out in a month.

At the time, I never fully grasped the costs, when all the medical expenses were tallied, associated with our military misadventure. For the cost of this terrible little incident—destroying one MRAP (mine-resistant, ambush-protected) vehicle and injuring four soldiers—we could have sent every single soldier in my platoon to a fully funded, private four-year university, including room and board and living stipend.

Despite my phone calls and desperate-sounding emails, which cited an ever-growing list of casualties, I sometimes received messages from friends and family that seemed absurd.

"Did you watch Tom Brady and the Patriots this past weekend? What a game!"

Did I watch Tom Brady and the Patriots? Did I watch Tom-motherfuckin'-Brady and the Patriots?

How did they not get it?

To evacuate injured soldiers, or to walk through a field of severed body parts—gummy mashed-potato brains spilling out all over the dirt—and return to the base to find this—it felt like that old joke: "Aside from that, Mrs. Lincoln, how was the play?"

I knew my family meant well, but it felt insufferable. Almost a taunt.

Not at the time, but now I empathize with their plight. How do you make small talk on the phone with someone who earlier that day watched a roadside bomb crush an Afghan National Army truck like a beer can on a frat boy's forehead? When one Afghan soldier stumbled out of the wreckage, clutching something that might have once been his eye, as blood rivered between his fingers? Or when U.S. and Afghan soldiers rocked the wreckage back and forth to get the last dead man out? Or when the soldier's body was extracted and it slithered over the truck's twisted metal frame like a snake because every bone in his body was broken.

What do you say?

It's lose-lose. Too much pity or gloom in your voice and it's a yearlong depression-fest. Too chipper and it would seem like life is going swimmingly without you. Both sides of the spectrum were bad, and with a volcano bubbling inside of me, the slightest miscue from a well-meaning family member could send the Richter scale into a tizzy. I was capable of erupting at any moment, darkening conversations with ash from the memories of cremated friends. I said some unkind things to people I cared about.

But the truth is that it's not the American soldier who would win the suffering olympics; it's the civilian victims of our so-called War on Terror. However bad we had it, we were war tourists; for them, it remains life.

I was not the only soldier who struggled with relationships back home.

If you want to have your heart shattered, go to an Army phone tent at a forward operating base in Afghanistan. Just sit and listen.

It's not uncommon to hear the sound of a marriage crumbling. And even if you didn't hear it firsthand, private matters like divorce inevitably become public gossip in the military.

I was in the corner, on the phone, talking at length with my then-girlfriend. If I went at odd hours, I could use the phone for over an hour.

One young soldier cooed reassuringly to his wife while another soldier, sardined together with him and separated by two feet and a plywood prison-style privacy screen, went berserk. His wife was leaving him, draining the deployment bank account, taking the kids, and moving back home with her parents.

"You're leaving me now," he said. "Now! When I'm in the middle of this." Shock transmuted into tragic desperation.

"Don't you know how much you mean to me? Can't you just stick it out? It'll work out, baby."

It was over.

"Well, fuck you! How fucking . . . how the fuck can you do this to me? I love you!"

When the hope of saving his marriage had flatlined, the young soldier smashed the phone receiver onto the desk until he grasped only jagged plastic and wires. He stood up in a fury, punched some stuff, and slammed the plywood tent door on his way out.

Deployment is an assault on all fronts; love is merely one more form of collateral damage.

I tried to push these memories out of my mind.

As soldiers continued to get injured, their belongings were packed up and stored in big plastic tough boxes, OD green in color like just about everything else. Little plastic monuments to tragedy, these boxes were stacked neatly in my tent.

To make the tent feel more like home, I had the dozen or so books I brought neatly aligned on a shelf beside my newly earned Combat Infantryman Badge. The badge, a Springfield rifle backed by a ring of laurel, had been bent concave from the force of all the fists hammering it into my chest during the blood-pinning ceremony.

Across from my bunk was a curtain, and next to it I had written in blue paint marker the words from a toast. It was the final toast that I had had in Colorado Springs before I deployed. Three of us: me, a Special Forces buddy, and Tyler, a West Pointer and my closest friend in our brigade, bought a round of tippity-top-shelf, I-might-die-soon whiskey.

To those who fought before us
To those who fight beside us
To those who will fight when we no longer can
Shoot Fast, Shoot Straight
Die, Fucker, Die!

Another early engagement sticks with me. One of my soldiers was injured, and as bad as that was and always would be, that's not what my mind returns to.

It was a searing-hot day and we'd arrived at a culvert on the edge of Hutal. A babbling brook with tricky terrain stopped us from checking the culvert from the relative safety of our armored vehicles. We were forced to check every opening, especially those that were hard to check, because insurgents had a history of packing upwards of 800 pounds of homemade explosives beneath the road. We had to dismount troops.

Dismounting near culverts was a dangerous job, but there was no reasonable alternative. It was the main paved route for coalition forces to use if they wanted to travel from east to west, from Kandahar to Helmand Province. Soldiers took turns.

This time, James, a team leader, and Ryan, an eighteen-year-old private, drew the proverbial short straw. To avoid setting a pattern, soldiers varied their approach: different sides of the road, different distances away from the culvert, never too close in case it was rigged to blow.

Ryan and James got out, using their optics to look beneath the road, when a pressure cooker filled with nails, bicycle chains, and homemade explosives detonated nearby. This type of bomb was command detonated, meaning there was a Taliban spotter at the end of the lamp cord, hidden, possibly hundreds of meters away.

The blast showered the area in shrapnel. Fortunately, a mud wall absorbed the lion's share of the fragmentation. James had his arm ripped up pretty good; his face was diced up, peppered with shrapnel. He couldn't hear very well. Initially, we couldn't rule out a perforated eardrum.

We whipped the vehicles around, loaded the wounded, and sped back to FOB (Forward Operating Base) Ramrod, an embarrassing five kilometers away—embarrassing because we couldn't control the only paved road just outside a major base. I called in an air medevac helicopter on the go, something that I had already attained considerable experience in.

Ryan, the eighteen-year-old private, was rattled but seemed OK—on the surface. No lacerations, no immediate signs of a traumatic brain injury (TBI), according to Army medics.

As if by ghoulish coincidence, we dropped off our injured soldiers at the aid station at the same time a memorial ceremony was commencing for three soldiers killed just days earlier, not more than a few kilometers from where we stood.

The second act to this story is what has stuck with me.

It happened when we went back "outside the wire." We had not finished sweeping the road for bombs. As ineffective and Sisyphean as the task was, it was ours.

We returned to the blast site with an explosive ordnance disposal team. They dismounted, scanning the site for any other nasty surprises with the aid of protective equipment and a robot.

An Afghan man on a motorcycle approached. He was on course to drive through our cordon of the bomb site—right by the bomb technicians on the ground.

My gunner began his escalation of force procedures, a series of escalating responses for when you couldn't control the Afghans.

First, hand and arm signals. Then a retina-scorching green laser pointer or pen flare. Then a warning shot from an M4 assault rifle. Then, in the case of an approaching car, one could rip a belt of machine-gun rounds through the engine block. Lastly, there was the lead-shower-to-windshield method. An effective albeit terminal solution. We had to keep those uppity Afghans in their place. Boot-to-neck, always.

The driver somehow did not see, or refused to heed, our warnings: wild hand signals, a retina-scorching green laser. He kept coming.

My gunner, German Hate Stick, ordinarily cool and brooding, seemed on edge. I took this seriously given his background and character.

German Hate Stick was a dual U.S.-German citizen who wasn't shy about his desire to fight and kill in combat. He had previously served in the German Army but switched to the U.S. Army because, as he gently put it, "The Germans have lost their appetite to kill people. I wanted to fight in Iraq. I knew I'd only get to do *real fighting* with the U.S. Army. And I got what I wanted."

The nickname *German Hate Stick* was interchangeable for both the man and the man's prodigious—almost equine—penis. In anticipation of porn stardom, he had prepared a shortlist of big-dick aliases: "Dick Van Damage" and "Daniel Castle-Cock."

But in this instance, he was all business.

He yelled down from the turret, "Sir—warning shot?"

Nervous, and still rattled from the casualties an hour earlier, I gave my answer.

"Go."

German Hate Stick carefully aimed and fired a single round from his M4 assault rifle. The round hit a rock and ricocheted, striking the motorcyclist in the femoral artery.

How incredibly unlucky.

The Afghan man veered off the embankment, where he crumpled in a heap. His motorcycle fell atop his already shot leg. The Afghan man now had a gunshot wound and a compound leg fracture. My platoon sergeant told me that he was squirting blood when our platoon medic arrived moments later. Our medic performed first aid. I called an air medevac—the second in two hours. After the Afghan man had been stabilized and was taken to Kandahar Airfield for treatment, my platoon sergeant, Ox, looked to me, camo blouse speckled in blood, and said, "Sir, you shoulda seen it—looked like someone slaughtered a sheep in the back of my truck."

Fortunately, both James and the Afghan civilian survived.

Only later, after James had returned to the United States to recover from his wounds, did I learn that he shouldn't have even been on this deployment. The Army had "stop-lossed" him. This meant that he was *involuntarily extended* beyond his expiration of term of service (ETS) to be sent back to war. Critics have referred to the program as "involuntary servitude" according to the Congressional Research Service.[3] This was James's second yearlong tour. James, tall, introspective, and quiet, didn't say much about it. No sense complaining, I guess. Would the Army listen?

What troubles me now, all these years later, and what was then only a flicker of consciousness, is that after the Afghan man had been airlifted to Kandahar

Airfield and I knew he would live, my next thought was not his recovery but rather how this incident would impact myself or my gunner in some way.

I was too caught up with our mission and our own safety to care about his long-term well-being. I didn't convey an apology. Even if I had cared enough to look into it, the value the military places on Afghan lives is pretty paltry.

An article by the *Intercept* titled "Our Condolences: How the U.S. Paid for Death and Damage in Afghanistan"[4] details the dysfunction found in the "pay-for-pain" condolence scheme: "An armored vehicle ran over a six-year-old boy's legs: $11,000. A jingle truck was 'blown up by mistake': $15,000. A controlled detonation broke eight windows in a mosque: $106 ... A child who died in a combat operation: $2,414 ... The average payment for a death was $3,426. Payments for injuries averaged $1,557."

If I had known about the condolence payment system and filed a claim on the man's behalf—not sure I would have—the claim would most likely get caught in bureaucratic purgatory. The *Intercept* article continues: "In all, the Army released 5,766 claims marked for Afghanistan, filed between Feb. 2003 and Aug. 2011, of which 1,671 were paid, for a total of about $3.1 million. Of those claims, 753 were denied completely, and the rest are in various kinds of accounting limbo."

The attorney in the Army's office described the condolence payment database as "G.I.G.O.—Garbage In, Garbage Out."

In the first months of my deployment, it was the thought of my soldiers—not the innocent Afghan people—that kept me awake.

I had learned through military indoctrination that "shit happens" in war. There is a higher tolerance for innocent civilian deaths than American soldier deaths. The moral math is that you heavily discount the lives of the Afghan local nationals relative to the lives of any other American.

Me, me, me.

Me, me, me—fuck you.

When the military can't deny their involvement in civilian casualties (sometimes they try anyhow), they begrudgingly conduct an internal investigation. In our case there was no denying that the 5.56mm full-metal-jacket round extracted from the man's leg was fired from German Hate Stick's M4. The weapons most widely used by insurgents don't use that ammunition. A summary investigation was conducted by a twenty-four-year-old officer from our battalion. The military decided, based on his findings, that our platoon and the military at large would bear no responsibility because we had followed escalation-of-force procedures. The injured civilian was no doubt unfortunate, but kosher.

I wish I had the power to reach through time and talk some human decency into young Lieutenant Edstrom. If you were in the United States and hurt an innocent person—a car accident, knocking someone over in the street—there would be a set of actions you'd take. The decent thing to do is to help them up, ensure they are OK, and, if you are responsible, pay for damages. Why should I have acted any different with an Afghan than an American?

For the rest of my life I will personally bear the responsibility for his injuries, for making the "call" that ultimately got him shot. Does each morning begin with pain? Could he go to work and earn a decent paycheck? Did his family suffer? Does he talk about that day as the moment that ruined his life's ambitions? This is but one awful little incident in a great compilation of tragedies.

THIS WAS MERELY the beginning of my journey. I had months and months of patrols to go. More stuff would be destroyed; more people would die. The coming year would be as much about physical survival as moral survival.

How much of this belongs with me? Would the same injuries have occurred if someone else had been in my boots? Was it my fault? How should I think of this?

With mercy of time and distance, I reflect on the young man who I was. I feel for him. In time he will come to the realization that the violence he has been asked to commit is not a mistake but a crime. He will lead his men to face the constant threat of death in patrols that he does not believe in.

In the night—dead quiet and full of stars—the cosmos was at peace. I felt infinitesimally small. It placed the war into perspective.

If only an alien life form were watching this war. How dastardly stupid we would all seem. Here we are, on a planet that's 4.54 billion years old, spending the tiny amount of time that we have alive on earth, the prime of our puny human lives, flying across the planet at great expense while simultaneously ignoring climate change, which threatens all organized life on earth, so we can bash in the heads of people we don't know, who pose no statistically significant threat, when we all evolved from the same matter anyway.

It would become harder and harder to find meaning in a war so meaningless. We were soldiers once . . . and young . . . and dumb.

Afghan Civilian Deaths Rose 40 Percent in 2008

—The New York Times, *February 17, 2009*

U.S. strikes killed 140 villagers: Afghan probe . . . According to villagers, families were cowering in houses when the U.S. aircraft bombed them. The incident has prompted anger across Afghanistan toward Western troops, and caused Karzai to demand a halt to all air strikes, a plea that Washington has rebuffed.

—Reuters, *May 16, 2009*

The US and Nato commander in Afghanistan, General Stanley McChrystal, who was boasting of military progress only three months ago, confessed last week that "nobody is winning."

—The Independent, *May 16, 2010*

Annus Horribilis

The War on Terror strip-mined my soul. The first few months hollowed me out; the rest extracted my once plucky, puppylike determination and innocence. And, like adding black to a can of paint, every emotional color, in every social interaction, became muted.

The time between May 2009 and June 2010 was my horrible year. It was a year defined by the horror of watching good people getting mutilated and dying terrible deaths. I experienced intense moral anguish, gnawing fear, boredom, aggression, hatred, envy, and butt-puckering anxiety. It strained my relationships, destroyed my notion of patriotism, eroded my support for American foreign policy, dissolved whatever faith I may have once had in religion or a god, and made me deeply sad.

For the entire year, my mind swam in a sea of doubt. Amid chaos and violence, I tried to reconcile the impact we were said to be having, measured in propagandistic images of smiling schoolchildren, with the actual impact we were having, measured in craters, displaced people, and flaming homes. Holding my thoughts and doubts at bay, I found an uneasy peace. I tried to shove those inconvenient thoughts out of the frame, hoping that I'd be too busy to look up and see what I was contributing to. I needed to lead patrols without a nagging conscience.

At the end of it all, when I was lucky enough to return home, I did so a worse person.

THE MEN AND women of 1-12 Infantry Battalion, 4th Brigade, 4th Infantry Division (of whom my platoon was a part) were deployed to the conflict in Kandahar Province, Afghanistan. Kandahar Province is one of thirty-four provinces of Afghanistan and contains approximately 1.2 million people. The city of Kandahar is the regional hub of the south and by rough estimate—according to "dwelling count"—constitutes more than one-third of the province's total population.

Despite U.S. best efforts to develop a political system in Afghanistan, those efforts have failed. An article from Brown University's Watson Institute for International and Public Affairs states, "The democracy and state-building model imposed [by the United States and its allies] on Afghanistan was stymied from the outset by critical foundational flaws. These include the return to power of discredited warlords reviled by most Afghans, the marginalization of particular groups including the remnants of the Taliban movement, and the concentration of power in an executive Presidency at the expense of a weak parliamentary structure."[1] By most conventional rankings and measures, Afghanistan remains one of the most impoverished, corrupt, unstable, undemocratic, and unruly countries on earth.

In 2017, sixteen years after the United States and its allies took control of the country, Afghanistan was categorized as an "authoritarian regime" and ranked at 149 out of 167 countries reviewed in the Democracy Index.[2] This is part of a downward trend since 2006, where Afghanistan has become progressively less democratic. And despite the multi-decade period of U.S. influence, Afghanistan ranks 111 out of 113 countries included in the 2018 Rule of Law Index[3]; similarly, it remains one of the poorest countries on earth according to the UN's multidimensional poverty index,[4] which measures deprivation using a cluster of health, education, and standard-of-living indicators. The Afghanistan I saw was a postcard of struggle and insecurity.

At the company and platoon level, we passed through Kandahar city frequently, but more often than not we operated in austere conditions within rural villages. Over the tour, we moved between two large bases and two small platoon outposts. Each of these locations touched unique districts. And with each new area of operation came new and different challenges in terms of landscape, mission set, and propensity to kill or be killed.

We spent between three and five months operating out of each location. Our unit started in western Kandahar Province and moved progressively eastward, closer to Kandahar city. But my introduction to combat started at our first home, FOB Ramrod, the base from which we set out daily to patrol the highway.

FOB RAMROD

FOB Ramrod was situated in the far western part of Kandahar Province, in a district called Maywand. Maywand was adjacent to Helmand Province, which had a reputation for poppy cultivation, cannabis and grape fields, criminal patronage networks, and the narco-economy. Helmand, like Kandahar, was a bloodbath.

As my boots crunched the ubiquitous gravel found at most American FOBs, it surfaced in my mind that I was literally standing in the same spot, inside the base, where Sam stood months earlier, before he was engulfed in flames. It was as if people came here on a pilgrimage, *to this very spot*, to leave scarred. Had Sam's vehicle not hit that antitank mine, I probably would have given him a bear hug. The observation was unsettling.

Sam was not the only person to be immolated in this unassuming, backwater dust bowl. On November 3, 2008, about six months before we arrived, Paula Loyd, a social scientist and member of a Human Terrain Team, was doused in fuel and lit on fire by a local Afghan man.

"By the time the fire was extinguished, all of Ms. Loyd's clothing had been burned off and only her helmet and body armor remained," according to an article in *Wired* magazine.[5] Ms. Loyd died from these wounds in early 2009. After capturing the Afghan man responsible for the immolation, Army contractor Don Ayala shot the prisoner in the head. Willfully executing a detainee is a war crime and violation of the Geneva Conventions of 1949.[6] Ayala was charged with murder—the first military contractor to be charged with such a crime. He received no jail time.

وینه په وینه نه پاکیږي

—*Afghan proverb, translation: "Blood can't wash blood."*

Ramrod was large—maybe two miles around, much larger than what the units occupying it required. The perimeter was surrounded by fifteen-foot-high HESCO barriers—modern gabions, or baskets, filled with dirt and rocks that acted as a blast wall. Afghan security contractors manned wood towers during the day; U.S. soldiers manned them at night.

Southern Afghanistan has been a bugbear for invaders of all flags throughout history. As if to prove it, Maywand maintained the skeletal wreckage of a British fort, located thirty meters from the main road, just on the outskirts of the village, Hutal.

It was a grand structure, and for its day it must have been majestic. After a century and a half and much fighting, the white earthen walls and arches looked like a bar of desiccated soap. Now explosives technicians destroyed bomb-making supplies and munition caches inside its earthen walls. It could still hold a blast without damaging the surrounding village.

It was here in July 1880, during the Battle of Maywand—one of the principal battles of the Second Anglo-Afghan War—that the British were obliterated by an Afghan force ten times its size.

According to the *Pashtun Times*, during this battle, the "Pashtun Joan of Arc" named Malalai used her veil as a banner to spur on Afghan soldiers to defeat the British.[7] Lore has it that she used a form of Pashtun poetry, called *landai*, which is composed of two lines and often twenty-two syllables, to spur on the troops:

> *Young love if you do not fall in the battle of Maiwand*
> *By God someone is saving you as a token of shame*

Malalai was killed in this battle but she remains a cherished part of Afghan culture. Many Afghan girls carry her namesake. Malala Yousafzai, the Pakistani activist who was brutally shot by the Taliban in 2012 and who was later awarded the Nobel Peace Prize, bears a derivation of this name.

Rumbling past the old British fort in our armored vehicles felt ominous—like passing the Alamo. *That could be us:* the "modern military," overstretched, out of position, without a plan, and vulnerable. The message was clear: this was not the place to fight a protracted war. Looking at this broken shell of military adventurism, it felt like Afghanistan really had earned its nickname, "the Grave-yard of Empires."[8] During one private conversation with a U.S. Army general officer in 2010, he looked to me and said, "I can't believe we are still there. It's a complete mess." He spoke as if he weren't working in the Pentagon. As if he weren't serving in one of the highest positions in the most powerful military on earth. As if he could not—or would not—resist.

Seeing so many monuments to military failure in Afghanistan—both historic and present day—I felt like my worst fears were coming true: The United States was not making any progress; the Afghans did not want us here, nor did they want what America wanted for them; our actions were not improving the security of America. But I could not hold these thoughts in my mind at the same time that I was patrolling. I needed to block them out. Initially, this was easy; surviving was hard enough.

It was made easier still by my unconscious incompetence: at the time, I only knew a fraction about the "big picture" I know now. All I knew was that the war was not going well, but the details of the havoc America's occupation caused—the torture, the global drone assassination campaign—these issues were outside my immediate purview. I was too fixated on the day-to-day workings of the platoon, leaving the question of foreign policy to politicians. What I knew was that I was attending memorial ceremonies for dead soldiers more than once a month.

FOB WILSON AND THE "HEART OF DARKNESS"

After about three months, our battalion was ordered to pack up everything and move from FOB Ramrod to FOB Wilson, about thirty kilometers to the east, closer to Kandahar city. We were glad to lay off babysitting for the chance to relocate. We packed our things and expedited our departure toward Kandahar, handing over our tents to an incoming Stryker unit.

Things were changing. Our unit was preparing to be at the coal face of the war, supporting General Stanley A. McChrystal's shift toward Kandahar.[9] During this "fighting season," U.S. military deaths hit record-setting highs. Month on month, we were getting torn up—the "deadliest month of Afghan war," according to Reuters in July 2009.[10] This was immediately eclipsed the following month.[11] And then again, in our final month of deployment, June 2010.[12] My soldiers were serving in one of the most dangerous combat roles, in one of the most violent districts, during what was the most deadly time to be there. We would operate from FOB Wilson full-time for about three months

and then span out, establishing smaller platoon outposts. Once these outposts were built, our platoon moved into these crude, earthen buildings. During those final five to six months of deployment, FOB Wilson acted more as a mothership for resupply than it did a day-to-day base.

Initially, my platoon relished the move to Wilson because it provided the prospect of getting out of the truck seat, off route clearance, and back in the dirt, on foot patrols. Living in villages. Trying to win over the primarily ethnic Pashtun population and provide security. "Real grunt shit," as some soldiers said.

We knew that the district we were heading to was the birthplace of the Afghan Taliban. We knew it would be a fight.

FOB Wilson was located near the intersection of four districts (Zhari, Panjwai, Arghandab, and Kandahar city). The small contingent of Canadians from Task Force Kandahar (TFK) occupying the base were drawing down with plans to exit the war in Afghanistan. They had had enough.

This area would soon become an American problem. And although the Canadians had worked tirelessly, faced serious fighting (such as Operation Medusa), and built high-quality bases from which to operate, they did not have the manpower to truly *lock down* the district.

According to a 2010–2011 Afghan census, for whatever the reporting is worth, Zhari District had an estimated population of about 81,000 people.[13] It was wide and thin—a pork chop of a district; roughly thirty kilometers from east to west and eight kilometers from north to south. Zhari was located on the north bank of the Arghandab River, which gave life to a mini–agricultural breadbasket in what was otherwise a desolate desert wasteland. The river fed a dense green belt of orchards, supported by smaller irrigation ditches known as wadis.

Outside the green belt, on the other side of Highway 1, the only paved road in the area, you stared into the abyss. Kilometers of moonscape. Powdery dirt as fine as confectioners' sugar would plume upward with each step, clogging nose and throat, turning snot hideous colors.

Earthen homes were mostly one story tall. There were no visible signs of toilets, running water, or medical facilities.

The districts around FOB Wilson were some of the most violent, least permissive in the country. Zhari in particular had a bad reputation.

According to ABC News, Zhari "was so feared by the Soviet Army it was dubbed 'the heart of darkness.'"[14] A correspondent from UK newspaper the *Telegraph* articulated the Zhari context:

> *The area forms a funnel of arms, fighters and supplies from rural Kandahar and Helmand to the provincial capital.*
>
> *Whoever controls Zhari, which sits astride the Highway One nation-wide ring road, has a critical hold on the western approach to Kandahar city.*
>
> *The district is also of historic importance to the Taliban movement, which grew up in Zhari's orchards and vineyards.*
>
> *Mullah Mohammad Omar, founder of the movement, taught at a small mosque in the village of Singesar after he and other leaders fought the Soviet army in the 1980s.*
>
> *His militia of religious students, or Taliban, were formed to fight the power of local warlords in 1994.*[15]

Coalition casualties in Zhari were highest in the greenbelt and along Highway 1.

First, the greenbelt. Here, there was plenty of cover and concealment setting the ideal conditions for all forms of attacks: RPGs, antipersonnel mines, snipers, and small-arms fire.

For its risks, the greenbelt acquired other names. As if to give it a Boston flair, a little taste of home, it went by "the Green Monster," a reference to Fenway Park—home of the Boston Red Sox. Lore had it that the Russians had a second name for it: "the Green Death."

The terrain was renowned for its difficulty, shifting from desert on one side of the highway to a spiderweb of orchards on the other.

Soldiers patrolling this farmland must scrabble over mud walls in 120F heat to avoid the paths seeded with homemade bombs. Visibility among the pomegranate trees is cut to a few yards.
The gardens are a patchwork of safe areas and battlegrounds, demarcated by streams, tracks and trees. Platoons can count [on] attacks from almost any group of trees.
In the labyrinth of alleys and sun-baked mud houses in Senjaray town, foot patrols have come under grenade attack from fighters no older than boys.

—The Telegraph, *July 2, 2010*

The second major threat was Highway 1, where you would get "nuked," as soldiers described being blown up, by the relentless back-and-forth game of roadside bomb minesweeper. Tactically, it was an unwinnable game of cat and mouse.

Insurgents hid IEDs in the drainage culverts. We got blown up.

We refined our TTPs (tactics, techniques, and procedures). We drove off road to check the culverts. They emplaced IEDs off road. We got blown up—again.

It went on and on, round and round. We were always made to be the fool.

WARS FOUGHT WITH roadside bombs have an asymmetry to them. A roadside bomb requires little money; it isn't particularly complex to make; it requires only a small team and, depending on the charge, only a small amount of time to emplace it; it is hard to defend against; it is wildly destructive; and it is difficult for coalition forces to catch the perpetrators to bring them to justice.

On the other hand, for coalition forces, detecting roadside bombs requires well-trained soldiers and bomb specialists; expensive vehicles and equipment; a large, platoon-sized unit for security; a significant amount of time; and, if the insurgents successfully detonate an IED on American soldiers, money to pay for medical and disability costs that will persist for decades.

In short, roadside bombs are an effective way of taking our lives, time, combat power, and public purse.

How do you defeat a foe who can destroy million-dollar machines with devices that can be built off the Internet for about the cost of a pizza, especially if that foe doesn't particularly worry about dying?

—Newsweek, *August 15, 2007*

Even for poor insurgents, this exchange rate—one of their dollars to destroy 10,000 of ours—is an exceptional deal. An injured soldier accounts for roughly $2 million of lifetime costs, according to research from the Harvard Kennedy School; as for damaged equipment, the fully burdened cost of an MRAP armored vehicle is likely in excess of $1 million.[16] Our battalion was burning through dozens throughout deployment. Similar to the Death Star in *Star Wars*, America spends billions of dollars on high-tech, super-sexy, super-complex equipment with vulnerabilities that can be easily exploited by ragtag Taliban militants with low-tech, low-cost weaponry. In the case of ground infantry units, we were being foiled by fertilizer, lamp cord, water jugs, and a car battery.[17] These were conditions that cynicism feeds on, and it would become increasingly difficult to keep that in check. Months later, further into my deployment, thinking—and then voicing those thoughts—was a liability that would threaten my career, but when the alternative was to die a meaningless death, risking one's career felt exceptionally cheap.

Over time, soldiers became jaded. We were not winning hearts and minds. The only Afghans we were winning over, it seemed, were those who were becoming fat on American treasure.

Because of the tempestuous security situation, the governmental outreach to the population, key to counterinsurgency, was minimal. And because the summer fighting months were so intense, many civilians either fled or were caught on the fence—in the crossfire, both literally and figuratively—between Taliban fighters and U.S. troops. According to a Public Radio International article entitled "Afghanistan: A Tale of Two Districts," civilians who were just trying to survive hedged their bets, "telling the coalition they are pro-coalition and telling the Taliban they are pro-Taliban."[18] It was a state of hopelessness. Soldiers were sustained by active denial and a stubborn fighting spirit to never quit, especially when that meant being defeated by what were in some cases teenage Pakistani boys. But to fight and kill Pakistani boys provided no sense of victory either.

The Public Radio International article compared the two districts we operated in, Maywand and Zhari, capturing, with considerable precision, the plight of the American grunt on the ground.

> *Soldiers here are all too aware of the catch-22 that prolongs the cycle of violence. They know that the only reason the Taliban is here is because the foreign troops are. And they know that the only reason the foreign troops are here is because the Taliban is. Often, soldiers wonder aloud, if they left, would the Taliban leave too?*[19]

NOT ONLY WERE we not winning, no one knew what we were doing.

Everything we did was a derivative, regurgitated version of a failed approach. As I write this in 2020, the Afghan War has been the longest war in American history by a country mile, stretching over six thousand days—longer than World War I, World War II, and the Korean War combined. This has given U.S. commanding generals plenty of time to create new names for the same old shit show. And after every crash-and-burn attempt, getting us no closer to that ever-elusive notion of "progress," out of the ashes emerges a new gee-whiz, good-idea-fairy framework. A fashionably new silver-bullet strategy that will *win the war*. The bullshit stew of rhetorical devices has included "Shock and Awe"—*Blitzkrieg*; "Hearts and Minds"—*touchy feely*; "Counterinsurgency (COIN)"—*persuade with guns*; "ends + ways + means = strategy"[20]—*who the fuck knows*; "Shape, Clear, Hold, Build"[21]—*Field of Dreams*; and a host of other gems. And let's not forget the oldies but goodies of yesteryear: "domino theory," "mutually assured destruction," and "countervalue targeting." I particularly like the

Orwellian euphemism behind "countervalue targeting," a U.S. defense policy that the *Encyclopædia Britannica* describes as "the targeting of an enemy's cities and civilian population with nuclear weapons."[22]

When I was in Afghanistan, the trendy thing was "Oil Spot Plus"[23] theory—a contrived framework advanced by the sociologist contractors attached to our unit. Battalion leadership bought into the idea that if you dump enough money, projects, and terrified young soldiers bristling with guns into a skittish and skeptical Afghan village, pro-American goodwill and security would flow out the other side. This was the "Oil Spot." And when one village saw *how great* the neighboring U.S.-bankrolled village was doing, the Oil Spot would spread outward. After you've built up one U.S. client community, you could shift your attention to the next. As compelling as the Oil Spot Plus theory may have looked in an academic white paper, it wasn't winning any fans. There was a general malaise among not only the enlisted infantry soldiers on the ground but also the battalion's officers. Midway through deployment, it was apparent that there was no coherent strategy. No objectives that started high and cascaded to subordinate units below. It was—not to mince words—a complete disaster.

If strategy can be defined as a series of hard-to-reverse decisions, with long-term consequences, made under uncertainty, I wondered what results we'd get from implementing a *no-strategy strategy*.

The officers from our battalion—about thirty of us—gathered together in the mess tent at FOB Wilson to "discuss strategy." Discontent was not solely the result of casualties; it was the futility of our *mission* that made it especially maddening.

Even the word *mission* felt like an impostor. If the difference between "doing stuff" and having a "mission" is the presence of a structured objective, understood and believed in by all, and directly linked to a guiding strategy, then we were merely *doing stuff*.

For months, no one knew what our AO actually was; in essence, the part of the map—communities, roads, and terrain—that our unit would be assigned to control.

The meeting involved much hand-wringing, well-worn platitudes, and the sipping of mango juice boxes:

"We don't have the people to cover that battle space."

"Our hands are tied by a strict ROE [rule of engagement]."

"The ANP [Afghan National Police] and ANA [Afghan National Army] are corrupt."

"Afghans aren't interested in taking care of their own country."

"That sounds great in theory, but it doesn't work on the ground."

There was, however, one captain who seemed to call the entire war into question for me. He said, "It's impossible to fight a war *based on terrain denial.*"

If the aim is to stop actual terrorists from finding a place to operate—if that is the point of America's occupation—then it is doomed to fail. You can't stop terrorists from meeting *somewhere* when their list of options is virtually *anywhere.*

It wouldn't matter if we occupied this village or that village, or if we brought in 35 million American troops—enough to watch every single man, woman, and child in Afghanistan—it wouldn't change anything. Maybe they operate with some sort of permission in Pakistan, Yemen, or Somalia—or underground, maybe a storage facility in Canada, an apartment in England. The list is infinitely long.

The War on Terror was doomed as soon as it started.

Placing legality and morality to the side, "going into the Middle East, by President Bush" was, as President Trump kindly reminds us, "the worst single mistake ever made in the history of our country."[24] The thought that was beginning to emerge in my mind—that my own actions, however well-intentioned, would fail in the long run—was psychologically devastating.

We continued to do more of the same, under a different name. First we did "presence patrols"[25]—walking up and down IED-infested trails to prove to the local community that we were still there. With time, the Army became allergic to the term *presence patrol.* It implied aimless wandering—which it was. It was rebranded. "Atmospheric patrols," they were called. Presence patrols with a feel-the-vibe angle.

Human terrain mapping was next.

According to the U.S. Army Research Institute for the Behavioral and Social Sciences, "Human Terrain Mapping (HTM) is an overarching concept . . . to systematically collect and catalog social and ethnographic information so that units can create and share a map of the human terrain in their area of operations."[26] There was a script with stock survey questions. Things like:

"What tribe do you belong to?"

"What is your occupation?"

"Where do you live?"

"How do you feel about the American presence in the village?"

"Who owns the most livestock in the village?"

"Do you own goats and sheep—if so, how many?"

Heavily armed, we encircled Afghan villagers, coercing them to give up their biometric data—iris scans, fingerprints, facial photographs—without consent. To this end, the Army Research Institute offers helpful tips on how to use biometric data to get better results from targeted killings:

> Sometimes not having the big picture view can lead to unintended consequences, as in this example: ". . . not having a complete picture of the network and taking the leader out too quickly without having enough information to determine who was going to fill his place . . . If we took longer to fill those gaps, if we had waited to take him out, we would have had more information to determine the second and third order effects."[27]

Coincidentally, Army-affiliated anthropologists objected to the moral efficacy of using their expertise for targeted killings.

Foreign Policy magazine stated, "In 2007, the American Anthropological Association called the Army's effort to embed social scientists with combat units 'an unacceptable application of anthropological expertise,' citing a moral conflict between studying groups of Iraqis or Afghans and advising troops who might end up killing them."[28] Ethics mumbo-jumbo didn't stop us.

Rebranding happened with other missions too. Originally, I took part in *small kill teams* (SKTs). We hunted people mucking around with the road at night, looking to kill anyone who dared to emplace an IED. When General McChrystal wanted to tamp down the stratospheric number of U.S.-caused civilian deaths, we did the same thing, under a lighter-touch name: *observation post* (OP).

THE OUTPOSTS

My platoon experienced this strategy whiplash firsthand when we pushed farther into the frontier, into rural villages. We started creating "oil spots" in virgin territory, never before occupied by coalition troops. To gain a toehold, we built two small, platoon-sized combat outposts (COPs).

Our first COP was a dismal choice, as was the order: Occupy an abandoned building five meters from the road—a terrible tactical location that constantly left us vulnerable to catastrophic car bombs and complex ambushes.

Furthermore, it increased risk to Afghan civilians. With so little standoff from the road, every car coming to our entry control point created a snap decision for the American soldier on guard. Was it a threat—or not?

We tried to make the best of it. We loaded up the roof with thousands of pounds of sandbags, equipment, and people, until I was terrified that it would collapse, killing the soldiers inside. But this was not the only health and safety concern.

Mold coated every ceiling in the house, and in order to make it "sanitary," the mold was bleached, leaving the ceilings blotchy and white. When people dropped equipment or moved heavy objects on the floor above, bleached mold flaked down onto you or your food. All day and while we slept, we were breathing in dust and bleached mold flakes. Soldiers tried to put a positive spin on it, saying that it was "snowing." The majority of my soldiers experienced respiratory issues.

> *The true count of Americans injured or sickened in the war is exponentially larger than the figures given on the official Department of Defense (DOD) casualty website. That official total includes only those "wounded in action."*
> *Not included are those suffering what are categorized as "non-hostile injuries" and other medical problems arising in theater, such as . . . respiratory problems . . . Toxic dust exposure and resulting respiratory, cardiac, and neurological disease represent another large segment of war zone-induced illness that has yet to be fully recognized.*
>
> —"U.S. and Allied Wounded," *Watson Institute, Brown University*

Despite the lousy conditions and our relative unpreparedness, the platoon coped well. Infantry soldiers slept cheek by jowl in tight quarters. Privacy was a luxury afforded only to leadership. At one of our mud-shack outposts, an

Afghan contractor furnished us with discarded Chinese mattresses that reeked of piss.

In such cramped quarters, even porn became communal. Soldiers circled around the gray-blue glow of a laptop, offering commentary.

"Look at that facial expression," said one. "She's getting bored."

Another chimed in: "How can you blame her? He's just noodling it. Pushing rope the whole way. He can't even get hard. Embarrassing."

A few more moments went by. "You call that a blow job? You're only licking the tip. Swallow that cock like it's your last meal on death row!"

"Gag, bitch, gag!"

Building outposts did not automatically build trust or goodwill, as the Oil Spot Plus theory was hoping to achieve. The Afghan National Security Forces were reluctant to do anything with Americans. We patrolled unilaterally—a big no-no—further undermining the narrative that we were training them to look after their own country.

Instead, the U.S. military established marriages of convenience with whatever nefarious warlords were willing to do America's bidding—sometimes reluctantly, but always for a price.

Corrupt officials or former warlords were power brokers and a fundamental part of counterinsurgency. Cooperation often required quid pro quo. But since the U.S. Army was reluctant to directly bankroll warlords responsible for human rights abuses, the money was laundered through "cash-for-work projects" run by the warlord, who, and known to all, took a fat cut. They needed "security," which seemed to be code for bricks of U.S. taxpayer money. I personally handed out racks of crisp, rubber-banded stacks of $100 Benjamin Franklin bills to one of the warlord's subsidiary companies. Perhaps America thought it could buy long-term, sustainable goodwill.

Our go-to power broker in the Zhari and Panjwai Districts was an illiterate, hashish-growing, bullet-riddled, purple-haired, forty-something, $100,000 SUV-driving, Russian-killing, ex-mujahideen *Godfather*-like Mafia don with three wives, named Haji Ghani.

I wish I still had the business card he passed to me; it was an artifact hilariously incongruous in rural Afghanistan. On the white card he had a middle name, something I had not seen before. I asked my interpreter what the symbols meant. "Death," he said, wagging a finger and shaking his head. "It means 'death' in Pashto." Yes, our battalion worked closely with an Afghan warlord whose middle name was literally "Death."

I was ordered to "build rapport" with Haji Ghani.

We always had meetings accompanied by chai and flatbread. The first couple of sit-downs were stilted, but it wasn't long before he was lifting his tunic to show us his bullet scars. He had five or six of them. Gnarly, twisted things across his belly, legs, and torso. He bonded with Ox, my platoon sergeant, over war wounds. Haji Ghani was delighted to find that Ox still had shrapnel stuck in his face from a bullet fragment that skipped off a road during the invasion of Iraq. From this point forward, he would, as a point of custom, try to hold hands with Ox, which made Ox extremely uncomfortable.

Haji Ghani was a convenient friend, because he wanted the Taliban to stop meddling on his turf: he lorded over three thousand acres in the lush Arghandab River Valley. We wanted his well-equipped personal militia and the plausible deniability that came with it.

According to the *Washington Post*, who interviewed Haji Ghani after we had built him up during our deployment, " 'I will clear this area, I guarantee,' Ghani said with a smirk. 'But during the operation, just don't ask me, 'Why did you arrest somebody? Why did you kill somebody?' "[29] He commanded a private

militia of about forty soldiers—but no one really knew for sure. He had armed pickup trucks, one with an antiaircraft gun mounted in the truck bed. He owned a stone quarry, farmland on which grew poppy for the heroin trade, and a racehorse dyed orange that was allegedly stolen from the founder of the Taliban, Mullah Omar.

Haji Ghani was a successful businessman and he fully intended to consolidate his own power and get extremely rich off U.S. contracts.

But despite being someone who's brutally killed hundreds and hundreds of people since before I was born, he was remarkably likable.

He played with his sons like any other engaged dad. He gently cooed to his caged yellow finches. He showed us renowned Pashtun hospitality: a warm welcome paired with spiced lamb, flatbread, cucumber, yogurt, and Red Bull lunches. Better fare than our ordinary shrink-wrapped Bulgarian space-program food. Over time, he liked us enough to introduce me during Afghan New Year's to a direct blood descendant of the Prophet Muhammad.

And when our sister platoon was struck by a suicide bomber that killed three of our soldiers, Haji Ghani rushed over to provide security and offer to carry stretchers. They came to FOB Wilson to attend the funerals for our dead.

When it was time for the U.S. military to create some social impact propaganda by building a school, it was no surprise that Haji Ghani won the contract. Money was funneled through him for construction of what quickly earned the nickname "The Haji Ghani School for Kids That Can't Read Good and Want to Do Other Things Good Too," after the film *Zoolander*.

In practice, opening schools was a complete *shit show,* but it did get our battalion on the cover of *Time* magazine.[30] On the surface, opening a school might sound like a good way to kiss-and-make-up for civilian deaths, but even something as politically uncontentious as opening schools should illicit skepticism from the American public.

Consider the costs and benefits.

First, imagine the costs. The "fully burdened" price of getting gasoline to some remote parts of Afghanistan can be roughly $400/gallon[31]; then factor in helicopter and fixed-wing "show of force" sorties (~$15-60k per hour, depending on platform)[32]; months of salary for multiple infantry platoons (by doctrine, 42 soldiers per light infantry platoon); the capital and operating expenses associated with the ground vehicles and personal equipment; the proportionate cost of support soldiers providing ancillary services—the *"tooth-to-tail ratio"* is about 9:1, or roughly nine support soldiers for every one combat soldier[33]; bloated contracts for American firms like KBR, a subsidiary of Dick Cheney's old employer; cash payments to slimy Afghan contractors presenting themselves as credible businessmen; the scrapping of destroyed Mine-Resistant, Ambush-Protected vehicles (MRAP, ~$1m each)[34] blown up during the school's construction phase; and the lifetime disability costs for medical care and pensions injured soldiers ($2m per injured soldier, average long-term costs; not representative of, "value of life"[35]).

Three or four destroyed armored vehicles, five or so wounded soldiers, season with operating expenses, and a quick back-of-the-envelope calculation reveals how a dirt *shit-shack* in rural Afghanistan costs more than an oligarch's penthouse in Manhattan.

Now, consider the benefits. You have built a modest mud and cinder block building, infested with spiders. It is intended for the teaching of a couple dozen Afghan kids. The quality of the education is low and comes dangerously close to finger-painting. There are no toilets, the learning materials are garbage, the educational outcomes, dismal, and the semi-literate teacher shows up occasionally. The school itself is used as a power-grabbing device for the local warlord who owns the land. In our case, we empowered Haji Ghani so that after he won one U.S. project, he won many more lucrative cost-plus projects, making him ever richer. Very little of this financial prosperity will "trickle down" to the poorest Afghans who need it. And as for the school—well—schools regularly get abandoned or destroyed, making their long-term value decidedly limited.

From a strictly economic perspective, if America's goal was to provide a quality education to Afghan children, it would have achieved far better social impact, at lower cost, with no suffering if the military followed these steps: Buy a used Gulfstream-IV private jet (~$4m[36]), pack it full of Afghan children, fly them across the world to Andover, Groton, Eton, or some Swiss boarding school, and pay for their entire education (~$4.7m for 24 students, all four years, with boarding). And after everyone is off the private jet, fill two briefcases with money—$1 million, each; $2 million, in total, in bricks of $100 bills—place them on the jet while it's still on the tarmac, and proceed to blow up the jet with high explosives. This is the effective cost of building a mud and cinder block shanty school in Afghanistan. But you will never be allowed to ask "why" because talking about the value of "defense" is strictly taboo in a world of lobotomized patriotism.

Because of lobotomized patriotism, America would rather spend money on low-impact education projects in Afghanistan than high-impact education projects in America.

Eager to ingratiate himself to the United States, and knowing that we didn't like the notion of poppy fueling the narco-economy, Haji Ghani ordered the peasant farmers on his land to raze their fields. In ham-handed, unstructured fashion with no concern for the second- or third-order effects, we spent a couple missions assisting with poppy eradication, tilling and destroying farmers' poppy crops. We did not consider how this could lead to impoverishment without providing "genuine alternative livelihoods." None of this was winning hearts and minds.

An ugly incident that took place around this time didn't help. The unit that relieved us at FOB Ramrod was responsible for a series of despicable civilian murders. Sport killings.

According to the military documents, Staff Sgt. Calvin Gibbs and four other soldiers were involved in throwing grenades at civilians and then shooting them in separate incidents. Three Afghan men died.

—CNN, *September 9, 2010*

American soldiers kept finger bones, leg bones, a tooth, and a skull from a corpse as sick war trophies. A documentary by Spiegel TV titled *Kill Team* illustrates how the U.S. Army kept images of soldiers smiling, posing over murdered civilians, one a fifteen-year old boy, under "lock and key out of fear it could result in a scandal even greater than Abu Ghraib." This incident received little notice by the American public, presumably to the relief of the U.S. Department of Defense.

According to the *Daily Mail*, Adam Winfield, a soldier in the Stryker unit, was so disgusted after the first killing that he sent Facebook messages home and "called the Army and a military hotline asking officials to investigate—to no avail." Unsurprisingly, an "Army spokeswoman declined to comment about whether the base received any tips about the case."[37] After American soldiers committed these brutal atrocities, FOB Ramrod was again rebranded. Its new name: Sarkari Karez. Perhaps the American brass noticed the unfavorable optics: maintaining the pretense of "nation building" when the name of the base responsible for housing alleged war criminals implied that something was going to be forcibly rammed somewhere, presumably unwanted.

Amid these reports, I tried to hold back my thoughts, deny what I saw, and soldier on. Remember: we are the good guys. We are the good guys.

Friend or Foe

"Would you fuck that dead and bloated sheep in the ass, then get a blow job from your wife and, without her swallowing, tongue her down for half an hour, lapping up the taste of dead sheep asshole and your own cum so you could leave Afghanistan right now?"

After my soldier posed this question to the truck, we watched as a wild dog approached the dead sheep on the side of Highway 1—ten kilometers away from FOB Wilson. For the next ten minutes it ripped and tore at the soft underbelly of the carcass. A strand of intestine hung from its gore-stained jaws.

All of the soldiers in my truck agreed. Totally worth it.

Our brains were addled from patrolling the same five-kilometer strip of road for fifteen hours on, fifteen hours off, for weeks on end. We'd been pulled back from our remote outposts to attend to a flare-up of danger closer to home. Again, we took to the road. The battalion's proposed solution to stop coalition forces from getting "nuked" was to do "hands across the highway." Sometimes we'd depart at noon, sometimes at 3:00 a.m., never sustaining a normal sleep pattern. All of our combat power was spent guarding this unremarkable strip of road, 24/7.

The soldiers dubbed it Operation Highway Babysitter.

Operation Highway Babysitter worked like this: the infantry secured the road, allowing the logistics convoys to resupply the infantry, so that the infantry could secure the road, so that the logistics convoys could resupply the infantry, ad nauseam, in perpetuity.

Such an operational strategy is mockingly referred to as "the self-licking ice cream cone"—a system with no purpose other than to sustain itself.

Another rarely discussed aspect of war-as-usual is that it may enrich the Taliban.

Here is how it works: insurgents blow up Highway 1 with a colossal IED that destroys the road and injures U.S. soldiers. The U.S. military pays a local Afghan contracting company to repave the highway. Then Afghan contractors reportedly paid tribute back to the Taliban to complete their work unmolested. Then the insurgents use this tribute money to buy more bomb-making materials—perpetuating the cycle.

This system of collusion between Afghan contractors, bankrolled by U.S. taxpayer dollars, and insurgents was well-documented during the time.

> *For months, reports have abounded here that the Afghan mercenaries who escort American and other NATO convoys through the badlands have been bribing Taliban insurgents to let them pass.*[1]
> *Then came a series of events last month that suggested all-out collusion with the insurgents.*
> *. . . "We're funding both sides of the war," a NATO official in Kabul said. The official, who spoke on the condition of anonymity because the investigation was incomplete, said he believed millions of dollars were making their way to the Taliban.*

—The New York Times, *June 2010*

Our mission was infuriating. We soaked up bombs with no one to shoot back at. It was sedentary, eye-wateringly boring, and deadly. Driving through the bad parts of Highway 1, you couldn't help but wince, wondering if it was your turn to get blown to smithereens. The impending feeling of doom—a raw, animal fear—was affectionately known as "puckering your butthole."

In the midst of taking this chaos, I was a long way from beginning to empathize with the enemy. We were too low on *Maslow's hierarchy*. This was about survival. Anything beyond your next birthday was icing on the cake.

With 100 percent of our combat power dedicated to highway babysitting, the number of IEDs on a couple main roads decreased momentarily, but at great financial expense and soldier burnout. None of our actions trained Afghan security forces or addressed the root causes of the insurgency. In essence, this approach ensured there would never be an end to this war.

When we stopped babysitting the road, the IEDs returned.

The great problem with IEDs—to restructure a famous Abraham Lincoln quote—was that we could watch some of the roads all the time, or all of the roads some of the time, but never all of the roads all of the time. And whatever you could not see was where the insurgents would slip the next one in.

The resistance was good at their craft. They presented easily recognizable dummy bombs to draw us onto a path littered with legitimately lethal bombs, or they'd distract us with "red herrings," forcing us to waste entire patrols investigating milk jugs with wire poking out of them, or burlap sacks filled with rocks.

We faced a dilemma: treat dummy bombs as a threat and be rendered entirely useless, wasting time on surface-level threats, or ignore the dummy bombs at our own peril.

Despite our best babysitting efforts, casualties continued to mount. In November 2009 I found a copy of the deployment newspaper, *Stars and Stripes*. On the front page, above the fold, was a photo of my West Point buddy Dan. The caption read, "The High Cost of Combat." Dan was sitting legless, in a wheelchair, staring out the window, looking at an overcast afternoon from his Walter Reed hospital room. He could not sit squarely in the wheelchair because the IED took both his legs above the knee, one of which included a "hip disarticulation"—a clinical-sounding term that meant he didn't have a hip to rest his weight on, which forced him to shift to one side.

Dan and I were part of the same Ranger School platoon, and, in a spooky coincidence, he had been injured not more than fifteen kilometers from FOB Wilson—the place where I was reading that newspaper article. The ceaseless attrition of friends became "the new normal."

But this experience was no bargain for ordinary Afghans either.

IT FEELS OBSCENE to use the word *accustomed* when speaking of Afghans' relationship with living in a war zone. Yes, they've faced decades of civil wars and foreign occupation. And yet, *accustomed* implies a level of comfort or being "used to it," when the truth is . . . there is no comfort in war, only a certainty that life remains precariously uncertain in all the wrong ways. IEDs merely multiplied the chance of random death.

The war placed Afghan communities on the proverbial torture rack. Every faction wanted loyalty; some demanded it. Tribes, local strongmen, the Taliban, the American-led coalition—each group pulled at the populace, with maximal force, in different directions.

Showing loyalty to the American-led coalition or to the Afghan National Security Forces would get you hunted by the Taliban, who possessed a long memory and showed no qualms about coming to your village to find you.

On the other hand, showing loyalty to the Taliban would get you hunted by the American military.

The dominant logic for most Afghans was to stay out of it. Be amiable, aloof, noncommittal, and inconspicuous. Tell both sides what they wanted to hear, but don't be welcoming beyond common courtesy.

That didn't stop us from trying to win them over. We wanted their support, not so much for their benefit, but for ours—so IEDs would stop blowing up American troops. We were willing to buy cooperation if necessary.

As U.S. soldiers, we'd go into meetings with our bravado and black Oakley sunglasses to proclaim we were "partnering with local elders to bring security." We promised to pump them full of money: "cash-for-work, local projects." But that wasn't all. We were going to "open schools" and, with their support, "destroy the Taliban this fighting season"—unlike the previous year, or the one before that, or the one before that, or the one before that.

After hugging and shaking hands, gushing that we were really just brothers from a different mother, we flashed those stereotypically American, max-whitening toothpaste smiles. But not yet out of earshot, American field-grade officers squeezed something into their hands. Something that made a distinct farting sound: a travel-sized hand sanitizer.

In this context, the American military overpromised and under-delivered. All sizzle, no steak.

So why would Afghans count on us to deliver against our word? How were we going to give 24/7 security assurance to a pro-U.S. informer in a remote village we rarely patrolled if we couldn't even secure the main road? To bet on America was to take a bad gamble with their lives and the lives of their families.

Afghans weren't reckless or stupid. In the villages it was a Mafia mentality. No one saw anything. No one heard anything. No one knew anything. In the case of the ANP, no one really cared.

We tried working with them, buying them new equipment, hoping they'd help patrol the roads. But for the Afghan National Security Forces, the war could wait. If the road was too dangerous, they'd refuse to cross. If they didn't feel like patrolling, they'd go home, trim their beards, and smoke weed. They were regularly high on drugs.

Reprimanding them, I found, was a waste of time.

One day we were ordered to "check out a possible IED," allegedly buried a hundred meters from an Afghan police checkpoint. Inside this checkpoint were goopy piles of fly-buzzing human feces, puddles of putrid-smelling La Brea Tar Pits sludge, and remnants of some rotten carcass—possibly goat.

As we arrived, the Afghan checkpoint came under fire from insurgents who had found cover in the surrounding grape field. It was small-arms fire—AK-47s and the like—nothing too serious. I ordered one machine gun team to each of the two guard towers that faced towards the insurgents. I went to one tower, Ox went to the other.

In my tower were two Afghan policemen. One was carrying a PKM machine gun, the other an AK. Both Afghans were visibly high. Both were standing up, above the sandbags, completely exposing themselves to enemy fire.

It was probably weed but we couldn't rule out something stronger. There was plenty of poppy in southern Afghanistan.

The one with the machine gun was standing up, firing from the hip, as if doing a Rambo impersonation. He swayed back and forth like a drunk man watering a lawn. His bullets impacted twenty-five meters in front of him, straight into the dirt, nowhere near the insurgents.

As he was ripping a belt of ammo, I heard the *ca-chunk!* The sound of his gun jamming. With the full belt of 7.62mm ammunition still draping out of the weapon, he began slamming his palm repeatedly into the charging handle, trying to clear the weapon directly into my face. Instinctively, I jerked back.

I started yelling, "Hey, don't fucking point that—"

My team leader, Sergeant Watson, rolled onto his side to see what I was yelling about.

I had one second before my head would become pink mist.

BANG!

I felt an overwhelming force and pressure. My body mainlined adrenaline and all of my limbs were shaking. My ears were ringing. For a moment, I thought we had been hit with an explosive round—maybe an RPG.

"I'm hit," yelled Sergeant Watson. "Fuck! I've been shot. Someone shot me. Who fuckin' shot me?"

Sergeant Watson coughed and spluttered. A spray of blood came up. Then the red burbled over his bottom lip, forming long, loose strings. He spat fragments of teeth.

The Afghan policeman stammered and hopped around, not sure what to do. He knew he was in deep shit.

He reached for his machine gun.

I tore his hand away and snatched up the weapon. "Don't fucking touch that!"

I looked down. Blood spackled my uniform, none of it mine. I looked at my rifle. The bulb of my SureFire tactical flashlight, which had been mounted to my M4 assault rifle, had been shot off. The entire light bulb, gone. The metal, jagged.

This meant that the bullet fired from the Afghan's machine gun had threaded the two-foot gap between my hands and face like a needle, then hit my rifle, then

hit Sergeant Watson. He had peppered metal fragments strewn about his neck, back, and face.

At the end of the action, we departed—everything left as a loose end. I have no idea if we killed any insurgents, and if so, how many.

Watson, unable to serve in the infantry any longer, was discharged.

DRIVING UP AND down the road, constantly getting bombed, unable to tell friend from foe, created an infection within the ranks. The malevolence we ordinarily reserved for the enemy was spilling over, changing the way U.S. troops viewed all Afghans.

We, the most powerful, professional, and expensive army in the history of the human species, were getting wrung out, balled up, and handled by an underwhelming number of goatherders who happened to moonlight as underequipped, part-time, seasonal fighters. To our battalion, we needed to take the gloves off and get tough on these "terrorists." Somehow.

Mid-deployment, my company, which had simply been referred to by its name in the military phonetic alphabet, Alpha Company, became known as Attack Company. Something more aggressive, something more suitable to match this war of aggression.

Even the battalion commander adopted a more militant tone. Before deployment he talked about "building rapport with local tribal leaders." Now he regularly referred to "cordoning off buildings and bombing 'em until all you need to do is count teeth and eyeballs." This catchphrase *count teeth and eyeballs* became his favorite rejoinder. It was now time to "stack bodies," as some soldiers proudly proclaimed with high-wattage smiles.

The battalion commander's paternal tone earned him the nickname "Dad" around the lieutenants. Whenever he talked about Oil Spot Plus theory, the eyes in the audience glazed over. Every veteran has heard the tired and threadbare promises of progress before. We had sat through too much "PowerPoint karaoke," too many razzle-dazzle slides, to care.

Another way we dealt with losing was by redefining "making progress" in Afghanistan. It required some definitional gymnastics, reducing the ambit of what "progress" meant so that it fit neatly—and conveniently—within whatever it was that the U.S. military was doing. Our battalion commander had an idea while holding dominion over his lieutenants one day in the mess hall tent.

"*Progress* means different things to different people," he said professorially, pausing dramatically to let the gravity of that insight sink in. "To Americans, progress is very different. By the time we are done, Afghanistan will not have a light-rail system and a Hooters on every block."

Duffel Blog, a military satire website (akin to the *Onion*) beloved by soldiers, captures this eyeball-rolling sentiment in its spoof articles: " 'We're Making Real Progress,' Say Last 17 Commanders in Afghanistan" or "Veteran Misses Simpler Time Fighting Unwinnable War Against Enemy He Unknowingly Helped Create":

> *Gen. Nicholson, the current RSM [Resolute Support Mission] commander, is looking to continue the progress made by his predecessors over the past 15 years. He has big shoes to fill, as at least two presidents and perhaps a dozen commanders have successfully won the war thus far.*[2]

As a platoon, we needed a place to put our anger and frustration. Boredom morphed from crude slapstick to the morally perverse.

The Would You Rather game, where one constructs a devil's bargain and forces others to choose the least bad forfeit, became increasingly brazen—well beyond bestial necro-sodomy and anal-to-oral fellatio.

One soldier posed to the truck, "Would you kill an Afghan kid to go home right now . . . or stay in combat for another year?"

Two of my soldiers offered their thoughts.

"Sir, you can't think of Afghans as humans. They aren't people. They're stupid, selfish animals. Fuck yeah, I'd kill a kid to see my wife again. Hell, I'd cook him up and eat an Afghan-kid burger. Just give me a few shakes of Tapatío. I'd even wear that kid's face as a hat if it got me home. You can't think about how they feel. They don't want ya to kill 'em; that's obvious. But think about home. We all know these kids have no future now. And they won't have a future whenever America's done here. Don't make a damn bit of difference."

Viewing Afghans as subhuman was not unique. It was systemic. A second soldier chimed in: "Sir, I'd beat an Afghani [sic] kid to death *with a brick* if it got me out of this country! We shouldn't even be here. We give these people billions of dollars and shit. Buy 'em trucks and loads of equipment. We built 'em an army and a police. And what do they do? Fucking nothing. They don't want it bad enough. They don't want to protect their own shitty country. Instead, we just keep on dying for them and none of these fuckers give a shit. Fuck 'em. I'm not dying for no sand nigger towel head."

As these conversations went further into the shitter, I took on a part-time stenographer role, capturing the otherworldly discussions in my journal. Years later, thumbing through those earth-stained pages fills me with a keeling sense of revulsion and shame. I look back on my words with disgust. My doubts might have been growing, my mind and emotions in the process of splitting, but I, too, was filled with hate. I'm certainly not proud of everything I did or said.

With so many casualties, I secretly started hoping for a "lucky" injury. Maybe I could be hit by a car and break something. Or maybe I'd slip on black ice and get a concussion during mid-tour leave. Or perhaps an MRAP would run over my foot. Or, after a run, maybe I'd feel a sharp pain and excitedly discover that I had torn my Achilles tendon.

I dreamed about going AWOL. During mid-tour leave I did the mental calculus, comparing a future banished from the United States relative to the probability of death, injury, or PTSD if I kept doing what I was doing. The vast majority of the world's population—billions of people—never step foot in the United States. Are they somehow deprived? Is the United States the only place where happiness exists?

Although almost anything seemed better than continuing on the same path, there was an inexplicable force that made it impossible to resist. The shame and dishonor that accompanied dissent seemed worse than actual death. The brainwashing I had received was remarkably effective. And so we performed our hallowed duty and gave ourselves to Operation Highway Babysitter.

ONE DAY A fragmentary IED in a burlap sack hit my vehicle. It detonated not more than two meters directly outside of my window. The armor held and it didn't breach the hull, but all of us were rattled. In the moments directly after the incident, my driver collapsed his head onto the top of the steering wheel, shaking with adrenaline. I still remember my gunner, whose face was nearly ripped apart by bits of bicycle chain, collecting the pieces that landed atop our vehicle. He looked at me, bewildered, holding the fistful of shit that had almost killed him, cigarette drooping from his cracked lips.

Another time, our sister platoon was struck by an IED that was large enough to corkscrew the platoon sergeant's multi-ton armored truck off the road, where it rolled several times before coming to rest.

This was all standard fare: nothing special to see here.

My friend and fellow lieutenant, Mark Wise, explained to me that he was ordered to "check out a suspicious compound, possibly rigged to blow"—a common request from a curious and higher-ranking officer, made from the safety of the operations center. Why you'd want a group of people who are not experts in explosives removal to check out a possible IED is beyond comprehension.

In an op-ed for the *New York Times*, Mark detailed what happened next:

> *While on patrol with 24 soldiers, we came under fire and I tried to maneuver squads to assault a machine-gun position. At one point during the fighting, I tried to switch places with my radio man, Pfc. Devin Michel, behind a mud wall. As Private Michel stepped behind me, he detonated a pressure-plate improvised explosive device. He was killed instantly.*[3]

Mark was grievously wounded in the explosion and awoke nine days later at Walter Reed Medical Center in Bethesda. He was bedridden, limbs fully immobilized, and on a feeding tube. He was incapable of pushing his own pain-medication button. Facial reconstruction and scarring, burns, partial hand and forearm amputation, and impaired vision were only some of the wounds.

A few months after deployment, Mark and his wife moved back home to Virginia. Into his parents' basement. I helped with the move, carrying cardboard boxes from the garage to Mark's room downstairs.

Mark was carrying an unwieldy bastard of a cardboard box, wrestling it with the 1.5 hands he had. He pinned it to the wall, recruiting a leg to push it upward, into a full nelson. I offered to help. "I got it, man. I'm not a cripple," he shot back.

Veterans don't want pity.

IT WAS UNCLEAR who deserved our discontent: our commanders for bad tactical and operational decisions; the commanding generals for bad strategic decisions and making false claims of progress; President Bush for lying us into two illegal wars; President Obama for escalating these wars and expanding the global drone assassination campaign, even after receiving the Nobel Peace Prize; ordinary Americans who hardly seemed to notice what violence was being done in their name . . . Or perhaps we should only blame ourselves.

But what was easier than looking inward to find a target for our blame was looking outward, blaming the Afghans.

The psychological strain of patrolling was further compounded by the ever-growing realization that few people wanted us there, sometimes not even the children.

Shopkeepers tended to their stands at scrappy, flea-market-type bazaars, peddling knockoff Fanta, flatbread, cigarettes, and sundry other items. Children—not in school—poured water on the dirt to keep the dust down. As we drove by, dusty kids touched bare hands to parched tongues, indicating they were thirsty. We were, at least in the beginning, moved by their abject poverty and offered water bottles or candy if we had it.

But our little trinkets of goodwill didn't buy deep appreciation. Little boys not older than ten would give us the middle finger. A tight little squad of Taliban youth stood by the road, yelling and shooing us away with the universal *Get out!* hand mannerism.

Some children armed themselves with imaginary rifles. They took careful aim at my soldiers, pulled the trigger, and even had the wherewithal to mime the force of the recoil. Another boy waved his arms wildly upward, making a *BOOM* sound.

How could they hate us so much?

But they already knew enough. Some gun-packing soldier just like me had been patrolling their streets ever since they popped out of the womb. I was just another extension of this infinite leviathan that never aged, never went away, and never learned. To them, we were the Empire from *Star Wars*—a huge, well-resourced, evil monolith that used its might and superior weapons to pulverize subsistence-farming Rebels who just wanted to be left alone on their distant, Wild West planets.

They were getting older—nearly old enough to fight—but the infidels were like vampires, forever composed of eighteen-year-old privates and twenty-three-year-old lieutenants. And every year we'd swap out and do the same thing again. The same "accidents," the same haughtiness. The self-acknowledged futility was noted in one Army saying: "We haven't been fighting the War on Terror for eighteen years; we've been fighting it for one year, eighteen times."

The United States behaves in Afghanistan like a colonial power.

—*Hamid Karzai*, Le Monde

Our presence was famously unpopular within the Pashtun strongholds of southern Afghanistan, where guerrilla tactics exploited our inability to identify the enemy—a hallmark of counterinsurgency. In places like this, everyone is "sorta the enemy."

Although the rules of engagement are fairly clear about when you may kill, the emotional threshold for classifying someone as "the enemy" in one's own mind as "killable" is, I think, naturally lower. In some villages support for the Taliban wasn't disputed; it was only a matter of degree.

How could you not harbor resentment for lookouts who alerted the Taliban to our presence? What of the farmers who welcomed the Taliban into their homes? And what of the suspected insurgent whose hands turned purple, testing positive for gunpowder residue, but without any other evidence there wasn't much we could do? Even if you hauled the suspect into the local Afghan police station, they'd either just release him or, worse, take justice into their own hands.

In one instance, a West Pointer in the battalion told me that his unit inspected an Afghan police prison to find a murdered suspect. He had been sodomized to death with a sharpened wooden stick.

I started to discover that many of the terrible things that happen in war are never reported. *Can never be* reported. *Will never be* reported. The ratio of journalists to infantry platoons is so low, and the facts so hard to check in a place like Zhari District, that the prevailing truth was whatever the U.S. military wants it to be.

As if by the transitive property of combat, since *the enemy is always evil*, and *every Afghan* is *sorta the enemy*, then *every Afghan is sorta evil*. In this way, ire spills from combatants onto the population more broadly and, taken to extremes—where thoughts and words become action—you become just like the American war criminals at FOB Ramrod who murdered civilians for sport and kept body parts as trophies.

It's shameful to admit, but I wanted people who I never knew to die horrible, horrible deaths. It crept up on me slowly, by degrees, but soon hatred was a familiar feeling, that inexorable force that tips your psyche toward malice and disgust and hate and racism. I began to feel contempt for *them*. The moral exchange rate of an Afghan's life relative to a U.S. soldier's was subconsciously downgraded by the day, edging ever closer to infinite worthlessness. I could feel hate at the exact moment when the bullet from the drugged-up Afghan policeman missed my face and hit Sergeant Watson.

My perspective was framed by the deep dehumanization promoted by the military's use of political language, which marginalized and diminished the dignity of *the other side*. With time, I became well trained in the use of incomprehensible, alphabet-soup acronyms and caviar-grade jargon to dehumanize the people the American military was killing.

Boys and men became "FAMs"—"fighting-age males," or, alternatively, "MAMs"—"military-age males." Or insurgents. Enemy. Compound-11 guy. Power brokers. Facilitators. Taliban. Criminal patronage networks. Militants. Islamic extremists. Islamic fundamentalists. Radicals. Terrorists. Local nationals. Militias. Cells. The only term that conferred a degree of humanity was *village elder*. Killing old people, however unintentional, was a big no-no.

Likewise, coalition forces never bombed, bulldozed, or occupied "homes" either. They were known by other, less-alive descriptions. Structures. Compounds. Built-up areas. Building Number B7. Suspected caches. These words described the structures without indicating what those structures meant to the people.

Military reports coldly assessed the hustle and bustle of the day as "patterns of life." Afghans were described by their "activities" or "behaviors," the same as you would describe lab rats under observation. Rather than saying that two Afghans were "friends," we'd say they were "connected" or "part of the same network." Afghans were zoologically categorized.

This way, no actual "people" get killed in war. No parents, or daughters, or neighbors. No households or homes are destroyed. Only funny-named entities. Names that would never describe someone in America. And as such, there is less remorse for the loss of anyone who goes by these detached monikers, which are accounted for in a completely different moral bucket and erased from your mind as soon as you return home—to the land of "people."

But enough with the *touchy feely*.

At its core, an insurgency involved cold arithmetic. It seemed simple enough: to stop an insurgency, you must create a net reduction in insurgents. Well, how does one do this?

As far as I can tell, there are two main ways: either by "removing enemy combatants from the battlefield"—an Army euphemism for homicide—or you get the insurgents to lay down their arms, "winning hearts and minds." This required either overwhelming force applied with scalpel-like precision, or immense and strategically applied goodwill. In Afghanistan, America possessed neither.

The attacks kept coming, and we were constantly barraged by stimuli that had to go through the Will-it-kill-me? filter. Everyday objects could be life-threatening. We became hyper-sensitive. Stepping on a seemingly innocuous piece of garbage that contained two saw blades could cost you your life, because, upon applying pressure, the saw blades would complete the circuit and you'd get blown to meaty bits from a victim-operated explosive device nearby.

Anything could be a threat. The intel reports of what to look out for were nightmarish: dead dogs stuffed with explosives; AK-47 magazines linked to directional fragmentary charges that exploded at face level if you picked them up; dog tags from dead American soldiers left at blast sites—a calling card letting us know the bomb maker had killed other American soldiers in the past.

Then there were suicide bombers. Pressure plates. Jerry-rigged homemade explosives (HME). A postcard of apocalypse. It's hard to show love and gratitude to the populace when everyone, it felt, wanted to murder you.

When it came to inanimate objects, if we registered a false positive, believing an unspun cassette tape, broken clay pot, burlap sack, or piece of metal rebar was an IED, the only consequence was that we had wasted hours of our time and tens of thousands of taxpayer dollars.

If, however, the stimulus was in relation to Afghan people and we registered a false positive, people died.

If a *youngish* Afghan man was carrying a shovel, he would immediately seem malicious.

Since shovels were used to emplace IEDs, it was thought of almost as a weapon by association. Soldiers—and not without reason, after getting blown up several times—were eager to shoot anyone with hand-on-spade, especially if they were milling about "too close to the road."

Seasoned NCOs flippantly joked about what happens if you accidentally killed a noncombatant: "Just make sure you use a drop weapon and sprinkle a bit of crack around the body."

Although one could hope this was hyperbole, the practice has been well-documented during the U.S.-led War on Terror.[4]

> *Keep AK-47s, or shovels, that you find in raids in your vehicle so if you accidentally kill someone that was innocent, you can throw down a shovel, or the AK-47, on him, and you call him an insurgent. You say "He was digging for an IED" or "He had an AK-47," you know? So this was the kind of world I entered in.*
>
> —Garett Reppenhagen, former U.S. Army sniper,
> 1st Infantry Division

Killing civilians was hardly the objective, but it seemed an unavoidable by-product of doing business.

A Nato airstrike against suspected insurgents has killed five civilians in Kandahar province in southern Afghanistan today.
. . . Air Chief Marshal Sir Jock Stirrup said the incident had damaged efforts to win the support of local communities, but . . . accidents were inevitable during conflict.

—The Guardian, *February 15, 2010*

When one of these inevitable accidents did happen, I received a second piece of advice. An NCO with several Iraq tours under his belt said, "When you kill someone who turns out to be a civilian, and the Army investigates, make sure you write in your sworn statement that you 'felt threatened' and that you 'saw suspicious activity.' Use those exact phrases. That's how you protect yourself. That's how you cover your ass."

Roger that.

The number of Afghans who think the US is doing well has more than halved from 68 per cent in 2005 to 32 per cent . . . A quarter of Afghans approve of the use of armed force against US or NATO forces, but this figure jumps to 44 per cent among those who have been shelled or bombed by them.

—Patrick Cockburn, *The Age of Jihad*

This was all part of a second recursive loop: Americans accidentally kill Afghan civilians; Afghans join the insurgency, creating more attacks on U.S. soldiers; U.S. soldiers become more guarded and register more false positives, which results in accidentally killing more Afghan civilians, which causes more Afghans to join the insurgency . . .

Never do we learn.

AS PART OF the strategy to get closer to the villages, our platoon was ordered to occupy an abandoned earthen building. The sergeant major nicknamed the building we were ordered to occupy "Hotel VBIED," which translates to "Hotel Vehicle-Borne Improvised Explosive Device"—basically "Hotel Car Bomb." *Comforting.*

My platoon sergeant and I had warned our company and battalion leadership in no uncertain terms that this building was a disaster waiting to happen.

The sergeant major was the only one on our side, but he was overruled by our battalion commander. The sergeant major knew that a van laden with explosives could park, day or night, in front of our base and detonate a charge that could breach our blast wall and demolish the entire outpost. But each time we brought it up, we were contemptuously dismissed.

Occupying this building posed extraordinary risks to Afghan civilians approaching the entry control point.

The road to the side-gate was too short, maybe ten meters of gravel, which did not provide soldiers enough time to react. It was apparent to me that by choosing this location, our battalion leadership was choosing to willfully ignore our own escalation of force procedures and regulations.

In simple terms: a nineteen-year-old soldier at the entry gate, whose thumbs were on the butterfly trigger of an M2 .50-caliber machine gun, would get only a split second to decide whether he was at risk. With such limited time to react, if it were an attack, he wouldn't be able to defend himself. Such a position incentivized the soldier on gate guard to shoot first and ask questions later.

And at the same time, a confused Afghan who accidentally drove toward our base, or who might not understand instructions given to him in a foreign language from a culturally incompatible person, had a high potential of being blown to bits, turning both vehicle and passengers into a scrap heap of blood, twisted metal, and broken glass. Increased safety for Afghans didn't seem to influence our battalion leadership's decision to order the occupation of this abandoned house.

My platoon made it out of Hotel VBIED in the morning, rotating back to FOB Wilson for routine vehicle maintenance and refit, when, not more than an hour or two later, we heard the hollow thud of a large bomb.

It happened—our fears realized. February 13, 2010—one day before Valentine's Day—my sister platoon was hit by a suicide bomber.

WHOMP!

I ran for the company TOC (tactical operations center—basically the headquarters). Staff Sergeant Ski, a squad leader at the base, was submitting a nine-line air medevac request. His voice was urgent but controlled. He enunciated each line of the report with the voice of someone shit-scared and full of adrenaline but attempting to remain calm.

"Mechanism of injury: a suicide bomber on a motorbike, pulling a trailer full of explosives."

The suicide bomber had driven up next to the dismounted patrol when they were returning from the nearby bazaar, while they were moving through the entry control point, located directly on the road—a concern cited by our platoon.

The radio crackled and Staff Sergeant Ski reported two dead American soldiers, five wounded. A few minutes later he called back, changing the figure: three dead American soldiers, four U.S. wounded, and four local national civilians wounded. All of the wounded were "urgent surgical, litter patients." This was very serious.

There was nothing we could do other than sit on our adrenaline and listen to the radio as our friends bled out on the other side.

I felt profoundly useless.

JB, our company executive officer, walked to the radio stand, grabbed a printed roster of names, and began highlighting in two different colors the dead and wounded. Both the platoon leader and acting platoon sergeant had been injured. A Ranger-qualified squad leader was dead. The platoon leadership had been decapitated.

The families of the dead were notified on the eve of Valentine's Day.

After the carnage had been cleaned up, the bloody equipment from the dead was brought back to FOB Wilson at night. It was grisly business.

Some of the weapons were blown to pieces. What was once an ACOG optic was now a handful of curiosities. A bloody Kevlar helmet that had belonged to one of the dead looked like it had peeled back in layers like an onion. I didn't even know that Kevlar helmets would do that.

After the bombing, we were ordered to return to the same house—Hotel VBIED—and continue on as we had before. The same risk. The same strategically irrelevant outpost. No new plan.

From this point, not only did we distrust Afghans, but we distrusted our own commanders. And unfortunately we weren't the only ones from 4th Infantry Division to be impacted by incompetent senior leadership decisions.

In one of the most embarrassing tactical blunders of the Afghan War, our sister battalion from 4th Infantry Division ordered soldiers to occupy COP (Combat Outpost) Keating, a base that the U.S. military described in a report as having "no tactical or strategic value," according to the *New York Times*.[5] It was built at the bottom of a mountainous ravine, offering dominant positions to insurgents from virtually any angle, allowing them to fire at will downward, into the base.

Camp Keating Officers Disciplined for Attack That Killed 8 U.S. Troops

—ABC News, February 5, 2010

U.S. Outpost in Afghanistan Was Left Vulnerable to Attack, Inquiry Finds

—The Washington Post, February 6, 2010

U.S. Military Faults Leaders in Attack on Base

—The New York Times, February 5, 2010

At daybreak, COP Keating was attacked by three hundred insurgent fighters. Half of the base's sixty American soldiers were wounded or killed.

Local Afghan villagers—the ones that the U.S. Army is supposed to be building rapport with—were alerted by the Taliban, but none of these villagers elected to warn the U.S. soldiers.

The daybreak breach of COP Keating remains one of the most shocking examples of gross incompetence in the Afghan War.

Our old company commander, Captain Langham, was asked to make way for an eager young officer, Captain Fillgrave (not their real names). It seemed like a peculiar decision by the brigade combat team: they took the man who led our company for the past twenty months and replaced him with Captain Fillgrave, a captain from Brigade staff who had spent the first nine months making PowerPoint slides. By his account, he seemed to be a desk jockey, cooped up in a shack, staring at computer screens for fourteen hours per day. Captain Fillgrave had no direct combat experience in Afghanistan and lacked on-the-ground experience in southern Afghanistan.

Fillgrave was prickly, willfully stubborn, and seemed to have something to prove. The men did not appear thrilled.

Given America's impressive record for killing Afghan civilians and our blatant disregard for the sovereignty of the Afghan people, President Hamid Karzai had issued a series of rules during the course of our deployment to protect his citizens' lives and safeguard them against the deep indignities of occupation, including the terrifying experience of having American troops break into their homes in the middle of the night. The set of rules were called the "Karzai 12."

According to the "At War" column of the *New York Times*, it was said that these restrictions were *"routinely factored into the planning for Western military operations* in the Afghan war" [emphasis added].[6] These rules were not "routinely factored" into our operations. Following these rules should have been the floor, not the ceiling, to respect the Afghan people—and to stem the ill-will of our occupation, which is the fire an insurgency feeds on.

The *Washington Times* compiled an informal list of some of these new rules:

- *No night or surprise searches.*
- *Villagers have to be warned prior to searches.*
- *ANA or ANP must accompany U.S. units on searches.*
- *U.S. soldiers may not fire at the enemy unless the enemy is preparing to fire first.*
- *U.S. forces cannot engage the enemy if civilians are present.*
- *Only women can search women.*
- *Troops can fire at an insurgent if they catch him placing an IED but not if insurgents are walking away from an area where explosives have been laid.*[7]

Captain Fillgrave systematically ignored these rules. We were never meaningfully "partnered" with the Afghan National Police or the Afghan National Army at any point during the entire deployment. We searched homes, people, and cars unilaterally and without warning. By and large, we never sought the consent of the Afghan people for anything.

Rules be damned, and with none of the patrolling conditions set, Captain Fillgrave pushed senior battalion leadership to build a second combat outpost, knowing that we did not have the support of the Afghan National Police or the village we were moving into. But he got his wish. We found ourselves, blueprint in hand, ready to build another shit shack in the middle of nowhere.

If the United States is treating Afghanistan as a sovereign country it has to prove it.

—*Hamid Karzai*

Building day arrived. The materials were stockpiled in our trucks as we prepared to capture a small, seemingly abandoned mud building in a village called Now Ruzi, located on a mountain hillside in Panjwai District.

But our company didn't make it more than a couple kilometers down the road before the truck commanded by my former squad leader—an RG-31 MRAP with mine roller on the front—was hit by an IED.

Our platoons were staged to leave at different times. My platoon was still on the main base, FOB Wilson, waiting to depart. But again we heard the *WHOMP* of an IED, followed by RPG explosions and machine-gun fire.

My former squad leader, inside the blown-up truck, had been concussed. Initial radio reports claimed his pelvis was broken and he had a compound fracture of his elbow.

The initial IED strike morphed into a complex ambush. After the vehicle was immobilized, machine-gun fire followed.

To help evacuate the wounded, my former team leader dismounted from his vehicle to secure a helicopter landing zone.

In the process, he stepped on an antipersonnel mine. A double amputation. Both legs, instantly blown off. One leg was lost above knee, high on the quadricep. One soldier who saw the incident compared the stringy bits of flesh that were hanging from the amputation to a "bloody fringe leather jacket."

Eventually the rest of the vehicles provided superiority of fire—using MK19 grenade launchers and M240B machine guns—to cause the insurgents to break contact and depart. The injured soldiers were evacuated. And, as always, the show must go on.

Soldiers, covered in their friends' blood, continued onward to build Fillgrave's platoon outpost.

My former team leader, the one with the double amputation, was evacuated to Walter Reed. He survived about ten days. Thousands of miles away, we were told that things were looking better for him—that doctors thought he would make it. But then a fungal infection flared up. His condition worsened suddenly. Then he died.

Only later did we hear about *the mix-up*. A communication error. We learned that on the eve of D-day for building the outpost, the battalion operations center used an observation device and allegedly watched insurgents emplace the IEDs that injured my former squad leader and killed my former team leader. We heard that the soldiers on guard saw people—presumably insurgents—digging in the middle of the night, but failed to tell us before we left the next morning.

Had they told us, we could have advised our soldiers to not drive down the off-ramp into the dirt, or to stick to the other side of the road. We could have called up an explosive ordnance disposal team to investigate, with proper equipment, from a safe distance, using a robot. But we were never informed.

Again, the military would never release the details of such gratuitous incompetence in the press, but it happens often, and good people die terrible deaths because of it.

The new outpost was established and abandoned almost immediately. We won no hearts and minds, but more were killed on both sides.

Funerals and the Tomorrow Pill

How many people thought you'd never change?
But here you have. It's beautiful. It's strange.

—*Kate Light,* "There Comes the Strangest Moment"

I never saw Ox, my platoon sergeant, cry. Not even after attending a dozen memorial ceremonies together.

One day we attended a memorial service for a Charlie Company soldier hit by an IED. He lost both his legs and passed away shortly thereafter. Two others were injured in the blast.

Charlie Company were owners of an outpost in Pashmul, an area within Zhari District that was in the heart of the Green Death. By comparison, Hotel VBIED seemed like we'd drawn the long straw.

Those poor bastards. They couldn't patrol more than two hundred meters outside their gate before they'd either step on an antipersonnel mine or get lit up by RPGs.

Mid-funeral, Ox looked on with monk-like stoicism.

"I don't usually get emotional at memorials. After dozens of them, it doesn't get to you the same way." He paused for a moment: "I take that back. It does affect you. It's just"—he paused again—"I've been to so many."

For me, tears decreased with each ceremony.

I got glassy-eyed but didn't cry. My soul was turning to ash. Every funeral features a soldier's cross: unworn tan combat boots, rifle, clean helmet, and dog tags. An official Department of the Army eight-by-ten photograph flanks the tribute. The equipment on the cross—sterile, fresh—never shows how the soldier died.

After each memorial service, a condolence line forms. Soldiers patiently wait their turn to approach and salute the memorial. If the soldier knew the deceased, they might take a moment to say goodbye. Some solemnly kneel; others grip the dog tags in their palm; some rub the helmet or boots; and others leave a favorite trinket.

With time and practice, memorial services became routine process and the crowd never seemed to stick around as long. *Back to business*—almost as if the duration one stayed at the ceremony was inversely proportional to the number of memorial ceremonies one attended.

We had scabbed over.

After one funeral, I sat a while. Incidentally, I observed some things.

Two specialists laughed, smoking and joking on their way to lunch. One said, "If I get whacked, all you motherfuckers better be there and you better cry your eyes out the whole time." They continued laughing.

But perhaps what got to me were two words spoken between first sergeants.

"Nice touch," said one, noting a particularly tasteful part of the memorial service, keeping it locked away in his mind for next time—for the next dead soldier.

Sometimes the leadership liked to use dead soldiers as a rhetorical prop for their own devices. It felt dirty, almost perverted. A field-grade officer would take the podium, becoming a ventriloquist; the fallen soldier his dummy.

Ambitions were twisted, dreams reimagined. And suddenly, almost by magic, the wants and desires of the fallen soldier conveniently aligned with the Afghanistan mission and the Army's talking points.

In many cases, the field-grade officer never *actually* knew the soldier being eulogized. He might interview some of the fallen's platoon mates, learning that this apolitical twenty-two-year-old, who could have been a big-time ballplayer, liked beer, Chevy trucks (hated Ford), rap music—especially Eminem and Tupac—and weight lifting, all of which he makes sure to reference in his speech.

But then he changes course, suddenly talking about the soldier's deepest convictions—what the dead soldier "believed in." About how he "would want us to continue with the mission." That we "should continue fighting to free the Afghans because it's a worthy cause," intimating, of course, that if we didn't keep patrolling, sacrifices like his would be in vain. That the fallen "knew the risks associated with being an American soldier"—the best our society has to offer—and "accepted those risks freely because he believed in protecting the American way of life."

Never do they mention the soldier's other sentiments: "I think the whole war is bullshit," or "Fuck these Afghanis—kill 'em or leave them here in the Stone Age." Never do they mention that the soldier may have joined the Army because it seemed like the only good option—the only way to emerge from society's cracks and claim dignity; the only way to feed his daughter; the only way to go to college and get an education. Never do they get to the crux of it: this person may have joined the military—and is now dead—because the alternative to joining the military and possibly dying for a war they had ambivalent feelings for seemed worse.

The product of being around all these body bags, bloody equipment, and memorials was a deep sense of nihilism and depression.

Our company XO (executive officer), a friend and fellow West Pointer, devised two new concepts: the "Wedding-to-Funeral Ratio" and the "Tomorrow Pill."

The Wedding-to-Funeral Ratio was a key performance indicator on the morbidity of our own lives. As I recall, JB thought he had a ratio of less than one—more friends buried than married.

The second idea, the Tomorrow Pill, derived from the slogan "Believe today never happened."

JB hoped pharmaceutical companies would commercialize something stronger than the "zombie meds" that were regularly fed by the fistful to soldiers. Something you could take when "the Zoloft prescription isn't strong enough." These were the pills the Army prescribed to make soldiers more docile and apathetic about dying. With the help of the Tomorrow Pill, you could completely eradicate memories of having lived that day. JB and I agreed, if it existed, we'd order enough for the entire deployment.

At the end, we'd be finished and a year older, or dead. Either way, we could move on.

Kill

I'm glad my guardian angel decided to punch the overtime clock today!

—One of my soldiers

Although I had experienced a spectrum of toxic wartime emotions—malice, depression, paranoia, bloodlust, and despair—there was one emotion that was conspicuously absent: grief.

Grief happens when pain comes to rest, when it slows down and eventually calcifies into something you can hold and observe in the palms of your hands. Grief offers an opportunity to apprentice the pain. To ask whether a life path that contains so many painful milestones is actually serving anyone's best interests. An emotion as powerful as grief can even cause you to redraft your life blueprint. And the military ensured we did not have time to grieve. We were kept busy.

Whereas garrison soldiers have about 140 days of leisure per year—100 days of weekends, a month of annual leave, and a slew of 3- and 4-day weekends—the deployed soldier had only 15 days of mid-tour leave for the entire year—roughly 10 percent of what they had when they were back home. We certainly didn't get special leave to return to the United States to bury our friends who died while we were deployed. Dead friends, like everything else, were stuffed in the "emotional backlog."

The nature of war: working seven days per week, waking and sleeping at erratic hours, facing constant threat, and doing it for months on end, turned brains to mush. But perhaps having mushy brains, whether it was incidental or planned, was the point.

In the short term, this may have even been advantageous for the military. First, soldiers in a deep state of grief, who become suicidal or have severe post-traumatic stress disorder, may be taken out of action, spending too much time with mental health professionals. Second, if we were not allowed to have time to think, we would be less likely to establish thoughts that were detrimental to our willingness to continue fighting.

When my subconscious escalated inconvenient questions, it was easier to look away than it was to confront the building realization that I had invested my life and first adult career invading and terrorizing an impoverished group of people.

I knew I was foolish. I didn't have to look hard for evidence. I knew the military-industrial complex was paying astronomical wages to legions of parasitic private contractors who incurred little risk relative to me or my soldiers. I saw my peers from high school who decided to take other paths, living better lives that were far happier, less traumatic, and more comfortable.

I was in a precarious position in relation to this war, simultaneously perpetrator and victim. I was dishing out violence and supporting hated warlords, while simultaneously being sent to do it by a government that lied us into war and contemptuously dismissed international law. I was fighting in support of the team that had a systematic torture program and a no-limits global drone assassination campaign. I was devoting my life to supporting acts that, if committed against Americans, would uncontroversially be considered state terrorism. Too much energy had been spent pursuing this path and too much had been lost for it not to have some grand meaning. I was seeking some sort of emotional refuge to lessen the sting of—the reality of—my poor decisions that had gotten me here. Although I couldn't delude myself any longer, I could still distract myself.

But if I knew then what I know now, I would not have been able to pull it off.

"Play it! Play it!" squawked my soldier, wearing a Cheshire Cat grin.

Every vehicle patrol started the same way: with Miley Cyrus's "Party in the U.S.A."

In ritualistic fashion, a soldier retrieved his phone, found the tune, and pressed "play," leaning it against the fuzzy-tipped headset microphone. The sound was lo-fi and tinny, but it supplied so much joy.

There it is—those wistful opening guitar chords. Something to *fire us up in the pants.*

"Awww, yeah, dawg! Turn that shit up!"

Even though we weren't the "home team" in Afghanistan, the song made our little starship truck, our *Nebuchadnezzar* from *The Matrix*, feel a bit like home. A four-wheeled American life raft amid an ocean of anti-American hostility.

Bubblegum pop didn't fit the seriousness of combat, and therefore, if only superstitiously, Miley doubled as a security blanket. Surely, any self-respecting Grim Reaper would be too embarrassed to take a life to this soundtrack:

> *I hopped off the plane at LAX*
> *With a dream and my cardigan*

Our four armored vehicles approached the berm at the rifle range, where we normally performed a test fire before going outside the wire. Another day, another patrol.

Joe Klein, a correspondent for *Time* magazine, shadowed our battalion and described the area that we regularly patrolled as "the enemy heartland . . . that was 80% controlled by the Taliban, an area the Russians called the Heart of Darkness and eventually refused to travel through." These towns, according to *Time*, "will be strategically crucial when the most important battle of the war in Afghanistan—the battle for Kandahar—is contested this summer . . ."[1] Our unit had become a regular feature of international news outlets.

"Test fire! Test fire! Test fire!"

Johnson, who was in the turret, fired four rounds—*thunk, thunk, thunk, thunk*—from the M2 .50-caliber machine gun into the dirt mound.

We passed through the entry control point, departing the relative safety of FOB Wilson—the mother ship—and proceeded, like so many times before, into the Afghans' world. For us, combat patrols were a source of fear, adventure, pride, and status—all at the same time.

We both envied and pitied the resort soldiers who never felt what we felt. They were merely enduring a boring overseas vacation at some cush-ass, fast-food-encrusted airfield or another. In the case of KAF (Kandahar Airfield), a personal pan pizza from Pizza Hut was accompanied by the lingering smell of an open-air sewage cesspool, colloquially referred to as the "Poo Pond."

In my journal, I wrote: "Support soldiers. They'd face greater risk of bodily harm, greater adversity, working the night shift at a Subway sandwich shop in Detroit."

The closest that "fobbits" came to being "warriors" was when they assumed the Warrior Two pose at an airfield yoga studio, pointing in the vague direction of a war they'd never know. And for this they had the gall to never correct anyone when they were called "warriors" or "heroes" in public. Probably embraced it.

Air-conditioning. Flushing toilets. All-you-can-eat buffets. Mocha chai lattes at Green Beans coffeehouse—the zenith of fobbit-ism and deployment privilege.[2] Hot showers. Video calls with the family. Salsa lessons. *Really roughing it, ya know.* In this moment I imagined their greatest crisis was a shortage of special sauce at the Kandahar Airfield Burger King, or a delayed shipment of chicken tenders at TGI Fridays.

I envisioned these support soldiers wearing their uniforms at the airport, aching for recognition; relishing that public pat on the back—that verbal hand job from society. If they milk it, milk it real hard, maybe a free drink. Maybe an upgrade to business class.

At the time, there seemed something stolen valor-ish about the whole thing. The image of the soldier throwing a *tanty* in public, attempting to shame the pimple-faced, twenty-year-old Putt-Putt golf worker who sheepishly apologizes that they don't offer a military discount.

Americans always remember their cultural training: Never confront a soldier about his or her service. Back down. Acknowledge that whatever you do couldn't possibly rival the gravity and sacrifice of the Kuwait Airfield tent setter-upper or the Fort Irwin motor pool handwritten-paperwork generator. Legions of people whose jobs exist to create work for other people. A second soldier to audit the handwritten chicken-scratch forms; a third to manually enter the data into the always-on-the-fritz *system*.

Dressing in camo might fool the rest of America to think they were badasses, but we knew the truth.

"Dick measuring," as the military so elegantly describes it, is common between combat troops and our doughier back-office counterparts. But, machismo aside, I realized that I was starting to wish, so long as I had to be in the military, that I could switch places with these support soldiers. If I had done so, I wouldn't have spent my time hunting and killing people who, had the United States not invaded, would happily be tending to their crops.

From the turret, Johnson, my gunner, was seeking attention.

"Hey, sir, check out my dance moves!"

He unfastened his thick canvas rigger's belt, undid the first couple buttons on his ACU (Army combat uniform) camo trousers, dropped his pants, and began dancing like he was using an invisible Hula-Hoop.

Helicopter dick. At eye level.

Cockwise. Then *countercockwise.*

Groans, laughter, and party-girl *whooooos* from the truck.

"What the fuck?"

"Shake it, girl!"

"Cut that shit out!"

The visual, auditory—and olfactory—experience of another man slapping his sloppy penis back and forth against his thighs—a foot from my face—inside an enclosed armored vehicle, in 105-degree heat, was unbearable.

"Oh. That is fucking *it.*"

I reached for the pouch that contained my Leatherman, ripped open the Velcro, and extracted the multi-tool. I twisted around from the passenger's seat, pliers at the ready.

Johnson, a six-foot-three-inch, 225-pound bear of a man, squealed, crossed his legs, and spun the turret around, showing me his furry ass, camo trousers still bunched at the knees.

The prospect of pliers clamped to the tip of his penis was the only thing that could bring him to heel.

I wonder if Afghans, idling in their colorfully painted jingle trucks, saw or thought anything of this.

Our vehicles bristled with machine guns, grenade launchers, and brightly colored stay-the-fuck-away signs.

The Afghans didn't test us too much. They were well trained in cruelty. And American excuses. They learned it the hard way: U.S. soldiers had itchy fingers.

When you looked at the stats on checkpoint and convoy killings, American soldiers had an impressive record. We machine-gunned a lot of people who were innocent or confused rather than dangerous. Since the previous year, American soldiers were reportedly batting 1.000. A perfect postmortem record for shooting civilians.

In April 2010, when our unit was preparing for the big summer surge into Kandahar, *New York Times* correspondents reported that "more than 30 people have been killed and 80 wounded in convoy and checkpoint shootings since last summer, but not one of the people killed was found to have been a threat, military officials say."[3] "We have shot an amazing number of people, but to my knowledge, none has ever proven to be a threat," said General Stanley McChrystal, the senior American and NATO commander in Afghanistan at the time.[4] During this same month, just a few hundred meters from our platoon outpost, the Arkansas National Guard hosed down a passenger bus with an M240B machine gun, killing five and injuring eighteen innocent Afghans.[5] It had all the trappings of yet another unforced error. Another *whoopsies* cold-blooded mass shooting of innocents gunned down by U.S. soldiers and excused by the U.S. military propaganda ministry.

Cars and trucks would be backed up for miles. Afghans, who probably didn't have better air-conditioning than us—*and ours was shithouse*—would bake in the sun and idle behind our convoys, visibly annoyed, gesticulating from their "Hajji Davidson" motorcycles, as soldiers called them. We didn't care if the delay caused the produce in their truck to spoil or if they were missing a family wedding. We didn't care if someone in that long line was urgently seeking medical care. We just didn't care—period.

Fuck 'em. If they blow up American soldiers with IEDs, then they'll just have to wait. Or, as my driver, Larry, delicately put it, "We get blowed up and these lazy motherfuckers won't get off their fucking prayer rug to fix their fucking shit-hole country . . ."

Our Afghan interpreter, code name Tyson, was in the back seat of the truck. Day in, day out, Tyson was treated to racist epithets, slurs, and disparaging remarks about his country, his culture, his religion, and his people, by

U.S. soldiers. Tyson just sat there and took it. He had to. He had no bargaining power.

If he stood up for himself, if he argued with U.S. soldiers or raised a complaint, he might be deemed uncooperative. His contract could be terminated, and, with it, any chance of getting a Special Immigrant Visa (SIV) would be terminated while simultaneously plunging him and his family into mortal danger if the Taliban found out that someone had previously worked for the U.S. military.[6] Nothing tempered Larry's worldviews. The best I could do was order him to keep the most overt expressions of racism to himself.

So when the Arkansas National Guard shot up the passenger bus, it hardly generated a twinge of anger or empathy. It was strange: on the one hand, we were in Afghanistan, allegedly to "free" them. On the other hand, and with much contradiction, Afghan lives mattered very little. Afghans could never expect justice from the U.S. military. Or tolerance. Or respect.

In typically misleading fashion, "a statement issued by the American-led military command in Kabul said that four people were killed. It said 'an unknown, large vehicle' drove 'at a high rate of speed' toward a slow-moving NATO convoy that was clearing mines," according to the *New York Times*.[7] It was first-rate victim blaming, as usual.

The passenger bus, the "unknown, large vehicle," appeared no different from the dozens of passenger buses we saw on patrol every day. What the statement failed to convey was that buses regularly drove off-road, around our road-clogging patrols. There was nothing suspicious or unusual about this activity. The Afghan civilians merely wanted to go about their day.

Furthermore, there was no precedent or pattern of using passenger buses as VBIEDs because the deliberate killing of civilians would undermine local support for the Taliban. Any reasonably trained platoon should have known this.

If you were so incompetent as to shoot a passenger bus, why not shoot out the tires or the engine block, or shoot only the driver? Something that would remove the threat—presumably the objective of shooting the bus in the first place. Why would you fire into the passenger part of the cabin?

American crimes are reimagined and conveyed in such a manner as to deceive the American readership into believing that there was a clear and present danger. "The governor of Kandahar Province, Tooryalai Wesa, called for the commander of the military convoy to be prosecuted under military law."[8] Excusing civilian deaths, refusing international investigation—it was sending a clear message to Afghans: the punishment for not seeing or not understanding a frantic signal from a panicky nineteen-year-old American soldier is death. The message for American soldiers was also clear: you won't be held accountable for your actions.

A slap on the wrist. A bit of "retraining." Maybe a single-grade reduction in rank for a corporal if the homicide was particularly brazen. American officers investigate American soldiers. Extenuating circumstances are almost always found. Little or no consideration is given to the Afghans' perspective. Few Afghans are meaningfully consulted or interviewed.

There were five dead Afghans, eighteen wounded—and no one would answer for it.

But, on the other hand, how could you fully blame the Arkansas National Guard? The capabilities required for modern warfare were beyond what most could expect from a small-town teenager armed with a machine gun. In 1997, Marine Corps commandant general Charles C. Krulak described these requirements in a memorable passage, referred to as "Three Block War":

> *In one moment in time, our service members will be feeding and clothing displaced refugees, providing humanitarian assistance. In the next moment, they will be holding two warring tribes apart—conducting peace-keeping operations—and, finally, they will be fighting a highly lethal mid-intensity battle—all on the same day . . . all within three city blocks.*[9]

These guardsmen were "regular season" dental hygienists, used-car salesmen, and motel night-shift managers who were armed to the teeth, had been given relatively little training, and then were sent to fight a politically sensitive, ethnically charged guerrilla war. To expect this figurative nineteen-year-old guardsman to fight a war and "decipher cultural narratives" when this may be the first time he has ventured outside the United States is probably an unrealistic request. Military buzzword bingo and regurgitated technobabble don't overcome an inconvenient reality: an invading foreign military that contemptuously dismisses international law and the will of the local people will not likely be the most ideologically sympathetic party.[10] Even under the best conditions, the number of hours required to become competent in combat remains hard to come by when you are, as active duty soldiers would snicker, a "weekend soldier."

I was angry. I was angry that whatever goodwill my platoon might have created had just been flushed down the crapper. I was most upset by how those dead civilians would come back to haunt us: how their bloodied, rigor mortis corpses would inspire new insurgents; how it would expose me and my soldiers to even more risk. My anger was misplaced.

Hundreds of angry Afghan demonstrators poured into the area. The U.S. military was backpedaling, on damage control. According to the *New York Times*, protesters "blocked the road with burning tires for an hour and shouted, 'Death to America!' and 'Death to infidels!' while condemning the Afghan president, Hamid Karzai, according to people there."[11]

The next time my platoon drove by the site, we could feel the emotion crackling within the community. Their hatred for us was urgent and palpable. I sensed the next chapter of insurgency coming. The Afghan people were fed up with their allegedly benevolent invaders.

In a separate civilian casualty incident, the *New York Times* quoted Naqibullah Samim, a village elder: "The people are tired of all these cruel actions by the foreigners, and we can't suffer it anymore . . . The people do not have any other choice, they will rise against the government and fight them and the foreigners. There are a lot of cases of killing innocent people."[12] The political backlash appeared in surveys too. The *New York Times* reported, "In a recent survey, Kandaharis favored negotiations with the Taliban by a margin of 19 to 1 over continued fighting. Five of six Kandaharis viewed the Taliban as 'our Afghan brothers . . .'"[13]

If there ever was a chance of winning "hearts and minds," that was lost when we stripped the Afghan people of their dignity and a route to justice.

THE MILEY CYRUS song—and the rest of our patrol playlist—had finished. We settled into the normal, back-aching, brain-deadening drone of vehicle patrols.

The fifteen-hour Operation Highway Babysitter patrols ran my men ragged. I gave Ox the day off to pay off some of his sleep debt. A squad leader stepped up to fill his place.

We drove our strip of highway—up and down, up and down—checking the day's pulse. Did anything feel "off" in the villages? Were there any new holes dug in the ground? Any suspicious garbage? Signs of tampering on the drainage culverts? Were any FAMs taking special interest in our convoy?

Satisfied, we pulled off the road and "circled the wagons," creating a defensive perimeter. We'd stake out an intersection for maybe an hour, do a lap of our piece of highway, pull into a patch of desert, do it again. This was the routine.

Boredom created hunger. I poked at a pack of lemon-pepper tuna fish with my brown plastic MRE ration spoon (Meals Ready to Eat: packaged U.S. military ration). I kept the standard-issue plastic spoon at the ready, strapped to my body armor, next to a flashbang grenade. In these parts, flavored tuna fish was a delicacy—a treat shipped in a care package from the land of milk and honey. Life felt like one of those daily tear-away calendars, the ones that have cartoon jokes or pictures of kittens on them. Something to perk you up. But in the War on Terror, there were no motivational quotes or relief, only new pictures of dead and injured friends. Each day's work crumpled in your fist and was thrown in the wastebasket with the others. I was wishing my life away. One day at a time.

When conversation about whose mom would likely give the best anilingus got tiresome, I would reach beneath my seat, grab a book, and read.

Something uplifting. Something easy on the soul.

Stalingrad by Antony Beevor.

It provided me with perspective and historical distance. But, above all, it made me want to stop bitching.

It was a distraction, and although World War II was more legitimate, as intense as my experience was—as bad as it got—I was luckier to be in this war than wars of the past. If you zoom out far enough, humanity is by and large a good-news story. I could draw some comfort knowing that, although society has not yet parted ways with political violence, it has, as a matter of historical fact, become more scrutinized.

I'd rather be sitting in my tin can, in the heart of Taliban country, actively being targeted by their best bomb makers, than have been a combatant in the Somme or Gallipoli, or one of the estimated 180,000 East Timorese who were killed by Indonesian troops, supported by "U.S. supplied weaponry . . . ," which "was crucial to Indonesia's capacity to intensify military operations from 1977" in that near-genocidal campaign.[14]

Although choosing the lesser evil remains evil, as philosopher Hannah Arendt reminds us,[15] the downward trajectory is hopeful.

Our stakeout was interrupted by the sound of gunfire. We buttoned back up and set our course directly toward danger.

When we arrived, the shooting had stopped. Just a little skirmish: no biggie.

A route clearance platoon was stopped beside the road. I hopped from my truck and found their platoon leader.

"We took potshots from the field over here, but it seems like they broke contact," he said.

I nodded, looking in the direction of the grape field he had referred to. It was huge—probably three football fields wide, at least two football fields deep.

"We're route clearance engineers, not infantry, so I'll leave it with you if you want to check it out. We're going to Charlie Mike" (phonetic alphabet for *CM*, code for *continue mission*).

I got back in the truck.

"Hey, three-six, my gunner's got eyes on about four guys walking in the field. Maybe farmers," said one of my squad leaders.

"Roger that. Let's pull into this dirt patch and dismount a squad-plus. We'll push into the grape field to interview these guys, check if they know anything."

About ten of us dismounted from the trucks, starting off toward the field in a V-shaped wedge formation. Fifteen seconds later our world erupted in gunfire. Immediately, I was mainlining adrenaline.

Machine-gun rounds cut through the grape vines, trimming the hedges around us.

My point man and team leader, Samuel, leaned into the ambush, firing back at the insurgents to get their heads down, which allowed the SAW (squad automatic weapon) gunner and the rest of us to move up and get into the fight.

In the madness, had Samuel not pushed forward into the attack, we might have gotten marooned and picked apart in no-man's-land, somewhere in the open between the trucks and the tangled brush before us.

To be on the receiving end of shots fired with intent to kill is to experience a quantum moment—being neither in body nor mind but being acutely aware of both simultaneously. Your body moves by itself, as if on tactical autopilot, commanding you to crouch and run to better cover, scanning the sector, and making snap decisions based on trained instinct. This frees your mind, which is still lagging two steps behind, stuck somewhere between tuna fish and the ambush, to catch up and think strategically, *What's next?*

Oh, shit! So this is what it's like to be in a serious firefight. Find cover! Think!

We pressed inward, shooting as we went, hoping to suppress the resistance fighters and gain *fire superiority*.

Some of my soldiers hunkered down behind the remnants of a crumbly mud wall; others found what cover they could: a little ditch, a mound—anything amid the grapevines.

I popped my head up: *Can't see shit.* The thickets and tightly packed rows made it extremely difficult to maneuver. You had two options: move along the canalized bowling alley that was your row or break through the scrub brush and clumsily flop into the next row over.

We were fighting in the Afghan equivalent of a wine vineyard.

We tried to move to solidify our position. I popped up a second time, took aim at the resistance fighters' last known position, and quickly popped off about eight shots before ducking down to avoid silhouetting my head above the bushes.

In the two-way fire, M4s, the M249 SAW, and M203 grenade launchers of U.S. troops were pitted against the rugged but imprecise AK-47s and PKM machine guns of the insurgents.

They're close, outnumbered, and the surprise of the ambush has worn off. Not good for them. It's time for tactical patience.

My squad leader reached into a pouch, fiddling with something.

"Prepping grenade."

He hucked it in the general direction of the insurgents before diving for cover.

"Frag out!"

The blast felt like getting mule-kicked in the third eye. The concussion reverberated around in my guts before making a swift exit out of my sphincter. I fought the urge to shit myself.

"Malfunction. SAW down!" yelled Private Tommy.

Desperate, now unarmed, he looked for help. "Anyone got a multi-tool?"

Some jams are so bad they require pliers to extract the bent round.

I reached down to my rig, undid the Velcro, and tossed him my multi-tool. When he caught it, he gave me a fleeting moment of eye contact—a "thank you" in a desperate moment—one that is hard to replicate.

Another team leader prepped his grenade and threw it.

There was an abnormally long pause.

Nothing.

"Fuck! I didn't pull the pin."

Awesome. Now there's a live grenade that can be used against us.

I looked over to my forward observer, Brock, a sergeant who was from rodeo and Stetson country. "Can we get rotary wing assets on station?"

"Roger. They'll be here in ten minutes. Two Kiowas."

Good. He's already made the call. My soldiers are killing it.

The crackle of insurgent gunfire continued, but seemingly from a more distant location.

We began taking small-arms fire—maybe a couple AKs—to our exposed right flank. It seemed to be originating from the nearby village, but it was hard to tell which building it was at a distance of four hundred meters.

I ran across the open area to our rear to get a message to the trucks.

"Hey, we need you closer to the action. We need the gunners to support us. You've got to move up here"—I pointed—"and here."

"Roger, sir," said Larry.

I returned to the men in the field. The trucks began to engage areas of the field where insurgents could still reasonably be hiding.

The rhythmic *thunk, thunk, thunk, thunk, thunk* of the MK19 grenade launcher improved the spirits of my dismounted soldiers. Meanwhile, Ryan started jack-hammering the buildings with his M2 .50-caliber machine gun, each hole the circumference of a can of beans.

We were drunk on adrenaline. This felt like black-and-white combat: we were attacked, we fought back.

I was feeling in control. There was a lull in the fighting—only a few anemic shots lobbed our way.

The NCOs checked on their men and sent up reports on casualties, ammo, and equipment. Aside from throwing a live grenade without removing the pin, this was a textbook example of *react to ambush.* I was especially proud of my soldiers and thankful for them.

I paused to look around. Everyone was profusely sweating. Sucking wind.

No injuries on our side, but we had burned through ammo: 1,500 rounds of linked 5.56mm machine-gun ammunition had been fired, the hand grenades were gone, and soldiers began redistributing magazines, ensuring everyone's assault rifle could put rounds down-range if things got hot again.

The sound of the approaching OH-58 Kiowa attack helicopters confirmed our survival. Jaws unclenched. Lips loosened. Eyes relaxed. My sweat-slick soldiers chortled in knee-jerk relief.

Today we live.

The pendulous back-and-forth swing—from *being alive* to certainly *being dead*, then back to *being alive* again—offered a sense, not of *being alive*—of having a pulse—but of *feeling alive*. My nips were hard as bullet tips. My arteries pumped electricity through my body, which activated a million-watt shit-eating grin. I looked to my soldiers. They smiled back, eyes glazed all the same.

But war, if it were a drug, would be a shitty one. A moment of survivor's elation followed by a lifelong come-down of sorrow and self-loathing.

We talked to the birds on station, marking our position in the grape field with a fluorescent VS-17 panel, visible from the air.

The pilots acknowledged our position. My M203 gunner shotgunned the barrel of his grenade launcher, loaded a smoke round, and fired it in the direction of the village from which we had seemingly received incoming fire. The smoke grenade landed and billowed upward, creating a nice purple plume. The pilots acknowledged the smoke and began their hunting expedition.

Over the radio, we explicitly mentioned to the Kiowas that we did not have PID (positive identification) on any more fighters—only occasional, sporadic, and ineffective small-arms fire. And at that point it was hard to tell where those ineffective rounds were coming from. We had to trust that the pilots, from their elevated vantage point, would be able to see and engage the armed insurgents.

The two Kiowas racetracked around the grape fields.

They must have positively identified the armed fighters, because they released a salvo of rockets on the nearby village.

The gun runs were punishing. Each Kiowa took turns flying nose up until they were right over their target, at which point, almost birdlike, they swooped downward, launching 2.75-inch rockets one after another into the fields and buildings.

The *whooosh* and impact of each sparkling incoming rocket could be felt by every soldier in the grape field, and we began to crack more smiles. The second

Kiowa followed a few hundred feet behind and followed the path of the first, strafing the entire area with its .50-caliber machine guns. They continued their attacks on the buildings until they expended all of their ammunition.

My soldiers in the field erupted in cheers:

"Fuck you, bitches!"

"Die, motherfuckers!"

"Yeahhhhh!"

I was feeling smug.

We had survived an ambush, reacted to contact, displayed tactical patience, used our assets, avoided unnecessarily risky moves, forced the enemy to break contact, called for close air support, then basked in the might of the U.S. Army as they obliterated our enemies. Might as well break out the deck chair and soak up a few piña coladas.

Eventually the sweat dried. The adrenaline had worn off. I had just survived my first real firefight. My NCOs seemed to have more respect for me. I felt that romantic "warrior" vibe. For a moment it felt like it might have been one of the proudest moments of my life: our small group of dismounts had performed admirably and I had done what I had been trained to do. From that point on, I would never need to second-guess how we would perform under fire. I knew.

* * *

It was evening when I returned back to FOB Wilson after we had finished that fifteen-hour patrol. I was looking haggard, worn, and bleary-eyed. Ox came over.

"Ox, how was the rest?"

"Pretty good. I didn't do shit yesterday. Slept all day. It was great."

"Oh, yeah? I'm sure you heard about the big firefight we got in."

"Yeah, I heard you guys were in contact so I went to the battalion headquarters to watch the live video feed from Scan Eagle. They had a TV screen so we could watch you guys while you were in the fight."

"Did you see how many guys were shooting at us? Where were they located?"

"Nope. I must have showed up a bit late, but neither Scan Eagle nor the Kiowas could actually see the enemy."

My heart sped up.

"Well, what the fuck were they shooting at? We had no idea where the insurgents could have fled to—only a general direction."

Ox laughed the nervous laugh he saved for terrible jokes and morbid happenings. "Yeah, the helicopters didn't have PID on anything. Scan Eagle was zooming in on some dead lady in a blue burka and the battalion XO said to Shamus [a helicopter call sign], 'What the hell are you shooting at?' Shamus said, 'Uhhhhh . . . we had reports of small-arms coming from this direction.' The XO gets back on the radio to yell at the pilots, '*Did you see weapons or have PID on anything at all?*' Shamus obviously didn't, so they said, 'Uhmmmm . . . negative.' The XO was pissed. He said, 'Well, I'm looking at three dead civilians right now. Do you want to explain that?' Shamus said, 'Uhhhhh . . . I guess they're enemy KIA.'"

The expression on my face must have looked like it could have fallen through the floor. How could they have made such a mistake? How could they justify the dead as "enemy KIA"?

I dropped my equipment in a heap inside my tent and walked to the company headquarters to fill out the debrief paperwork. I looked at the SIGACT (significant activity) whiteboard to see what the Army chose to report. The report was vague. Small-arms fire, grid location, calling for helicopter air support. When I saw the final column—the punch line—I was fuming. The column header was "BDA," or "Battle Damage Assessment." In bold capital letters was written: "UNKNOWN."

There was no mention of these civilian casualties in the reporting. I felt urgently sick.

Everyone knew that civilians had been killed that day and no one had recorded it as such. Where was the honesty? Where was our morality? Where were the "Army values" that I had been taught at West Point?

Where was America?

To understand things we must have been once in them and then have come out of them; so that first there must be captivity and then deliverance, illusion followed by disillusion, enthusiasm by disappointment. He who is still under the spell, and he who has never felt the spell, are equally incompetent.

—*Henri-Frédéric Amiel,* Amiel's Journal

The Awakening

The International Coalition Against Terror is largely a cabal of the richest countries in the world. Between them, they manufacture and sell almost all of the world's weapons, they possess the largest stockpile of weapons of mass destruction—chemical, biological and nuclear. They have fought the most wars, account for most of the genocide, subjection, ethnic cleansing and human rights violations in modern history, and have sponsored, armed and financed untold numbers of dictators and despots. Between them, they have worshipped, almost deified, the cult of violence and war. For all its appalling sins, the Taliban just isn't in the same league.

—*Arundhati Roy,* "Brutality Smeared in Peanut Butter"

I was reeling after the conversation with Ox.

If the Kiowa helicopters had properly identified and killed only combatants, I would have felt a bit smug. Proud that I'd done my part. Initially. Until "victory," that ephemeral feeling, wore off and the big picture starting creeping in again. And with more time I'd start further down the path that I'd already begun to start down, marked out by doubt, lies, and my attempt to bury it all. Then I'd be confronted with the legitimacy of their defense, creating a checkered sense of moral remorse. Resistance fighters were fighting us because we illegally attacked and invaded *their country.*

But without an impartial investigation—the let's-absolve-ourselves kangaroo court—we could only speculate that the Kiowas shot up the village without positive identification as punishment for civilians allegedly housing the insurgents.

It had either been *an accident*—and, instead of accepting responsibility, the military deliberately was looking the other way, horse-trading integrity for plausible deniability—or the civilian murders *had been deliberate*—a war crime.

Either way, a conscious decision had been made to do something truly terrible.

There is no such thing as war without war crimes. I felt like an unwitting accessory.

If the military was acting in good faith—not trying to cover up a possible atrocity—and I raised the issue to my battalion commander, surely he would launch an investigation. *Right*? I clung to that puerile thought.

I paced my living quarters, a metal cocoon, when I was overwhelmed with an urgent need to shower. To wash the murder off in a dank linoleum box that maintained a bouquet of stagnant piss and the sour musk of sweaty dicks. Looking past the flecks of dental floss food and globs of popped pimple pus stuck to the shower trailer mirror, I saw a greasy young man. He looked different. Disturbed. Depleted.

I wondered if the man in the reflection was, in a more abstract way, partially at fault for all of the victims from America's longest war. He had joined when *military service* was synonymous with *War on Terror*. He had actively sought out roles where he'd be given the great honor of maiming people. Could it not be said that his year-on-year complicity in such a cause was a declaration of his own values? And if so, what, if anything, did he stand for?

I really wanted to give the military the benefit of the doubt. Perhaps logging the civilian deaths as "unknown" was just a *really convenient* clerical error. Made at the exact moment when it could cover up homicide. But thinking about deployment as a whole, I had already given so many other incidents a pass. So many things that had once seemed permissible no longer were. Everything that I had been holding back rushed forward, creating a crisis of conscience. I could no longer repress, forget, or delude myself any further.

The brainwashing I received made it easy to aim weapons at people I knew nothing about. I could stare through my optics and finger the trigger, still equipped with the arrogance to believe I was the protagonist in this never-ending saga.

I was not the protagonist.

In one second, and armed with a weapon, I could strip someone else of all human dignity. In one second I could make someone feel like everything they ever worked for was about to be disposed of. In one second I could make someone transform from father, steward of the land, and member of the community into a "target." As easy as it was to aim a weapon at another human, I also knew the hatred I felt for those who aimed weapons at me. Becoming a target creates a potent and near-unavoidable hatred. A hatred that creates fresh enemies.

In that fetid shower trailer, I rinsed the suds from my body—a body molded by thousands of workouts done at all times, from predawn PT to midnight foot movements. I trained more, and with greater intensity, than what the Army asked of me; one product of this practice was a body designed to hunt people and take lives. It was a warrior's body. I was proud of it. Proud of the fact that, in a pinch, I could "move further, faster, and fight harder than any other Soldier": that's the Ranger Creed. And, like soldiers throughout history, I, too, had been fooled by nationalism to believe that murdering people and sleeping alone was the best way to expend the prime of my youth.

The breaking points for body and mind are different. Pushing an exhausted body past its limits may reduce you to a crawl, but whipping one's conscience past its limits eventually backfires in fierce rebellion. Subverting one's morality is a different force, one that doesn't slow you down but rather makes you want to stop, turn around, and run as fast as you can the other way. I was less equipped to carry a fully burdened conscience.

After the shower I went for a run. My thoughts moved so frantically that the only reasonable thing to do was match its pace.

Working out was my usual way of coping with tragedy. I was a fiend for that special out-of-body, drunk-on-exhaustion feeling. It was a way to process what I had been through. I used fitness to distort my reality, and up to this point the emotional enema worked wonders.

For this particular run I didn't know what I'd do, but it needed to be longer and more painful than usual—so painful that I wouldn't be able to think of anything else. I cinched up my trail shoes, grabbed my headphones and headlamp, and went to therapy.

I could run for hours without hardly noticing. The only indication of the passage of time was the looping of my playlist, which roused me from somnambulism, but only momentarily.

I mostly ran at night because it was the coolest; it was also the time when we were least likely to get mortared by insurgents. Incidentally, night running is hypnotic. With each stride, the light from my headlamp bobbed gently and the gravel gave a satisfying crunch like biting into toast. Not even the beady, sapphire-eyed scorpions and spiders interrupted my flow. I hurdled the critters and kept going.

And in this trance I had the opportunity to unpack and make more sense of my thoughts. By the end, my muscles, tendons, and ligaments were screaming.

I ran for four hours and thirty-eight seconds.

When I stopped trusting what the military was telling me and started interrogating the claims, I found that none of it would ever stand up to rigorous inspection.

Think about it: How could we, after so many years, the expenditure of trillions of dollars in military spending, and the building of a coalition of the most powerful armies on earth, allegedly with the support of the Afghan people, not be able to get rid of a few thousand ragtag Taliban fighters?

How was that possible?

And worse still, never mind defeating the Taliban: How could such an overwhelming force not be able to control the road we needed for resupply?

Why was it that Afghan resistance never led to an inconvenient but possibly more reasonable explanation that we were not "helping the Afghan people" and that we didn't hold their interests above our own? Ordinary Afghans—the ones who weren't getting rich off U.S. contracts—did not want us in their country; we were terrorizing these people, and no amount of further intervention coming from armed invaders was going to change their mind.

> *Many of those who are keenest on the conditional sovereignty of others*
> *resist strenuously the slightest diminution of their own sovereign rights.*
> *The ghastly horrors of the American Civil War might have presented a*
> *case for humane military intervention by outsiders, but as William*

*Shawcross put it: "If the prospect of having their conflict 'managed'
for them by foreigners (however well intentioned) would have been
unwelcome to the American people then, why should it be more acceptable
to other peoples in the world today just because the motives of those who
believe fervently that 'something must be done' are often decent?"*

—*C. A. J. Coady,* Morality and Political Violence

It's one of America's blackest ironies: in efforts to "prevent terrorism" in our country, we commit far larger acts of terrorism elsewhere. Foreign-born terrorism, one of America's greatest and most irrational fears, and the images that come with it—targeted assassinations, bombings, drone strikes, secret "black site" prisons, torture, and wanton civilian murder—is precisely what we inflict on others. What is also galling is America's special arrogance when we expect that the same treatment won't come back to haunt us, even when we've historically proven that we will destroy far more for far less.

What Americans are truly raised to believe: Terrorism isn't a crime—when America does it.

Once you begin to realize that America's fetish with political violence is unjustifiable and immoral, can you still support a military apparatus that intimidates, threatens, and oppresses other people because it is supposedly in our country's best interest? To kill, you need moral certainty. You need to believe that the people you are killing *deserve it.* And when this dries up, what are you left with?

"Doing my duty" had already forced me to compromise my moral code; the only question was whether I would tolerate it further.

I decided that it was time to do that politically charged thing: "blow the whistle." I worried as I imagined how this would work, what my first move would be. I would seek out my battalion commander and boldly declare that our response to civilian deaths was morally flaccid—a violation of our own values. I would refuse to commit violence on behalf of the U.S. military, noting that my participation in this war was no longer consensual.

My solution was to request an immediate transfer, completing my mandatory service obligation elsewhere. But the stakes were high. I knew if I didn't manage the tone the right way, I could end up in prison. But, truthfully, even that—prison—would be a step up.

I took out some paper and drew up plans for my rebellion. I needed a strong rejoinder to punctuate my request to be transferred. "I agreed to give the Army *five years of service*, nowhere did I volunteer to *hand over my conscience for a lifetime*." Maybe it came off too earnest or melodramatic, but it felt about right.

I realized that one could argue that serving in any part of the military, even in a support role, would still be supporting the same war of aggression—just at an emotional arm's length. But I had a contract that I would honor. So I'd honor it in a different capacity that would be less overtly immoral.

I was brave and full of piss and vinegar, but only in my mind.

Saying no to superiors requires a type of *courage* the military doesn't *encourage*. Dying for nothing felt easier than staring down my boss's boss, a lieutenant colonel, and telling him that the war was bullshit. My visceral reaction to the war—the thing he had dedicated his own career to—might make him feel threatened. He might realize that, even as the battalion commander, he was playing a middle-management role in a low-value war in which his unit couldn't even temporarily secure a little fiefdom and defeat amateur peasant fighters on the field of battle.

I imagined something terrible would happen to me if I spoke up. I'd be dragged out to the nearest stone wall and shot for mutiny or something. I had the hunch that the military is vindictive. They would go after me for any embarrassment I caused.

And yet, it was such a curious contradiction: How could the military claim it has principles when soldiers are so actively discouraged from taking a principled stand for anything?

In the coming hours and days, I seemed to be assaulted by a kaleidoscope of images and memories that were only half-buried.

My platoon had been driving along Highway 1 when insurgents attempted to hit our convoy with a roadside bomb. Rather than using a basic command wire, which creates an insulated path to detonation, coming directly from the firing point, they tried to activate a remote-controlled device.

Fortunately, our vehicles were equipped with electronic countermeasures (ECM), an apparatus that jams radio and cell phone signals within a certain

radius. (This is not a state secret: one can google it.) This offers a bubble of protection against certain types of IEDs. As a result, only after we passed the "kill zone" was the bomb successfully activated by the insurgents. The result: rather than striking its intended target—our heavily armed convoy—the bomb was ready to obliterate the next unlucky vehicle that crossed its path. In this case, the victims were a group of Afghan civilians riding in a pickup truck roughly five hundred meters behind our convoy.

Whommmmp!

The bass from the explosion shook my truck. A dust cloud billowed. Pieces of stuff fell from the sky, landing in the dirt. A human meat shower. About nine people were killed in the blast, although it was honestly hard to tell. We did our arithmetic, walking through the yard sale of body parts. We counted severed limbs and headless bodies.

"I think this slab plus that torso equals one."

Meaty goo, cooked rare. No survivors.

As I was about to step out of the truck, Larry, my driver, offered a macabre joke. "Hey, sir, only hop and skip on the body parts. At least you know there isn't an AP [antipersonnel] mine beneath it. Just do a little hopscotch, ya know?"

The phrase stuck in my mind.

"Hey, sir, only hop and skip on the body parts . . ."

"Hey, sir, only hop and skip on the body parts . . ."

"Hey, sir, only hop and skip on the body parts . . ."

What had we become?

After I tiptoed through the yard sale of shredded flesh, I found one more body. A boy, maybe ten. He lay on his back, next to a jingle truck. The dirt next to his body had been stained dark from urine.

A man was crying over the body. He told us he was the boy's uncle and that they had taken a break from trucking so the boy could take a leak. At that exact moment, the fated pickup truck, maybe thirty meters away, hit the roadside bomb intended for my platoon. Shrapnel struck the boy directly in the heart.

The uncle watched as blood geysered from his nephew's chest, creating throbbing red lumps seen through the fabric of his all-white tunic. The boy lost blood pressure, blacked out, and died before we could treat him.

It was as if he had died ceremonially, presented for burial from his last heartbeat. *Biblical* is the word I'd use to describe it. Almost Christlike. Rather than being splayed out in grotesque angles, the boy's legs lay neatly side by side like railroad tracks. Aside from the blooming red spot on his chest, his white tunic hardly looked mussed. His arms were spread loosely apart, palms upward to the heavens, as if he were meditating or offering himself up to some ethereal being. One more human sacrifice in tribute to an infinite nothingness.

A lone sandal lay in the dirt beside his lifeless body.

If he had been dressed in jeans with a school backpack, he would have looked like a schoolboy. In a different setting, he could have been walking to an elementary school in Stoughton, Massachusetts.

I was seeing him—*them*—as the people they were.

They were *lives*, no longer the lesser *Afghan lives*.

AND SO I finally got my audience with the battalion commander. I awaited it nervously.

The BC was flinty-eyed and had raptor-like facial features with a haircut like the top of a nailhead. His pristine salt-and-pepper flattop was a time capsule unto itself that hearkened back to *Rocky IV*.

The BC and I didn't share much common ground. The last interaction I had had with him was when he stepped out of "Shangri-La," the name for his living quarters, as coined by other lieutenants, and hopped in the chow line at FOB Wilson.

The disparity in rank gave our relationship an avuncular dynamic. I found that a chuckle at his dad jokes and casual bigotry helped keep my war humming along. I learned that his kryptonite was his own homophobia, and sometimes I deliberately pushed his buttons.

I draped my arm over the shoulder of another male infantry lieutenant in line. "Hey, sir, I've been thinkin' about it . . . When I go on leave, I'm going to marry this man right here. San Francisco. Whaddaya think? Would you do the honors? Would you be our master of ceremonies?"

"You need to cut that homo shit out. What are you trying to say, Edstrom? You want to suck another man's cock? As soon as gays are allowed into the Army, you'll see me with a baseball bat . . ." He trailed off, becoming aware that he had shifted from garden-variety homophobe to full psychopath.

When he arrived, subordinates greeted him with the feigned but obligatory level of chirpiness that is expected from their lower station. He made his way to my container.

With limited options for seating, he pulled up a folding camp chair, putting him in a less-than-regal posture. There was no head of the table, and, perhaps because of it, he shifted his orientation, more "bedside manner," less bulldozer. He dropped the aristocratic meathead facade: the Brahmin-like entitlement, the speech sprinkled with frat boy *fuck*s and out-of-date prejudices, to better relate to his audience.

He maintained a neutral expression when I spoke of dead civilians, wisely avoiding his usual shtick of "counting teeth and eyeballs."

I recounted the story: the way the Kiowas had strafed the village and unleashed their full payload of rockets; how they landed at FOB Wilson, restocked munitions, and did it all again when, after the first gun run, the insurgents had already lost the will to fight. The second gun run was superfluous—the beating of an already incapacitated person. I described how the helicopters punished homes with salvo after salvo of rockets without positively identifying the targets; I spoke of the flames and smoke that exuded from the burning fields and mud homes. I told the BC about what others saw on the drone footage: the woman in the blue burka, face to dirt, in a lake of blood. I talked about the "unknown" report on the battle damage board and the moral spinelessness of the Army for not launching an investigation to seek truth when it would likely lead to an embarrassing or potentially criminal outcome.

I was not holding up well. This felt like a vulnerable and desperate moment. There is no incentive for the military to release gratuitous details about scandals or war crimes when the truth is unlikely to be discovered. The military's values are subordinate whenever there is a violation of those same values.

Whatever happened in that grape field on Halloween 2009 in Zhari District, Afghanistan, will be locked away in the digital vaults of shame, along with all the others, never to be shared with the American public, who paid for it to happen, allegedly on their behalf.

The BC appeared pensive. His longer-than-normal pause encouraged me to believe that my words had struck a nerve. After a minute he admitted to blood on his own hands. How he, too, had made decisions that were responsible for dozens of dead innocents. It seemed to me that he wasn't proud of it, but he told me that he went to bed soundly, believing that our efforts were "setting the conditions" for the next unit.

I told the BC that I wanted to be transferred to staff somewhere else— anywhere else. I didn't want to lead troops in a war I would never believe in.

Then something unexpected happened. He acquiesced.

Before I could finish my thought, the BC agreed that he would transfer me without punishment, but only after a qualified lieutenant was available to take my place. He conceded it might take a month or two.

The BC's tempered approach deflated my resistance. The civil disobedience montage that I had built up in my mind during the run never happened. There were no handcuffs, no time in the clink from where I'd fight *the real War on Terror*—communicating to the world the wrongness of America's ineffective and self-perpetuating global violence campaign.

Before he closed the door to my container, the BC turned to look back at me. "Your concern for civilians is admirable. I'm surprised more people haven't come to me to talk about this."

Teetering on the verge of insanity and enlightenment
Introspective, microscopic thought

Beaten and exhausted, nerves, shot
My world is tattered, torn, and forlorn

With heightened emotions, reality haunting
Cremated innocence, shattered urn
Ashes whiskeyed away, Humpty-Dumpty
Caffeinated heart, thumpty-thumpty

60 days to go, 60 days to go
All I want is to make it so

—*My journal, Afghanistan, spring 2010*

Months passed. I continued patrolling. Nothing changed. There was no murmur of an investigation into the civilian deaths. No peep of an update for when I would be transferred. Plenty of qualified lieutenants sat around in the stables, itchy, waiting to get a platoon. I was itching to leave.

I was trapped.

When you sign up to the military, you are buying into the future morality of America's politicians, the military-industrial complex, and the military. There is a responsibility to honor that contractual obligation, but there is a categorical difference between serving your country and being lied into serving your country in a way that forces you to subvert your morals. The Army takes no action to distinguish between the two.

Each discrete step of the way, you measure your options and may think that your actions make sense until they don't any longer—and then you're stuck. At that moment you realize that the noble ideals that you were sold on the day you signed up aren't being lived up to in practice.

Deployment is not a consensual agreement—you will go—and you may be responsible for murder in a morally repugnant, illegal war. If deployment to Afghanistan had been offered to me as an option, I wouldn't have gone. But there is no way for soldiers to protect themselves, even if they discover that they are supporting state terrorism on behalf of a "rogue state."[1] Even after the secretary-general of the UN, Kofi Annan, declared the war in Iraq "illegal" in 2004, there was no way out. Army regulations and the Supreme Court (*Gillette v. United States*, 1971) ruled against objections to specific wars as grounds for conscientious objection:

> *Such expressions must be given no consideration . . . based on objection to a certain war. [Army Regulation 600-43, Conscientious Objection]*

It's all-or-nothing: either you oppose all war and are not willing to defend your-self—to include self-defense—or you must serve wherever you are ordered to go.

Americans are already hyper-patriotic, and I'd wager that few soldiers would terminate their contracts if we actually fought in direct defense of our borders. But getting "trapped" is a design feature of military contracts. There is no opportunity for soldiers to align their moral code to the violence they are ordered to commit.

If the Army were to include a safety net in its contracts, giving soldiers a chance to "defend" America, but avoid participation in the enrichment of Dick Cheney's cost-plus, no-bid, *Halliburton broskis*, under the auspices of self-defense, perhaps it would incentivize governments to avoid war altogether—undertaking legal wars only as a last course of action.

But instead, people considering military service should know that they will be exposed to extreme and unmitigated moral hazard. Weigh your career deci-sions accordingly. Given America's misuse of the military, it's a gargantuan risk.

Furthermore, once you are sent to a war you don't support, there are inade-quate provisions made to protect soldiers' psychological integrity. With sadness and more than a little irony, despite the support-the-troops rhetoric, refuge is hard to come by when you express feelings of moral remorse. I learned this the hard way, through personal experience with Captain Fillgrave.

I CONTINUED WAITING, hoping I'd be replaced, as we built Fillgrave's new outpost, COP Durkin. The name of the outpost was derived from the name of my former team leader who was killed on the first day we commenced construc-tion to build that dump. Now we were squatting in two mud hovels: Hotel VBIED and COP Durkin.

The platoons in our company regularly alternated between the two outposts—six days outside the wire (three days at Hotel VBIED, three days at

COP Durkin)—then three days back at FOB Wilson to shower, do truck maintenance, refit, and perform administrative duties.

Back at Hotel VBIED, we built knee-jerk protective measures in response to the suicide bomber. These protective measures included razor wire, incremental improvements to the front gate, and a few speed bumps on the paved road that touched the wall of our compound.

Most of it was for show. The speed bumps didn't actually provide any tactical benefit. There was no need to come racing up to our outpost to kill us all. Instead, an insurgent could have leisurely pulled up next to the outpost in a car filled with eight hundred pounds of explosives and blown us all to shit.

One day, when my sister platoon was manning the outpost, an Afghan man inexplicably went over to the speed bump, rolled it up, and carried it off to his tractor, seemingly with the hope of keeping it for himself.

Seeing that the speed bump was being removed, a soldier from my sister platoon yelled from the guard tower, hoping the bump stealer got the message. It's unclear if the Afghan man heard or understood.

Maybe he thought it fell off a truck? Maybe he didn't know what it was, because Afghanistan is a country without speed bumps? Maybe he thought it was a lucky find—a curiosity he could sell? Maybe he thought it was an obstruction in the road and he'd do everyone a favor if he removed it? Maybe he didn't have all his marbles?

There certainly was no indication that removing the speed bump was part of some elaborate plot to attack our base. But the point is, we will never know what he was thinking. First, because *we didn't care* about his perspective—how an Afghan farmer might draw meaning from experience. Second, because our company shot him to death. He died on the spot.

Not without some sort of dark humor, the death was celebrated, printed as a military case study for others to read. Another parable-ish Army vignette. Shooting an unarmed man for putting a plastic speed bump in his getaway tractor was proudly heralded as a proportionate, textbook response to "defend protective equipment." These vignettes were handed out as learning materials across southern Afghanistan so that soldiers could do the same elsewhere.

Imagine how Americans would react if an invading army did the same thing to an American citizen on American soil.

If petty larceny got you shot, the entire U.S. Army would be decimated. Soldiers got arrested so often, you'd wonder if they enjoyed it. Drunk on duty. Drunk on extra duty. Domestic violence. AWOL. Drugs. Drunk driving. The whole gamut. Weirder shit, too.

Is this what a "global force for good"[2] does?

Not once during deployment did I hear military leadership say any of the following phrases:

"What do they want?"

"Are we putting their interests above our own?"

"Are we respecting their habits and culture?"

"If we were in their shoes, how would we see America's occupation?"

The truth is the U.S. military would never treat Americans the way it continues to treat Afghans. And since Afghans know they'll never be treated with equal dignity, doesn't it seem ridiculous to expect *their cooperation* with *our vision* for *their country* during *our war*?

At the end of our lives, how will we answer the question "How did we treat our Afghan and Iraqi brothers and sisters?"

I didn't have a good answer for it, so on the day I found an acceptance email from the ARSOF (Army Special Operations Forces) board, stating that I would be transferred to the Special Forces branch to begin the Special Forces Qualification Course (the "Q Course") after deployment, I knew what to do.

Had I received this email one year earlier, I would have accepted without hesitation. Now, war-rattled and disillusioned, it took five minutes to respectfully self-detonate five years of work and ambition that started when I passed the twenty-four-day Special Forces Assessment and Selection at the age of nineteen and continued my training with the 10th Special Forces Group's Commanders In-Extremis Force the following summer.[3] It was the first time I said no to what others kept telling me was a "great opportunity."

Decoupling myself from the military was deeply refreshing. Like smokers who kick the habit, regaining their sense of taste, I was regaining my ability to think clearly. I even started doing some thinking of my own.

I looked for the cushiest non-deployable two-year exit plan I could find. Enter the Honor Guard in Washington, D.C., the premier ceremonial unit in the national capital region. It was a plum job with the right ingredients. Major city. Time to think. Despite knowing I'd spend two years as an impeccably dressed human lawn gnome with a bad haircut, being a stage prop was one of the best jobs a departing soldier could hope for. All you had to do was stand completely still, sweating for dignitaries who rarely acknowledged your existence, and bury your best friends in Arlington National Cemetery.

I applied and fist-pumped the air when I was accepted.

But first there were complicating matters: getting through Fillgrave and keeping my platoon alive.

Fillgrave kept ordering us to play no-win games of human minesweeper, wandering around the same tactically useless patch of dirt where mine-resistant vehicles kept getting nuked.

The military uses jargon-y acronyms and official-sounding words like *missions* and *phase lines* to give shocking incompetence and stupidity the illusion of structure and thought. We do random activities and drive around, claiming we are "disrupting enemy operations" without any evidence to prove it.

People who think and stand up in the military don't go far; as a test, name the high-ranking generals who have vociferously condemned America's wars in uniform and were promoted further. Can we believe that all generals are in favor of the war when this same war had the largest protest march in history? Generals who oppose the war, who think it's a complete debacle, do exist; I've met some. They just suppress their comments, because undermining Army talking points to tell an inconvenient truth would be a career-limiting move and viewed as "unprofessional." People like Fillgrave bring in others who don't ask questions and get more people killed. That's how it works.

Although they would probably never admit it, I imagine that general officers probably dream of being the nation's savior. Their legacies depend on saying yes to war. Where are the bronze statues, military bases, and *Time* magazine covers dedicated to great generals who *didn't go to war*? They don't exist.

I wanted answers. Why must we continue to get blown up for nothing?

Fillgrave's answer: "If we don't show the enemy that we are willing to patrol anywhere, they will be everywhere. Soon they'll emplace IEDs here, at our doorstep."

Not a smart answer. It was the same stupid logic some Americans use when they say we need to occupy Afghanistan to stop attacks in America.

Doing more unilateral bomb-trawling patrols wasn't advancing any greater objective. Fillgrave's Russian-roulette missions were destroying lives and equipment and wasting taxpayer money.

I pushed back.

"We are only doing the Taliban a favor if we expose ourselves to areas we can't overwatch, especially when we don't even have any follow-on objective once we take on that risk. We aren't tough guys because we repeatedly march into a known IED hot spot; we are only proving that we are flamingly stupid."

Fillgrave was livid.

He ordered me to patrol it.

I refused.

I told him that if I was forced to go, I would go to the site but stop short, using my judgment to overwatch the road; but so long as I was the platoon leader, no one from my platoon was going to walk down that dirt path and get blown up for no reason.

Fillgrave pulled rank. He threatened to have me removed from my post, replaced by another lieutenant.

"Sir, I *want* you to transfer me. This isn't a secret. Thanks for letting me know the conditions are set. The BC approved a transfer months ago. I look forward to handing over to someone that you find more . . . cooperative."

Fillgrave looked like his mind had exploded. It wasn't the response he expected. He expected supplication. He expected subservience.

He wanted to punish me. He didn't want me transferred; he wanted me to be given a "relief for cause"—an Army-ism for being fired.

Fillgrave continued: "If you get transferred because of your *convictions*," he said mockingly, shoehorning as much contempt into the word as possible, "then it sets a precedent where any soldier could do the same. Any coward who thinks war is too hard could just pull out—or maybe that's what this is about for you. You're a coward and it's just too difficult."

"Sir, if this was about defense—if Boston was bomb-ravaged and I was hiding in rubble—I'd happily shoot invaders in the face all day. But that's not this war, is it? *We* are the invaders. If I were them, I'd shoot me too. We aren't helping anyone out here. How can I fight a war like that?"

"You don't get special treatment because you're an officer who can make flowery arguments. If you leave your role, it's because I'm relieving you for cause. Think about the specialist who thinks the same way as you: Do you think anyone cares about his moral compass?"

"Don't know. But it'd be pretty fucked up if we don't."

"If anyone in war could opt out, how could America fight a war?"

"Have you ever considered that this is a problem? If you can't get soldiers to fight for the war willingly once they know what it is, it's a bad war. I mean—I'd support anyone who chose to object to this war."

"No, you won't! You'll do no such thing. Tell me: Are you going to do your job or am I giving you a relief for cause?"

"I'm going to do my job. Elsewhere. As already agreed."

"Are. You. Going. To. Do. Your. Job?"

Fillgrave teed up the relief for cause. But just to ensure it wouldn't get kicked back, he made sure that he took the necessary steps to drop the hammer. Hard.

First, I was forced to fill out several sworn statements. These statements explained my moral positioning, and one was written to ensure I couldn't claim conscientious objector status. I believe in defense, which made me ineligible to be a conscientious objector, and no consideration would be given to my objections to the War on Terror specifically.

Next, Fillgrave ordered me to attend a psychiatric evaluation with a female colonel who was the leader of the 467th Medical Detachment in Kandahar. The evaluation yielded a signed memo, and in it the colonel stated,

> *In my estimation as a field grade officer with 30 years of both active duty*
> *and Reserve military service, there would be no benefit to any negative*

repercussions levied against him, given his performance throughout his deployment [ranked in the top 1/6 of officers on previous Officer Evaluation Report, two weeks prior] . . . 1LT Edstrom is completely willing to fulfill his service obligation to the Army admirably, but to do so in his current duty position would be detrimental to his mental health.

After receiving this memorandum, Fillgrave, a captain with five years of experience—twenty-five fewer years of experience than the colonel, and infinitely fewer years as a mental health practitioner—refused to heed the colonel's recommendation. Instead, he deliberately kept me in my position and began regularly issuing me a trail of negative counseling statements.

He counseled me on what felt like a biweekly basis. He was trying to build a case to prove I was a fuckup.

Later, when it was time to have my performance review, Fillgrave gave me the worst officer evaluation report of my career by a country mile. In one rating period I went from "top block" performer to total failure. Thankfully, the BC did not concur with Fillgrave's rating and wrote an opposing statement in the comments block, making Fillgrave look like he was guilty of a personal attack. He was.

When Fillgrave failed to get me fired, he switched to coercion, whereby he threatened me in order to satisfy his personal vendetta. One day in the summer of 2010, Fillgrave took me into his office, closed the door, locked me up at the position of attention, and explicitly threatened to destroy my final duty assignment in Washington, D.C., unless I promised him something.

Fillgrave looked me in the eye. "I had a tough time sleeping last night," he said. He enjoyed mocking me in the next sentence, his lips twisting upward. "I think I was having a crisis of conscience." He continued, "I've come to the conclusion that you do not deserve to wear the uniform or represent the country. For that reason, I want to call the commander of the Honor Guard and tell him it would be a mistake to take you. I don't want you to get what you want. The only way I'd feel comfortable with you serving in that role is if it is the last job you ever have in the Army. Unless you want me to start emailing negative counseling statements from Afghanistan to the commander of the Honor Guard, which will likely ruin your final posting, then I want you to promise that you'll never serve in the Army ever again after this assignment. I want to ensure you don't slip through the cracks and start commanding troops in the future. They deserve better."

I accepted his "offer" and made the promise. I would not change my mind and stay in the Army.

The new unit from the 101st Airborne Division arrived, ready to do the same old patrols. The "cherries" even looked excited about it. Poor souls; I did not envy them.

We were informed that Chinook helicopters would land in waves, exfilling us to Kandahar Airfield, where we would begin the long journey back to Colorado.

I checked on my men. Their bags were packed. Plastic boxes were sealed. Final photos were taken.

We gave one another long hugs, fist bumps, and bro-style shoulder pats. A rock of despair was lifted, but joy was not beneath it. Deployment ended not with a bang but a whimper—a feeble moan of relief. It was not time to celebrate; it was time to pick up the pieces of our lives. It was time to start over. Or at least try.

As I looked at my soldiers, I realized that there is something profoundly unifying about traipsing through forests, carrying double basic load in a hypothermic rainstorm, soaked down to my pale, miserable gooseflesh. It did something to rekindle the sense of struggle faced in the natural order. It made me feel like a real person. As senseless and violent and dehumanizing as war often is, there is something remarkably humanizing about sharing a dwindling food supply with a fellow Ranger student in a swampy bivouac with a storm rolling in. Or when there is a weapon malfunction during an intense moment in a firefight and your soldier, now completely defenseless, yells out for a multi-tool; in that brief moment, as you toss the pliers his way, making fleeting, I've-got-your-back eye contact, you know you have forged a new type of bond. I shared the most intense versions of these experiences with the men who stood in front of me. We were individuals with our own shortcomings, but we made a pretty good team.

It was almost tribal the way we worked together. We didn't trust "Big Army" or the "Oil Spot Plus" theory or the lofty strategies that had sent us here. We didn't have time for that. We cared about each other. And for that same reason, subjected to an Afghanistan's worth of stress and danger, I understood why

Afghans operated in tribal communities. I understood why they were especially skeptical of their government institutions, a Western construct thrust upon them, and why these government institutions would continue to fail.

As tight a team as we were, there were gaps in our ranks from those who had become casualties. The number of soldiers boarding the "freedom birds" was conspicuously fewer.

Up, up, and away—the Chinook helicopter hovered, finding its balance before it lumbered to Kandahar. The noise of the engines drowned out the chatter. The vibrations shook us violently. I looked to the porthole window to see what we had left behind.

For starters, we left our interpreters. "Abandoned them," more like it. And to this day thousands remain marooned by the U.S. government. To thank them for their service to American troops, our government has let them rot in administrative purgatory for years, capping the number of Special Immigrant Visas, which has caused interpreters and their families to be murdered by the Taliban.

The rest of the trip home showed me the full "value chain" of war—in reverse. First you see the suffering and destruction the war has caused and the living human beings who are subjected to live in permanent war; then you see the military-industrial complex that sells fear and this season's killing accessories; and finally you see the Americans whose complicity props up the whole thing.

My platoon was getting away. Going home to a flawed but immensely better place. But the Afghans, they were here to stay. The "Heart of Darkness" was their home. There was no alternative to living, raising children, finding a clean well and a meal, and trying to survive in "the Green Death."

People from poor countries don't get a choice—or a voice. The poor are indirect objects: things *happen to them*. They did not have a choice when they were invaded. They did not have a choice when Obama ramped up the bombing or the global drone assassination campaign. They did not have a choice when we tortured them at "black sites." And whatever freedoms America was supposedly protecting by going to war superseded whatever claims Afghans had to be treated with decency by America.

I looked past the Chinook door gunner. Two farmers prodded their goat herd with sticks. Other men lay on mats in the shade, drinking chai. They were just trying to make do.

As we passed overhead, women, fully covered despite the heat, slunk away into hiding. They have learned that American soldiers bring fear and "accidents."

You could see how the familiar highways were blown to bits here and there, and as we flew farther away from our AO, the destruction was less familiar. Next to bazaars where sweets were sold and children played in mud puddles were burned-out vehicles.

The Afghan National Police outposts were dilapidated. The main structure riddled with bullet holes. Recoilless rifles and RPGs had turned the walls to Swiss cheese. Protective sandbags were shredded from bullets and years of disrepair.

I saw the most powerful country on earth obliterating subsistence farmers from mostly Muslim countries. (Today the known number of countries we are bombing is seven.[4]) And in one year I observed this place go from suffering to more suffering, from violence to more violence, from hatred to more hatred. No one was saved. No goal advanced. Only waste and tragic loss. And after each bombing, the dead children were carried out in blankets.

The US Has Bombed at Least Eight Wedding Parties Since 2001 . . .
Estimated total dead from the eight incidents: almost 300 Afghans,
Iraqis and Yemenis.

—The Nation, *December 20, 2013*

We passed the grape fields, the Arghandab River, dusty mountains, and dozens of poverty-stricken villages. Out of the $6–8 trillion that America is estimated to have spent on the War on Terror, little, if any, benefited these people.

After landing, my soldiers and I ate at TGI Fridays—a new addition to the "boardwalk." It was nestled in among Burger King and Tim Hortons and the shops that sold scary-looking, not particularly useful, knives and brass knuckles to young fobbits who would never leave the airfield. The people who bought these things were the ones you felt least comfortable about wielding them. The shops looked like a combat scene designed by a fifteen-year old boy who played too many first-person shooter video games. Camo netting. Heavy metal music. Velcro hats. Everything was "black ops." "Special Forces" this, "commando" that.

My soldiers and I bought cheap trinkets and wandered, taking in the circus.

A soldier must want to do the things we had to do—or at least be satisfied
with them. I couldn't find good enough reasons for killing men and
women, nor understand the reasons when they were explained.

—*John Steinbeck,* East of Eden

It was a funny thing, arriving home. It didn't feel like home. Most things were the same, which felt rude, given how much we had changed.

Relative to where I was coming from, it felt like most Americans had it easy—and were still complaining about it. And while everyone was too busy wallowing over stubborn belly fat, America just kept on screwing up the world for everyone else. We've contributed more to the climate change crisis than any other country. We consume more plastic per capita. We sell the most arms. We empower autocratic strongmen to do violence against their own people.

Bald Eagle America, the version I was raised to believe in, the one I had risked it all for, didn't feel like America anymore. It felt like "'Murrica," its loutish, inbred, belligerent cousin, featuring George W. Bush driving a bright yellow Hummer H2 on his way to Panama City, eating a Taco Bell Chalupa Supreme® and blaring Toby Keith.

It was late. One a.m. on a small Colorado Springs tarmac. A smiley, leather-fringed biker gang was there to greet us. Harleys grunted in the background. Their appreciation felt good.

I lugged my baggage to the airport hangar and was given a folder filled with don't-kill-yourself brochures. I had never seen so many suicide prevention phone numbers.

I thumbed through the rest of the folder, wishing to find an Honorable Discharge. No luck. All I got was a coupon for a "Free Baconator"—a triple-stacked bacon cheeseburger from Wendy's.

Soon we were bombarded by American businesses looking to get their hands on our war money. Tax-free pay in a war zone meant more money to spend on trucks and motorcycles in America. In fairness, it was the perfect time to "penetrate the market." We were vulnerable and suffering from fiscal bulimia. We had binge-saved our paydays and we were willing to do anything to feel fortunate. Impulsive, discombobulated, and hedonistic—the perfect storm.

The sales and marketing departments of America's most American companies were out in force: Harley-Davidson, Ford, Chevrolet. Everyone had veteran discounts with financing a few basis points lower than usual. Biceps and fake breasts, generously doused in self-tanner, gave us pamphlets detailing the latest model of whatever-it-was. The rest of the synthetic salespeople, seeing dollars, did the rank-to-pay calculation, finding the perfect product that verged on unaffordable. I didn't know it until then, but I looked like a man who belonged behind the wheel of a Ford Super Duty F250 King Ranch quad-cab fossil burner. *'Murrica!*

Months later, the soldiers earning $27,000 a year sold off their $49,000 trucks at a huge loss. Some slept in them.

Despite the safety briefs, our unit didn't make it more than forty-eight hours in the United States before one soldier was killed in a drunk-driving disaster. Another soldier decided to drink liquor while cleaning a loaded pistol, firing a round through the apartment wall, where it whizzed by his unsuspecting neighbor.

One aspect of "redeployment," as it's called—that is, returning home from war—is to go through a slew of processing stations. One of those stations is for mental health.

Sitting in one of Fort Carson's on-base gymnasiums, I looked down at the clipboard and questionnaire in my hands. It had a whole bunch of barometer-type questions to assess how fucked up you were.

- *Have you ever been frightened in the last year?*
- *Have you ever witnessed Afghan civilians either injured or killed?*
- *Have you ever witnessed American soldiers either injured or killed?*
- *Were you ever afraid that people were actively trying to kill you while you were deployed?*
- *Have you ever been attacked by indirect fire?*
- *Have you or your vehicle ever been struck by an IED?*
- *Have you been abnormally angry or irritated in the last 3 months?*
- *Do you feel abnormally angry or irritated at the moment?*
- *Have you felt emotionally numb or detached in the last 3 months?*
- *Do you feel emotionally numb or detached at the moment?*
- *Do you find yourself having more frequent arguments with the people that you care about?*
- *Have you had trouble sleeping during the last 3 months?*

My life, in questionnaire form, was a dark satire. Every box I checked "yes."

Perhaps it was due to not heeding the memorandum from the colonel—or perhaps the damage had already been done—but upon returning from Afghanistan, the Department of Veterans Affairs diagnosed me with post-traumatic stress disorder. I was given a disability rating and monthly disability pay for life. Sometimes I feel bad about receiving it. Sometimes I don't.

I would speculate that my experience with mental health in Afghanistan would have been different had the mental health professional been male. If the colonel had been male, he would have been "a colonel"; but since the colonel was female, she was marginalized behind closed doors, called "that crazy female psychologist" or "Colonel Dusty Crotch" by infantry soldiers. No respect was given for her professional experience.

This systemic marginalization manifests itself in action too. Women in the military find themselves exposed to a high likelihood of sexual assault. According to the *Washington Post*,

> In a recent VA survey of 1,500 women who deployed to Iraq and Afghanistan, one in four said they experienced sexual assault—defined as any unwanted contact from groping to rape—during their deployments.[5]

COURTHOUSE MARRIAGE

The emotional costs of war take many forms. Although I had it better than many soldiers and officers I knew, I wasn't entirely spared either.

Less than a year after returning from combat, I got "courthouse married."

It lasted a week.

One calendar week before we were officially separated.

I demand a distinction. "Courthouse married" isn't "real married." I keep *that shit* separate. Cold. Administrative. There was no ceremony. No reception. "Real marriage" was never going to happen. It's easier for everybody if "courthouse marriage" stays a terrible clerical mistake made by a someone, not us. We signed those government forms in Arlington, Virginia, for a number of reasons—all of them bad.

The lesser reason was that she struggled to find decent-paying work that would provide health insurance. I knew that if we got "courthouse married" the military would provide both healthcare and additional pay for "dependents"—several hundred bucks per month. Because America doesn't have universal healthcare, the benefits offered by the military equated to a perverse financial incentive for marriage. It made me wonder: if America offered universal healthcare like other wealthy countries—Australia, the UK, to name a couple—how many others could have avoided the turmoil and embarrassment caused by the other, ugly-named thing I had to do: "get divorced?"

The greater reason for the "courthouse marriage" was the belief that if we signed those papers, a magical life raft would appear to rescue our cement-shoed relationship. It had been less than a year since I returned from combat when the two of us hit a rocky patch, caused by our fundamental incompatibilities. It took me less than one calendar week until the same arguments resumed—until I realized that marriage, courthouse or otherwise, was no salve for diverging souls.

Returning home alive—and physically whole—distorts reality. And judgement. If my girlfriend stuck with me through deployment, couldn't we make it through anything? I was so wrong.

Years passed.

After you learn something, you never look at the world the same way. With each phase of understanding, we shift our frame of reference, generating an entirely different mental image.

In military training, "a gun" is named "a weapon," which later becomes "an M249 squad automatic weapon." It's difficult to go backward, to "un-see," "un-hear," or "un-taste" what you have learned to sense.

The way in which I think about this war, about political violence more generally, has evolved with time and the mercy of distance. I began to *see through* the mirage.

Not only did I have the shallow expertise to distinguish between weapon systems (a component of the Reconnaissance School curriculum) or understand, from on-the-ground experience, that war is far more ugly and clumsy than it is portrayed in the movies, I realized that I—the war—wasn't defending anything.[6] I was *offending*. I was just another heavily armed militant, head down and deep among the scrum. I was an accessory to state terrorism and a tool for America's

Middle East agenda, which involved yanking and dislocating these people from their natural state of being.

Once upon a time, I used to feel pride when I watched those empty-calorie patriotic action flicks. That has changed. Films like *American Sniper* and *Lone Survivor* that depict American soldiers as badasses and heroes make me feel sad, alienated, or revolted.

And I get it. I understand the tug-the-heartstrings, I'm-no-hero, just-a-simple-steak-eating-American-soldier-doing-my-job story arc. But should we choose to listen and divorce ourselves from the biases that favor the geography we were born in above all others, we'd probably find that Afghans and Iraqis have more sympathetic story lines.[7] Every time I hear Americans cheering at combat scenes in the movies, I can't help but think they are cheering for ignorance. If Americans knew what I knew, they wouldn't act the same way. It's as if many ordinary Americans don't notice, or don't care to notice, that they are cheering for the invader. The man pumping bullets into people who are defending *their* country *from him*. We are the bully. The storm troopers. The leviathan that ignores international law.

This Memorial Day, I hope you consider what Memorial Day might look like in the countries we have attacked. For starters, these events would be much larger, not in pageantry or self-congratulatory stories about one's own righteousness, but rather in terms of human suffering. From the perspective of the countries who have been attacked by America, our impact may best be measured in civilian body count.

PART III

IMAGINE THE COSTS

What else might we be doing?

You count upon the heat of battle and the enthusiasm of patriotism to faster fetters upon our people . . . It is in time of war and under the cloak of patriotism that the most vicious schemes of legislation obtain a foothold upon our statute books and the most infamous conspiracies of public plunder are carried into execution.

—Edward W. Carmack

What Has Been Lost?

*The power to do good goes almost always with the possibility to
do the opposite.*

—*Amartya Sen,* Development as Freedom

In the beginning of this book I suggested that before we decide to go to war, we should be accompanied by three visions: First, the vision of one's own death in that war; second, the vision of experiencing the war from the other side; and third, the opportunity cost—what could have been *but was not* because of the war.

In the preceding pages, I've offered my own story, sharing my reality of the first two in a war that had already been declared, and in which I was a combatant.

These three imaginings are supposed to take place before our nation has committed to war, but it's clear that I would have been unable to formulate my visions as a sixteen-year-old, when I applied to West Point.

I lived in post-9/11, hyper-patriotic America.

I did not have adequate information.

I was a kid.

War helped me to devise these questions; only the tragedy of war and a decade of reflection have helped me to answer them.

I have asked you to conjure visions, but for me these are not visions at all. They are violent realities.

My vision of death is informed by the memories of bloody, ketamined soldiers carried on litters to Black Hawk medevac helicopters; of a wounded friend asking if I have a needle or something to drain the blisters on his leg stump; of flowers and stacked pebbles or miniature Johnnie Walker nips resting in tribute against gray cemetery headstones; of soldiers rendered joyless; of soldiers who can't get a job, can't keep a job, don't want a job, but need a job; of soldiers who, over a break during classes at an inpatient mental health ward, avoid eye contact, referring to life like it's a rudderless affair; of soldiers who have committed suicide; of my former soldier's Facebook posts as he risks death by kidney disease, exacerbated by alcoholism—"deaths of despair,"[1] as they're known.

> *Family and friends, I've kept it in long enough, I'm stage 5 kidney disease. I lost my left kidney in 2012, and have slowly been losing my right . . . I also have a problem with alcohol . . . this is my acceptance . . . Please forgive me . . .*
>
> *—A former soldier*

My vision of empathy—to imagine the "other side"—is informed by memories of burning fields and OH-58 Kiowas firing rockets overhead; of mud homes caved in from high explosives; of Afghan civilians and soldiers clutching various bloody stumps and holding their lacerated faces; of a dead baby brought to our outpost; of the boy in a white tunic, dead, on his back with the bloodsome stain over his heart; of broken glass beside a passenger bus, shot to Swiss cheese by the U.S. military. Not all of the destruction was due to the U.S. military—far from it—but all of it was on account of us being there. In their country. Illegally. It's still surprising to me when I look down at my hands, typing this sentence, that these same hands were responsible for a small part of the total devastation.

My vision of opportunity costs is more complex. It's not simply imagining the direct costs of war—the number of dead, injured, or traumatized. It's the act of imagining the negative space—the hole in the universe created by the absence of people—and the substitution of physical health for physical pain and disability; or of spending trillions to create war debt instead of putting those funds to better use almost anywhere else.

I have approached this final vision—opportunity cost—in two parts.

In this first chapter, I will explore the human costs of this war—how it affected me personally and how it affected the world more broadly.

In the second chapter of part 3, I will explore the economic costs of the War on Terror, conceptualizing alternatives to never-ending war and ever-growing military spending.

For everyone's sake—and for the sake of unborn generations—I hope America reimagines its relationship with the military, military spending, and never-ending political violence, putting to better use the spirit and resources of the American people.

IN THE SAME breath that I encourage us to reflect on the things that will be lost by going to war, I concede that we are woefully ill-equipped to do so. Recruits and civilians are not encouraged to think too much or too deeply about the gory, unglamorous details. About killing or being killed in a realistic, non-Hollywood way.

I needed a book like this when I was weighing the decision to join the armed forces. I believed in the patriotic war fantasies so favored by the American Right.

Twelve years ago I crossed the graduation stage at West Point. I nervously collected my for-show empty diploma tube from Dick Cheney and shook his hand. Cheney was a soft-handed man, and he carried his CEO's girth with gravitas. It was clear that those soft hands would never carry out the rough deeds ordered by his administration. He was leaving that dirty work for us.

But that's not what I was thinking in that moment. I was taught to respect and revere our government leaders and avoid speaking ill of our commander-in-chief and vice president no matter what. So what I spluttered in that moment was something like "Sir, it's an honor to serve under your leadership." It came off puppy-ish, and childlike. At twenty-one I was a dipshit.

My views of the world were not grounded in reality. I had not heard the words of Representative Barbara Lee of California, who stood alone in opposition in a 420-to-1 vote for the Authorization for Use of Military Force, a resolution that was as broad as it was vague.[2] In the congresswoman's words, the resolution was "a blank check to the president to attack anyone involved in the Sept. 11 events—anywhere, in any country, without regard to our nation's long-term foreign policy, economic and national security interests, and without time limit."[3] Unfortunately all of what Congresswoman Lee feared became true. For her courage, "Lee was deluged with rancid insults and death threats."[4] Nor did I know that President Bush rejected a Taliban offer to hand bin Laden over in October 2001. Afghanistan's deputy prime minister told reporters, "If the Taliban is given evidence that Osama bin Laden is involved" and the bombing campaign stopped, "we would be ready to hand him over to a third country."[5] Of course, America continued bombing. Likewise, I didn't know that legal scholars claimed the U.S. war against the Taliban government could not be justified as an act of self-defense under Article 51 of the UN Charter. Geoffrey Robertson, human rights barrister and author of *Crimes Against Humanity: The Struggle for Global Justice*, writes, "[Article 51] certainly permitted an incursion on Afghan territory and sovereignty to flush al-Qaida out of its caves and to capture its adherents, but did not extend so far as to allow the overthrow of the Taliban."[6]

Iraq was no better, and probably worse. "The assault on Iraq had been undertaken without UN Security Council approval, and could be justified on no traditional doctrine of international law. The belligerents were not under imminent threat from Saddam, and neither the United States nor the UK claimed to be acting pursuant to any right of humanitarian intervention to stop civilians being mass (or even individually) murdered . . . If 'the US rides rough shod over international law today, we will create precedents that will surely come back to haunt us when invoked by our enemies in the years ahead.'"[7]

Nor did I know that atrocities inflicted by the "coalition of the willing" were almost never reported with sufficient outrage, for fear that sincere and courageous journalism would be a career-limiting move. Dan Rather, the former anchor of *CBS Evening News*, spoke of these post-9/11 extreme psychosocial dynamics: "There was a fear in every newsroom in America . . . a fear of losing your job . . . the fear of being stuck with some label, unpatriotic or otherwise."[8] Nor did I know that there was tremendous pressure placed on members of Congress to open up the public purse to the military-industrial complex. Perhaps it was driven by fear of being seen as un-American, or maybe the Faustian bargain was too hard to resist: offering to support America's permanent war footing in exchange for new security jobs in the home district during lean Global Financial Crisis years.

As Harry Stonecipher, then Vice President of Boeing, expressed the
corporate confidence in an interview with the Wall Street Journal,
"the purse is now open," and "any member of Congress who doesn't vote
for the funds we need to defend this country will be looking for
a new job after next November."

—*William D. Hartung,* "The Military-Industrial Complex
Revisited: Shifting Patters of Military Contracting
in the Post-9/11 Period"

Nothing, it seemed, could check the war's inertia.

Looking back on it, I feel like it was a perfect storm: culturally ingrained nationalism, a desire to wage war from the earliest days of the Bush-Cheney administration,[9] fear of another 9/11, and the military-industrial complex became the tinder, kindling, fuel, accelerant, and spark needed to engulf the Greater Middle East in conflict. The Bush-Cheney administration was adept at wielding fear. They got what they wanted, and with considerable success. Lawrence Wilkerson, the chief of staff to Colin Powell during his infamous 2003 UN speech, said in an opinion piece in the *New York Times*, "The sole purpose of our actions was to sell the American people on the case for war with Iraq. Polls show that we did."[10] Once the Pandora's box of the War on Terror was opened, nothing could stop the momentum of what was released. Paradoxically, goaded and cowed by threats of more attacks, the American people sacrificed their best interests before the altar of the national security state.

War is the health of the State. It automatically sets in motion throughout
society those irresistible forces for uniformity, for passionate cooperation
with the Government in coercing into obedience the minority groups and
individuals which lack the larger herd sense . . . Other values, such as
artistic creation, knowledge, reason, beauty, the enhancement of life, are
instantly and almost unanimously sacrificed, and the significant classes
who have constituted themselves the amateur agents of the State, are
engaged not only in sacrificing these values for themselves but in
coercing all other persons into sacrificing them.

—*Randolph Bourne,* The State *(1918)*

And once the War on Terror was in full swing, the broad interests of the American people were traded for the short-term interests of the administration, their political party, and a narrow group of economic elites. According to the *Guardian*, since 9/11, America has developed a "national security industrial complex that melds together government and big business and is fuelled by an unstoppable flow of money."[11] The strength of this could hardly be better illustrated than by seeing the trillions being spent on wars across the Greater Middle East while Congress cuts billions from core social programs and simultaneously gives tax breaks to the wealthiest Americans.

I wish I had been able to see though the mirage of these forces. I wish someone had taught me to hold the government to the highest standard of proof in all matters pertaining to armed conflict.

What did we get from stealing sovereignty from the people of Iraq and Afghanistan? Global terrorism deaths increased 4,000 percent from 2002 to 2014 (from 725 to 32,727).[12] The Taliban now hold more ground in Afghanistan than at any point since the invasion of 2001.[13] TSA airport screenings fail to detect mock weapons in 95 percent of tests.[14] The U.S.-friendly client regime established in Iraq looted billions of dollars in American aid.[15] And that's just the beginning of a long, long list. In the words of longtime war correspondent Patrick Cockburn, "The United States has failed in Afghanistan. They will leave a deeply divided country in which reconciliation will be very difficult. The war may soon be over for the Americans, but not for the Afghans."[16] Similarly, the invasion of Iraq by the United States "destroyed Iraq as a united country and nobody has been able to put it back together again. It opened up a period when Iraq's three great communities— Shia, Sunni and Kurds—are in a permanent state of confrontation, a situation that has had a deeply destabilizing impact on all of Iraq's neighbors."[17]

Now, at thirty-three years old, when I think back to the moment when I shook Dick Cheney's hand, I have an entirely different reaction—not as a moment of pride, but of loathing. Dick Cheney is a man who unapologetically condones torture[18] and in 2018 autographed an at-home waterboarding kit with apparent glee.[19] The architects of the War on Terror are still owed their day with the International Criminal Court for the crimes they committed against the people of Iraq and Afghanistan.

And this is how most of my memories are—same memory, two very different reactions based on the level of information I had. This one moment, a microcosm of my moral and emotional transformation.

Now I can see the hole in the universe left by our wars.

If we are going to reimagine America's relationship with the military, military spending, and war, we need to muster political will. And political will seems to come only from sufficient outrage, shame, or embarrassment. If we look at the damage, it is beyond comprehension. It can't be undone.[20]

DEATH

We shoot the sick, the young, the lame,
We do our best to maim,
Because the kills all count the same,
Napalm sticks to kids.

Napalm sticks to kids,
Napalm sticks to kids.

Flying low across the trees,
Pilots doing what they please,
Dropping frags on refugees,
Napalm sticks to kids.

—*"Napalm Sticks to Kids," U.S. Army marching cadence*

A 2015 report from Physicians for Social Responsibility, a physician-led organization that was awarded the Nobel Peace Prize, concluded that "the war has, directly or indirectly, killed around 1 million people in Iraq, 220,000 in Afghanistan and 80,000 in Pakistan, i.e. a total of around 1.3 million."[21] If other war zones such as Yemen were included, the figure would be higher.

A different report, from Brown University's Watson Institute, cited that direct deaths in the United States' post-9/11 wars in Iraq, Afghanistan, and Pakistan have killed between 770,000 and 801,000 people.[22] This number does not, however, include "indirect deaths," which "include factors like disease, collapsing infrastructure, environmental degradation, and child malnourishment.

" 'A reasonable average estimate would be a ratio of four indirect deaths to one direct death in contemporary conflicts,' " according to the Geneva Declaration

Secretariat.[23] Meanwhile, during the War on Terror, direct deaths in major war zones have claimed the lives of 7,014 U.S. military service members and 7,950 U.S. contractors and DoD civilians from October 2001 to October 2019.[24] Not including journalists and humanitarian workers, among others, this leaves the direct death toll of those serving U.S. state interests at 14,792. For the U.S. soldiers who died in direct combat, roughly half were killed by rocket-propelled grenades or improvised explosive devices. Vehicle crashes, electrocution, friendly fire, heatstroke, and suicides were additional contributors.[25]

According to CNN, "2,977 people were killed in New York City, Washington, DC and outside of Shanksville, Pennsylvania" during the 9/11 attacks.[26] This means that roughly five times as many people serving U.S. interests have died in a war allegedly waged to prevent another 9/11. Arithmetically, if the goal was to prevent another 9/11's worth of American deaths, America failed miserably.

More than 312,000 civilians have been killed by "direct deaths" as a result of the fighting.[27] Roughly 255,000 opposition fighters and 175,000 national military and police have been killed.[28] The American-led coalition and the insurgents have killed these people in markets, in their homes, and on roadways, especially at checkpoints and entrances to U.S. military bases. They are killed by bombs, bullets, IEDs, and drones[29]; deaths are completely random, and other times, well-rehearsed and excitedly prepared for.

Applying the previously cited four-to-one ratio of indirect to direct deaths, roughly 1,220,000 civilians have died on account of the war.

Putting civilian deaths into perspective, in absolute terms, the America's War on Terror caused *over one hundred 9/11s' worth of civilian deaths.*

If we adjusted this damage relative to Afghanistan's population, it would, of course, be much larger.

9/11 was one of the great crimes since the new millennium, but any elementary appraisal would show that Bush's War on Terror against the people of the Greater Middle East is a far larger crime by an order of magnitude—that is, unless you believe *their lives* are worth pennies on the dollar relative to American lives. Aside from being a moral obscenity, such an extreme devaluation of human life sets the standard for despots to follow. America does not want to be on the receiving end of its own precedents, especially if another country surpasses America's military and economic might.

INJURED

More than 52,000 DoD personnel have become battlefield casualties.[30] As in every war, the wounded are far more numerous than those killed. Although the Pentagon counts only those injured as a "direct result of hostile action," this is only a fraction of the total human costs—something we are not regularly encouraged to think about. "Non-hostile injuries" and other medical problems arising in theater, such as heatstroke, suicide attempts, respiratory problems, and vehicle crashes, are not counted.

Many ailments are not diagnosed until the injured return home. Some ailments are not diagnosed at all. Toxic dust exposure and resulting respiratory, cardiac, and neurological disease represent another large segment of war zone–induced illness that has yet to be fully recognized.

American soldiers have been injured in a myriad of ways. Gunshot wounds, burns, broken bones, shrapnel lacerations, spinal cord injuries, paralysis, loss of sight or hearing, and PTSD, to name a few. More than 327,000 GWOT veterans have been diagnosed with traumatic brain injury as of August 2017.[31] Of course, not all injuries are immediately diagnosed. Amputations from having limbs blown off, shot off, or ripped off constitute a sizeable number of injuries.

"More than 1,600 soldiers who fought in the post-9/11 wars Iraq or Afghanistan have had battle-injury major limb amputations as of late 2015."[32] Gruesome, AK (above-knee) leg amputations can involve having one's genitals severed or damaged in such a way that sex, or sexual fulfillment more broadly, becomes completely out of the question. Large parts of the human experience that gave value to existence are gone or deeply impaired. Although the devastation of Iraq and Afghanistan has made it difficult to conduct reliable polling, there are a few things that are certain: civilians have been wounded and killed in far greater numbers. They have been killed by crossfire, IEDs, assassinations, indiscriminate coalition bombing, and botched raids on homes of suspected insurgents.

Although the war has affected me deeply and personally, legions have experienced far, far worse. Everyone who has been to combat knows the stories—the stories from their battalion, or platoon, or maybe even squad—so fucked up that the act of recollection takes you to the verge of tears.

There was an Air Force joint terminal attack controller (JTAC)—an airman who is embedded with infantry troops to coordinate and communicate with fixed wing jets—in our AO who lost both eyes and his entire jaw when an IED ripped them off. He will be mute and blind for the rest of his life. How he will navigate once-simple tasks—or communicate—is a mystery. The human costs of war are not extracted all at once.

According to Pew Research, injured post-9/11 service members are more likely to survive their wounds than during any other American war dating back to the Revolutionary War.[33] Wounded veterans now have the pleasure of living, but that comes at the cost of living with far more horrific war injuries. For a group of vigorous people, whose existence is inextricably intertwined with physicality, war wounds are the thieves not only of physical freedom but of identity. What sort of person are you if you are no longer able to do the things that made you *you*?

For service members whose jobs required rough-and-tumble living—climbing mountains, open water swims, rappelling cliffs, wading across rivers, jumping from perfectly good airplanes—new limitations must be daunting.

Imagine a map of the globe with all of its twisted, craggy terrain and roiling oceans. Now, place an overlay on top, based on one's own physical constraints. How much of the globe is actually *accessible*? Now, as the map lies before you, what percentage is left for the curious wanderer inside a soldier's mind?

The world remains broken into squares, but of a different type. They are not an expanse of grid squares to be walked, or swum, or sailed, or cycled, but rather boxes—a box you drive in, a box you sleep in, a box you exist in. What grand adventures live within the walls of hospitals, cars, malls, movie theaters, and restaurants? The map of the world only captures a set of concrete veins and asphalt arteries, predesigned to accommodate handicap vans and wheelchair-accessible paths.

A million disappointments, interred with a sigh. Although some human costs are easier to measure—in body bags, in prostheses, in trips to Walter Reed—the psychic cost of lost hopes, the burden of care placed on loved ones, missed opportunities, also count.

TRAUMA

Since 2001, the War on Terror has required 3.1 million troop-years of life from roughly 2.7 million service members, who have deployed across the globe.[34] Of the 2.7 million service members, more than half "struggle with physical or mental health problems stemming from their service, feel disconnected from civilian life and believe the government is failing to meet the needs of this generation's veterans, according to a poll conducted by the *Washington Post* and the Kaiser Family Foundation."[35]

Mental illness and depression is another scourge of war. According to the *Washington Post*, "The wars have caused mental and emotional health problems in 31 percent of vets—more than 800,000 of them."[36] But however much mental health awareness is raised to support U.S. soldiers, however much emphasis is placed on the 20.6 veterans and service members who committed suicide every day, American soldiers are just not in the same league as Afghans when it comes to sustaining mental health trauma.[37]

First of all, more Afghan citizens were exposed to war. And for these Afghans, there is no *post-* in post-traumatic stress disorder, because these traumas have persisted for decades without respite.[38] Whereas U.S. soldiers got to *go home* at the end of a combat deployment, a combat deployment *is home* for Afghans. Brown University estimates that 10.1 million people across Iraq, Afghanistan, and Pakistan have become refugees or displaced persons (IDPs). Being a refugee at the hands of a country who won't accept you is fraught with dangers, including food insecurity; unemployment; homelessness; and lack of adequate health care, water, electricity, and sanitation. It is a trauma of both the body and the mind. And whereas a whole host of mental health services exist for U.S. soldiers, mental health services for Afghans are nonexistent. For Afghans, there is an acute shortage of qualified mental health providers and the general situation in

Afghanistan is one in which "chronic mental illness has been left unattended . . . for decades."[39] Providing mental health services to U.S. service members, especially post-9/11 veterans, is not a politically contentious issue. I'm thankful that leaders across the spectrum offer their support.

President Donald J. Trump signs Executive Order to Improve Mental Health Resources for Veterans Transitioning from Active Duty to Civilian Life

—Office of Public and Intergovernmental Affairs

But the United States is responsible for, and should claim ownership of, the lifelong rehabilitation costs for the mental wounds we have inflicted not just for veterans but for the far larger number of people across the Middle East suffering from mental health issues caused by America's wars of aggression. Bernie Sanders once said: "If you can't afford to take care of your veterans, then don't go to war."

I don't think Bernie went far enough. Such a declaration should extend to the civilians who America has hurt or killed on account of our wars of aggression. If you can't afford to take care of innocent people who have a right to not be killed by the U.S., then don't go to war. "Although on average only 5 percent of the world's population will meet the criteria for PTSD at any point in their lives, an estimated 29 percent of Afghans meet the definition now."[40] Given that Afghanistan has a population of roughly 35 million, about 10 percent of that of the United States, this means that approximately 10 million Afghan people suffer from PTSD. To put this into context, on a relative basis, if that much PTSD were inflicted on America, it would be the equivalent of about 100 million Americans.

What I've learned is that war has a long tail. Some of my friends died in Afghanistan; others died in Afghanistan but it took a couple years for them to realize it, at which point the bullet finally caught up. When they were at home, drunk, with a gun.

Some were with me—in the platoon, in my truck; others were old friends, from a different unit, on a similar path. I called them my brothers. We were very close. And yet, in some cases, things changed so drastically inside of them.

War affected everyone differently, but these are the human costs of war through my eyes.

PORTRAITS OF LOSS

Ryan

More than 45,000 veterans and active-duty service members have killed themselves in the past six years. That is more than 20 deaths a day—in other words, more suicides each year than the total American military deaths in Afghanistan and Iraq.

—The New York Times, *November 1, 2019,*
"Suicide Has Been Deadlier Than Combat for the Military"

Ryan. Private Ryan.

Ryan was eighteen when he deployed to combat. Just two or three months into deployment he was subjected to being near a pressure-cooker IED when it detonated. Luckily, Ryan's body was mostly protected by a wall, but he watched from meters away as one of our platoon's beloved team leaders, James, was torn up and peppered with shrapnel made from nails, jagged metal, and bicycle chains. Ryan was rattled but had no observable physical injuries.

The medics gave him the "green light" and a rub-some-dirt-on-it pep talk. Ryan finished the tour, still the giggly, joking morale booster of the platoon. All of us were "broke the fuck off" by the time we went home. Combat didn't seem to wear on Ryan harder than anyone else.

Back safe in Colorado, Ryan posted to Facebook the obligatory tough-guy war photos. One had him manning a .50-caliber machine gun, kitted up with Oakley shades, with a caption fitting the soldier genre: "i mean mug the shit outta every towelhead fucker."

Another year passed and Ryan's unit geared up to deploy again. But this time Mental Health flagged him as "non-deployable," according to friends who knew him.

As a "non-deployable," you're jerking off, helplessly safe on rear detachment, a stigmatized unit with the reputation for being the "lemon lot" for soldiers. Rear-D hosts the flunkies, the druggies who "pissed hot," the discipline-issue kids who are awaiting trial and prison, the "broke dicks," and the basket cases.

For soldiers, a lot of self-esteem rides on one's ability to deploy. And when some shrink tells you you're unfit for duty, forcing you to watch your friends load their kit and come back again, some in metal boxes—well, that can be a real blow to one's self-worth.

I was a thousand miles away and in my final week in uniform when I got the call. Ryan committed suicide. I was told that he shot himself in the head with his personally owned firearm in August 2012.

I didn't know that he was struggling. I feel ashamed that I didn't have a chance to intervene, to try and get him help, to be there in some useful way.

His last public Facebook post shared a mini-documentary titled *The War Within*. This short film featured one of my former team leaders who was struggling to find peace at graduate school after serving two tough combat tours—one in Iraq and the one with us, in Kandahar.

Ryan wrote, "I'm re-posting it because people should know what is going on with our men. This 12 minute video explains our problems when we come home."

A friend's response: "heavy shit man."

Ryan's last public response: "life as i know it bro."

In 2012, more active-duty soldiers killed themselves than died in combat. Ryan was one of these soldiers.[41] But that refers only to active-duty soldiers. In the same year an astonishing 6,500 former military personnel killed themselves— more than twice the number of soldiers who have died in combat during the entire War on Terror.[42] It's hard to isolate the number of soldiers who were affected by war so dramatically that life no longer seemed worth living. Had our military not gone to war, how many would still be living their dreams, leaving a positive impact for others?

When it comes to Ryan, I don't know what he would have gone on to do in life. He had not lived through his formative years when he made the decision to kill himself. I know his family misses him and how grateful all of us would be to have him back. There are no words for that.

Nathan

People do not join the military to be submerged in philosophy, history, current affairs, UN charters, etc. . . . They rely on the reputation of the state. And when they are let down, when they realize they have been recruited by a hoax, it becomes one of the greatest disappointments in life.

—*John Kay*, Other People's Money

Even some of the best soldiers struggled.

In 2018, an unexpected letter arrived at my office. It was from the mother of one of my former soldiers, Nathan.

I spoke with Nathan every couple of months. Although he was clever and motivated, rebuilding his life post-Army was a struggle. Nathan told me that he had received misdemeanor assault charges in college, one for an incident at a college house party where derogatory things were said about the military, an American flag was hung upside down, and a brawl ensued. The other was for putting a guy into a medically induced coma, outside another house party. In the second fight, Nathan threw a punch that knocked the guy out in one, but on the way down without reflexes to instinctively soften the blow, the other guy's head hit the asphalt, causing extreme brain hemorrhaging. The victim's injury allegedly impacted him for years after this incident. A secondary effect was that Nathan's legal fees drained him of the money he had saved in Afghanistan.

To his credit, Nathan dug himself out. He went through house arrest, took anger management classes, and earned a 3.98 GPA in undergrad.

He was accepted to and completed graduate school and, after working in city planning, got a job at Tesla selling battery storage units. Things seemed like they were on the up-and-up.

He was keen to do something about climate change and he did. Then, Nathan got laid off. A restructuring got him, I was told.

After a bad breakup Nathan moved back home. He stopped looking for work and started looking for the bottle.

> *Dear Erik,*
>
> *My name is Peggy, I am Nathan's mother . . . Nathan is an alcoholic; he has been drinking for 8 years beginning with his return from Afghanistan . . .*
>
> *Additionally, the VA has prescribed medications for sleeping, anxiety, depression, and ironically, alcohol withdrawal. The combination of medications and alcohol is sure to be deadly for him. Nathan rarely connects in person with anyone. He is spending days on end isolated in our downstairs guest room watching war movies. At night he calls friends and typically screams at them for any number of reasons . . .*

Nathan is out of control. Would you please call him and speak with him? The best time to reach him is in the morning before he starts drinking (which seems to be about 8:30am or 9:00am). By late afternoon or evening, Nathan is inebriated and would not remember your conversation so I do not recommend speaking with him after 3pm or 4pm. I am saddened to share this information with you, but do so in hopes of saving Nathan's life.

Nathan and I had exchanged a string of messages around the same time, when I was absorbed in a new job. He wrote: "I am in dream state now. I have no phone . . . I am in dream state now . . . My family has some land and I walk it bare foot and I feel good."

I was panicked—not only for Nathan, but for how his depression, in a different way, made sense to me. I, too, was depressed, just better at hiding it, didn't cope with alcohol, and had more distractions. It was easy to see how, if circumstances had been different even just a little bit—or if I wasn't blessed with healthier habits for processing the experience of war—I, too, could have fallen into a state of malaise.

From work, I called Nathan's parents and explained that Nathan was on the ranch—probably drunk—and walking barefoot to Mexico.

Nathan's parents rushed to the farm and found Nathan in time, which might have saved his life.

In an email to me, Nathan resolved to seek help.

Tomorrow my entire family and I are walking into the VA and demanding help. I don't know why I carry such sadness. I just do . . . I need medical help to get out . . . I want out. I want out so badly. I don't know how it got to this point, but if I don't get out I'm going to die.

Nathan was accepted into a VA inpatient mental health clinic in Los Angeles, where he had formally started to process his backlog of emotions.

I took some vacation time and flew out to visit him. We'd spoken a good amount over the years, but eight years changes a person. We both looked older. More tired. We went to LACMA, the Los Angeles County Museum of Art. Nathan liked art, and sketching, and writing, and playing music, and doing skits, but even going to the museum—one of the things he liked most in life— brought little joy to his face.

The next six months was a tough slog for Nathan, and recovery never happens all at once. Nathan remained sober for about a year. Then he relapsed. The war within rages on, and today, he still wrestles with alcohol. Sometimes he is winning, sometimes he is losing.

One day in December of this past year, I gave Nathan a call to catch-up. He had just come off a multi-day bender. He paused mid-sentence to throw-up in the toilet. Eventually we got back to discussing war and the upcoming Memorial Day. It occurred to me that it had been almost a decade since the two of us returned home from Afghanistan. A lot has changed in that time, with one notable exception: America is still at war in Afghanistan.

I asked Nathan what burden of responsibility ordinary American citizens should bear for this never-ending war.

"The American people need to save the 'sad'-button Facebook emoticons and Memorial Day, 20%-off mattress sales for something, or somebody else," he said. "It's not helping, and that's no way to 'support the troops.'"

The takeaway: Soldiers and veterans don't need priority boarding, 10% discounts at gimmicky chain restaurants, or a few crinkled bills stuffed in a charity's coffee can; they need a nation that can find the courage and conviction to stop misusing their service.

AJ

Then there was AJ Nelson.

AJ Nelson was one of the soldiers who was injured in the first four days of deployment in that initial IED strike where we "earned" our Combat Infantryman Badges.

After his traumatic injury, the Army stitched him up, rubber-stamped his bill of health, and sent him back to war six or seven months later. After deployment, AJ became a murderer in the most horrific way, according to the *Eugene* (Oregon) *Register-Guard:*

> *[AJ] Nelson was 22 when he and the then-18-year-old [Mercedes] Crabtree traveled from Portland to Eugene to rob a bank with [David Ray] Taylor, who had spent 27 years in prison previously for a 1977 murder in Eugene.*

> *The trio was en route to a Siuslaw Bank branch in Mapleton when their getaway car broke down. They then set in motion a plan to kidnap and kill a stranger in order to use the victim's car in the robbery.*[43]

The female accomplice, supported by Nelson, lured the twenty-two-year-old victim to his death after pretending to have been stranded in the parking lot of a tavern on Highway 99 in Eugene.

> *After Nelson and Crabtree staged an argument in the parking lot of the Brew and Cue tavern, Gutierrez gave Crabtree a ride to Taylor's nearby home.*
>
> *There, Nelson tied up Gutierrez, shoved an arrow into his ear and pounded it into his head with a railroad spike, then choked him. Taylor then wrapped a chain around Gutierrez's neck and pulled on it until the victim had no pulse, according to trial testimony . . .*
>
> *Taylor and Nelson dismembered Gutierrez's body in a bathtub after killing him. Hours later, they used his 2010 Toyota Matrix in the Mapleton bank robbery.*[44]

AJ Nelson is currently serving life in prison without parole in Oregon.

This wasn't the first murder AJ Nelson was involved in. AJ and Specialist Frank Miller, another soldier from our company were involved in a "2010 drive-by shooting outside a Colorado Springs Wal-Mart [where Miller] told his accomplice to 'shoot the first person you see' . . ."[45] That means that at least two soldiers in Alpha Company, 1-12 IN, returned home to the United States to murder two of their own countrymen, killing more Americans in America than they did Afghan opposition fighters in Afghanistan.

When it comes to American soldiers committing heinous crimes, the American public hardly cares to notice. If these same crimes had been committed by Muslims who had not served—*well now,* that would elicit an entirely different reaction.

AJ wasn't always a menace to society. Certainly wasn't born that way. When he was in my platoon, he was an average soldier with some promising qualities. A bit immature, sure, but he was eighteen, thrust into a desperate situation.

It made me wonder: Did the Army admit a complete psychopath into its ranks without noticing or checking? Did I miss a red flag? Did Nelson's experience of being injured warp his psyche? Did the military not adequately screen him for mental health before they sent him back to war a second time? Was he not adequately screened when he returned to the United States, after deployment? Or did AJ just acquire a taste for murder independent of the Army?

One of the roles of the military is to train people to kill without thinking about it too much, so why are we surprised by the results when they bring it home? In an alternate universe, had Miller and Nelson not been radicalized by the military's culture of violence and traumatized when that same culture was put into practice in war, I would guess that neither of these men would have become murderers, and the innocent Americans, their victims, would still be alive.

Rock

With equal parts passion and frustration, I have spent four years helping one of my interpreters (code name: Rock) fight America's bureaucracy. Rock's application to acquire a Special Immigrant Visa for the United States has taken roughly four years without an end in sight. Despite jumping through every infuriating hoop, including a final interview at the U.S. embassy in Kabul, Rock has been told that he must continue to wait, which is code for "You and your family's lives will remain threatened because we don't possess the political will to do anything about it."

I went to what some may consider unreasonable lengths to get Rock to America. I wrote letters to my congressman, Stephen Lynch. I wrote letters to the Special Immigrant Visa team. I contacted the State Department. I spoke to Congressman Lynch's migration policy expert on the phone. And when none of this made a difference, I flew to Washington, D.C., to meet with Stephen Lynch in person, at the Rayburn House Office Building, to discuss the issue.

None of it helped. Congressman Stephen Lynch did not take the necessary steps to ensure the safety of our interpreters, nor did he draft policy to ensure that interpreters receive the same benefits as every other military service member.

Our Congressional leaders have abandoned our allies and abdicated their Constitutional duty to declare war. And because Congressional leaders are too timid to take a stand—to demand that acts of American violence be accompanied by a declaration of war, we have arrived where we are, today—in 'forever war' purgatory.

Meanwhile, the Taliban continue to look for Rock and have already searched his home; luckily, Rock was tipped off and escaped. At the time of this writing,

Rock and his family remain in hiding, in a permanent state of limbo, waiting for the moment when America has the courage to do the right thing. He may be waiting a while.

The United States government has shamefully abandoned the interpreters that served beside us—during *our war,* in *their country.*

I, as do many veterans, have strong bonds with the interpreters we worked with. In many cases, soldiers consider the interpreters they worked with "brothers"—in a *Band of Brothers* sense. And despite their importance to the war effort, our government has left them for dead.

Rock's situation is not the exception. He is one out of tens of thousands who have been completely shafted by this national injustice. America has abandoned "more than 17,000 Afghans" who remain in the pipeline, according to a State Department official.[46] There are roughly 60,000 Iraqis waiting to be processed, according to *Stars and Stripes.*[47] In the meantime, Afghan interpreters are killed at a rate of one "every 36 hours," according to an article published by the Foundation for Economic Education.[48] An article from Harvard's *Kennedy School Review* states, "Statistics from the *Armed Forces Journal* indicate that interpreters in Iraq were ten times more likely to be killed than the Americans they supported."[49] It is probably safe to assume a directionally similar risk for Afghan interpreters. This same Harvard Kennedy School publication provided gory details of what this looks like in reality: "The Taliban decapitated the heads of my uncle, my cousin, and my best friend, Ateeq, all because I supported the infidels," said Fahim Muhammad, an interpreter who served the U.S. Army.[50] Had America not waged the War on Terror, the interpreters—or "terps," as they are nicknamed—would not have been killed serving American troops, or assassinated, or beheaded when they were discovered to have worked for coalition forces. These interpreters and their families—good people—would still be alive.

Andy

My friend Andy—Captain Andy Byers—was killed on November 3, 2016, in Kunduz, Afghanistan, in a place not far from where the United States mercilessly bombed Doctors Without Borders roughly a year earlier.

I first met Andy when I was a Yuk and he was a Plebe. We became friends when we joined the crew team. We rowed our first race together in western Massachusetts in the fall of 2004. Over the next couple years and hundreds of practices later, we were good friends.

On my graduation day, I bid farewell to Andy and my former teammates. Aside from seeing him at the odd wedding or two, we lost touch over the years.

It did not surprise me to learn that Andy became a Green Beret detachment commander in the U.S. Special Forces. What did surprise me was the notification that he had been killed.

I reluctantly searched for details of his death.

An article by the U.S. Central Command titled "Until Dawn: The Battle of Boz Qandahari"[51]—a dramatic and romantic-sounding name—provided a rah-rah account of the mission and contained many in-person interviews from soldiers in Andy's team.

Andy was said to have been killed in a mission to "target known enemy safe havens and disrupt the refit operations of several high-level Taliban leaders"—an offensive mission.

From the reporting, the mission turned sour quickly.

Canalized in an alley, surrounded by gates and high walls, insurgents threw grenades over one of the walls and opened up with small-arms fire, injuring and killing Afghan and U.S. Special Forces soldiers.

In an attempt to consolidate the fifty-nine-man force, Andy looked for a secure place to treat casualties and create a perimeter.

Andy, "determined to get his team out of harm's way, attempted to kick the gate open himself. It held fast, however, secured by an object . . ." Andy reached over the gate, "and that's when I watched the rounds rip through the gate and into [Byers]," said one team member.

Those shots, fired by an insurgent, were the ones that killed Andy.

From the reports, it appeared as though the Special Forces Team was faced with a decision: use air strikes to "build a wall [of fire] between us and anyone out there" or face a seemingly hopeless situation.

The team went with the air strikes, successfully building a wall of destruction around them. If I had been in that situation, in their boots, I would have done the same thing.

The article said that the U.S. Special Forces had inflicted "catastrophic damage on multiple Taliban enemies." One Air Force combat controller, attached to the unit, was "recommended for the Air Force Cross Medal for his actions, [having] spent the night calling in precision air strikes on enemy positions." The mission that killed my friend Andy was described as "a bittersweet victory," and one Green Beret from Andy's team "felt content with the effects that we had on the enemy that night." "Three Silver Star Medals, three Bronze Star Medals (two with Valor), four Army Commendation Medals with Valor, and six Purple Heart Medals" were awarded to team members.

But as I continued to read more—and very different—accounts of the incidents from other news sources, like Al Jazeera and the *New York Times*, I came to realize that the type of "Army news" I received during my career was complete propaganda. It was deliberately misleading and minimized collateral damage.

It's almost a rule: to avoid moral dissonance, the military does not like to publish accounts that mix "awards with valor" with "dead children."

The article by Al Jazeera had a completely different tone. It was titled "US forces Admit Killing 33 Civilians in Taliban Clash." One Afghan resident whose family was killed by the bombing said the attack "only killed innocent people" and the houses were targeted based on "speculation."

At the end of America's air strikes, "residents carried more than a dozen bodies, including children, towards a local governor's office in a show of anger . . ."

One resident of the village said, "We don't even know if the Taliban were actually killed in this attack. All we saw were dead bodies of the innocent people . . . We saw dead bodies of children as young as three years old. What was their fault?"[52] The atrocities inflicted on the Afghan civilians was also recorded by the *New York Times*. "This was an act of oppression . . . We are also humans. It should be investigated by an international court, and we need to be compensated for our loss."[53] After Andy was killed and the civilians had been bombed, protesters filled the streets. According to reports by Al Jazeera, Afghan citizens "were chanting 'Death to America', 'Death to President [Ashraf] Ghani' and they were [vowing] to take revenge."[54] Reality and what the U.S. military says do not match.

As deeply tragic as the death of American soldiers is, there was no mention of the thirty-three civilians killed by American air strikes—more than ten times the number of U.S. soldiers killed. The collateral damage made the tragedy of Andy's death all the more tragic.

The methods America uses to achieve "peace"—presumably the goal of warfare—assures that it will never happen. If General Stanley McChrystal's "insurgent math" is directionally correct—for every innocent person you kill, you create 10 new enemies—the raid that killed Andy created another 330 insurgents.[55] Given this 10:1 ratio, it means that the American military would need to kill more than 10 insurgents without a single civilian death just to keep the insurgency from growing—not to beat it; just to stop it from growing—a seemingly impossible task in modern warfare. Grégoire Chamayou's book *Drone Theory* captures this sense well: "Kill enough of them and the threat goes away ... However, the 'kill list' ... never gets shorter, the names and faces are simply replaced.' Caught up in an endless spiral, the eradication strategy is, paradoxically, destined never to eradicate."[56]

Had Andy not been sent to this war, he'd still be alive, making the world better with the compassion and zeal he applied to all aspects of his life. He had a good moral compass, strong work ethic, a clever mind, and there could hardly have been a better person to fill the role of Special Forces Team Leader. The tragic killing of thirty-three civilians, including children, does not dilute my memory of him.

Although I've never met the Special Forces men in Andy's team, I'd still wager they, too, are distinctive, good people. I don't blame them for bombing known or suspected enemy positions while carrying their dead friends to the helicopter.

It's rational to want to live.

It's rational to shoot back when someone is shooting at you.

It's rational to prioritize the protection of friends who are in imminent danger over possible risk to innocent people you don't know.

Even someone as averse to political violence as I am cannot find fault in these actions, because war is a special kind of madness that puts people in a position where the rational choice and the morally repugnant choice are the same. Decisions that most people would agree are rational lead to conclusions that no one wants to support.

For all the same reasons that it was rational for Andy's Special Forces team to do what they did, it was rational for the Afghan opposition fighters to do what they did too. To fight back.

We don't want to believe that the "enemy" we are bombing is, like our military, composed of a cross-section of society that includes loving fathers, husbands, and sons who never wanted to commit acts of violence, who are kind, and who feel compelled to fight only as a last resort to defend their homes. Had America not waged these wars, we would not have forced them to defend themselves from us. In effect, the Afghan version of ourselves would still be alive.

If I grew up in Afghanistan and was inculcated with a different set of values, and my family was bombed by American air strikes—what happened during this botched raid—I, too, would fight against the invaders. When you arrive at this conclusion, it's not hard to imagine a parallel universe where Andy was trying to kill me and I was trying to kill Andy. And when you see the futility of war in this way, you can't go back.

In this story, you can imagine the vision of your own death, you can imagine the other side, and you can also imagine the opportunity cost, all at once.

If America hadn't gone to war, Andy would still be alive, the Afghan children, killed by American air strikes, would still be playing outdoors, and those who knew the deceased could have been saved an ocean of anger and sadness.

Tyler

As a rule, when you are deployed and someone asks you to call urgently, and when they answer they are crying, the next words out of their mouth are going to Fuck. You. Up.

On September 10, 2009—one day before the eighth anniversary of 9/11—I received a cryptic email from Tyler's then girlfriend, asking that I call her ASAP.

I called from behind a cement T-wall barrier at FOB Wilson—as soon as time allowed. She picked up and was already crying.

Fuck!

Due to the FOB's piss-poor internet connection, I could make out only every other word of what Tyler's girlfriend was saying. It was so bad that I needed her to repeat herself. Saying it once was hard enough. She was openly crying at an airport. But I got the main message: Tyler had been killed in Konar Province.[57] I returned to my living quarters, closed the door, heard the click of the door shutting, and immediately fell apart.

But this—receiving notification that a friend had been injured or killed—was becoming hauntingly frequent. At twenty-three, I had a lot of friends in the

obituary pages. I had a sinking, I-want-to-throw-up feeling every time I opened my email and saw in the subject line:

"[distr007] Graduate Death Reported . . ."

This was West Point's way of notifying you that a classmate had died.

Tyler's death was a profound reminder of the ephemeral nature of life.

Like an hourglass with the top painted black, we see only the part of our life that has passed, that which is over. There is no telling how much more sand is left in the hopper. You can only ever have ten summers in your twenties. No more. Maybe less.

Tyler had five summers. Four were spent in all-consuming military training; one was spent at war. Only Tyler can judge if these summers were well spent. We will never know how he may have reflected on this—or how that answer may have changed with time, much like mine has—because he is dead.

During deployment there is no time to deal with grief, to figure out what the fuck any of it meant. I could not be sidetracked by the natural grieving process. The show must go on. Additional leave to attend friends' funerals is not permitted.

And so I treated grief and sadness like nuclear waste: I found a deep, dark emotional mineshaft, poured these natural but now toxic emotions into rickety, self-made barrels, and cast them into the depths below, hoping the hole was deep enough, the barrels strong enough, until I could deal with it later. Back in America.

Only a handful of Afghanistan's 35 million people were responsible for killing Tyler. Only a handful. But it didn't feel that way. In that moment it felt like the whole country was giving us an omni-directional beat-down.

Like so many other fallen American soldiers, Tyler was a good and gentle man—not a violent man—and yet he died a violent, violent death. His body raked with bullets—shot over and over on the side of an exposed mountain escarpment, according to an officer from his company. Ordered to ascend a rocky path without cover and concealment allowed insurgents to pelt his unit with small arms, RPGs, and machine guns with near impunity. Fish in a barrel.

First Lt. Tyler E. Parten, a native of Arkansas, died Thursday in Konar province in a firefight where insurgents used rocket-propelled grenades and rifles. He was assigned to the 3rd Squadron, 61st Cavalry Regiment, 4th Brigade Combat Team, 4th Infantry Division.

—The Denver Post, *September 12, 2009*

Defense Department death notifications read like an Orwellian ledger—deliberately insincere, making the reader feel informed without the inconvenience of feeling anything.

Two years after Tyler's death, his family decided to bring his ashes to rest in Arlington National Cemetery, Section 60, next to so many other service members who died serving in the War on Terror.

By this time I was serving in my final role, at the Honor Guard. There I earned my living, listening to extreme grief at close range. The sound a family made when they saw their loved one in the casket for the first time made me wince and bite down on the back of my molars. Showing emotion was not permitted. It was grim work, taken very seriously.

To shield myself from seeing the aggrieved faces, I'd cant my dress blues hat real low. I didn't allow my eyes to connect with those of the grieving family. Doing so would create a human connection where they could pass their sadness my way. I didn't want that. I had enough.

To be truly empathetic with the day-in, day-out funerals would be too depleting. I would give them the thousand-yard stare, never focusing on them. If I inadvertently did, and tears started to well beneath the brim of my hat, I'd tilt my head lower still so all I'd see was a wad of tissues clutched tightly, hand gripping hand, or tremoring against the leg of a freshly pressed black suit; I'd try to stare at the arrangement of sympathetic funeral flowers—often lilies or gladioli.

And on the day of Tyler's funeral, we marched in slow cadence to the site of the grave. The firing party and escort platoon moved to their predesignated locations. The body bearers unloaded Tyler's urn from the caisson, which was led by six white horses. Tyler's family looked on, through tears.

I stood near the grave. The chaplain delivered his sermon. I tried not to look at Tyler's crying mother and grief-stricken father, knowing what I was going to have to do next.

I stepped in, filling the chaplain's place, rendering final honors. I saluted Tyler's urn while the firing party delivered the three distinct cracks of the twenty-one-gun salute. The Army band played a hymn and the body bearers began to fold the flag into its triangular form. The flag was passed crisply from soldier to soldier until it reached me at the head of the grave. I waited for the body bearers to leave the grave site, keying me to do the final and most difficult task: delivering the folded flag to Tyler's mother.

There is a protocol for giving a flag to the next of kin. It is scripted and robotic. It's as personal as a call center recording, telling you: "Your call is important to us. Please hold."

I stepped up to the chair where Tyler's mother was seated. I extended the flag as an offering, allowing her to take it and hug it to her chest.

"Ma'am, this flag is presented to you on behalf of a grateful nation for the honorable and faithful service rendered by your loved one."

To give a standard-issue condolence to a friend's mother felt unfitting. I added more.

"Tyler was one of my best friends in Colorado Springs. It was an honor to have known him. He truly was the best of us. I'm so sorry for your loss."

As I choked out the last quivering sentence, tears began to run down my cheeks. I rendered the final salute and returned to my spot at the head of Tyler's grave, watching over it until his family left.

When the family left, I stayed. I let the enormity of a Tyler-sized hole in the universe sink in.

JUST AS WE are conditioned to think little of the weight of reflexively killing others, so, too, we are taught not to consider the weight of risking our own lives or sending others to risk their lives. When we are sent to occupy a backwater village or secure a miserable little fragment of Afghan road, we are programmed not to question if the objective is worth dying for. We put our faith in the government's master plan: that it will be worth it no matter the cost in American flesh. We are inundated with ideas about sacrifice and the honor of dying for the American way of life, until we are incapable of stripping them away and truly imagining dying for the sake of getting a handful of insurgents to leave their village for two days, and who return fresh, ready to emplace new IEDs for us to step on. We do not demand en masse that after the deaths and disfigurement of so many servicemen and women we should have something to show for it. In the failure to do so, we devalue our own lives and the lives of our fellow soldiers.

I worry that the training the military has given to soldiers has, in a different way, been given to all of American society. To some extent, we are all recruits in the U.S. military, inculcated with the same taboos and mythologies in schools, in newspapers, and at the dinner table. We are pressured to fall into formation, because failure to do so would be *un-American*. Ordinary citizens are pinned with various terms of abuse if they question the military, or dare to assert that their job is equally as important, or demand diplomacy over political violence. I maintain that none of these sentiments are helpful.

Often when good people die, out of love and respect for them, we canonize their character and actions. However, in the case of political violence, if we don't make a distinction between the character of the individual and the war itself, we only preserve the belief that our illegal war of aggression was good, perpetuating violence for longer, inadvertently creating more victims. To describe injury and death in combat as unromantic, sudden, and ordinary earns you no friends. To posit that our endless wars are a form of state terrorism earns you many enemies. And so we continue indefinitely, urged forward by our self-perpetuating education in nationalism, militarism, and *terrorphobia*.

One of the many great tragedies of the War on Terror is that an entire generation of people were deluded and misled by their own countrymen. As soldiers, we did our job, freed no one, made global terrorism worse, were accomplices to state terrorism, buried our country in debt, buried our friends in graveyards, and in the end were, as Sam once described it, "ejected like empty shell casings back into society."

But "tragic loss," rebranded as "patriotic sacrifice," is a recursive, intersubjective belief, passed back and forth, on and on.[58] It is handed down through school, parents, and friends. Country songs, action movies, and beer commercials. Holidays, decorations, and cultural artifacts. Everything in America coalesces into a singular theme: those who serve in the military are deemed to love their country just a bit more than everyone else. They are slightly "more American"—and therefore better—than the special education teachers, park rangers, and sewage treatment workers whom they serve to protect. This belief is shaped with adulation, privilege, shame, guilt, honor—all the extreme emotions that nations at war are meant to feel.

If Americans did not believe that militarism and endless wars were somehow patriotic or romantic, then we would be less likely to plunge ourselves into needless war, and as a result a lot of good people would still be alive and a lot of needless suffering could have been entirely averted.

Costs, Opportunity Costs, and Opportunities

So long as states waste their forces in vain and violent self-expansion, and thereby constantly thwart the slow efforts to improve the minds of their citizens by even withdrawing all support from them, nothing in the way of a moral order is to be expected. For such an end, a long internal working of each political body toward the education of its citizens is required. Everything good that is not based on a morally good disposition, however, is nothing but pretense and glittering misery. In such a condition the human species will no doubt remain until, in the way I have described, it works its way out of the chaotic conditions of its international relations.

—Immanuel Kant

If America were actually concerned with safeguarding its citizens, it could have stayed home to deal with far larger threats, at a far higher return on investment.

If America were actually concerned with reducing terrorism around the globe, it could have stopped the acts of terrorism we have the greatest ability to control: our own.

If America were actually concerned with justice and equality, it could avoid the double standard of calling a drone strike against America "terrorism," meanwhile calling America's global drone assassination campaign, as if by some form of sorcery, "counterterrorism."

If the American government's action in the Middle East were concealed by a fig leaf of plausible deniability, it would have been removed a long time ago. Now, we as the American people have the hard work of confronting the facts of what our government, military, and intelligence agencies have done.

> *Secret CIA "black jails" like as the infamous "Salt Pit" also operated in Afghanistan, where prisoners . . . were interrogated and tortured. Khaled El-Masri, for example, was an innocent German citizen arrested in Macedonia, transferred to the "Salt Pit," then tortured and sodomized for four months. The U.S. held him for an additional five months after realizing they had mistaken him for another person, then released him at night on a desolate road in Albania, without apology, or funds to return home . . . The U.S. role in their rendition and torture is beyond dispute.*

> —*Brendan Fischer and Lisa Graves,* "International Law and the War on Terror"

It's hard to say what the world would be like if we didn't have a War on Terror, but it's not much of a leap to say it would be better. More stable. Happier. And without a War on Terror, we could have applied ourselves differently.

Although it's easy to mourn the what-could-have-beens, the things we should have done instead of obliterating the Middle East are still worth doing. According to the Chinese proverb, "The best time to plant a tree was twenty years ago. The second-best time is now."

Still, enabling alternatives to never-ending war won't be as simple as flipping on a light switch. Even as our soldiers are drawn down in the Middle East, they ramp up in other places, like Africa. The almost two-decade-long War on Terror has reconfigured the way our nation operates—the way our nation thinks. Should we ever aspire to goals besides self-perpetuating wars, we must first reject the fear that was wielded to get our nation to support these wars in the first place.

We will need to confront the characteristics of lobotomized patriotism that emerged in post-9/11 America—paranoia, xenophobia, fear-mongering, surveillance, militarism, and blind nationalism—and redirect our energies toward more positive ends. As former vice president Joe Biden highlighted, putting the right assets on the right problems at the right time is hard even in the best of times:

> *So the hardest thing to do, I've found in 44 years [in government], is prioritize the most consequential threats and concerns, and allocate resources relative to the nature of the threat. There is a tendency to respond to the "wolf at the door," but [policy makers] tend to sometimes over-respond and not leave enough assets to deal with the pack of wolves out there in the field ... Terrorism is a real threat, but it's not an existential threat to the existence of the democratic country of the United States of America.*[1]

Ok, Boomer.

Although Vice President Biden hit a valid point—that politicians must become better at prioritization—his remark comes across as a rich hypocrisy when you consider that during Biden's forty-something years in government, the United States took no meaningful action on climate change—an existential threat. Even if every country fulfills its current pledges under the Paris Agreement—and many, including the United States, Brazil and Australia, are currently not on track to do so—the Emissions Gap Report found average temperatures are on track to rise by 3.2 degrees Celsius from the baseline average temperature at the start of the industrial age.

For years, capital *T* Terrorism has irrationally been labeled as the Big Bad Wolf at America's door. However, the threat of terrorism in the United States has been sensationalized—used as political clickbait to distract from any number of threats that are far larger concerns. To put terrorism into context, in 2010, the year I was in Afghanistan, "obesity and related illnesses killed about 3 million people, [whereas] terrorists killed a total of 7,697 across the globe, most of them in developing countries. For the average American or European, Coca-Cola poses a far deadlier threat than Al-Qaeda."[2] Likewise, the *Atlantic* cited that Americans are as likely to be killed by their own furniture (i.e., crushed by their TV) as by terrorist attacks.[3]

War is the perfect cover and rationale for people to cede decision-making authority to the state, which is controlled by plutocrats and special interest groups, including the military-industrial complex. Be that as it may, the many, and not the few, will have to shoulder the debt burdens from this war. And a terrible price it has been—and will be.

THE COST: WHAT DID WE SPEND?

The worst single mistake ever made in the history of our country: going into the Middle East, by President Bush ... Obama may have gotten [U.S. soldiers] out wrong, but going in is, to me, the biggest single mistake made in the history of our country ... Because we spent $7 trillion in the Middle East. Now if you wanna fix a window some place they say, "oh gee, let's not do it." Seven trillion, and millions of lives—you know, 'cause I like to count both sides. Millions of lives.

—*President Donald Trump*

The current estimated cost of America's War on Terror is $6.4 trillion, or, as *Newsweek* mentioned, roughly $23,000 per U.S. taxpayer.[4] But what's happened is a bit different from "buyer's remorse," in which someone overpays for something and regrets it afterward. This is worse—more akin to "debtor's remorse," because we haven't yet paid the bill.

According to a paper published by Brown University's Watson Institute for International and Public Affairs, "War appropriations for Iraq and Afghanistan were not funded with new taxes or war bonds, but by deficit spending and borrowing."[5] In effect, America has locked itself into paying for something deep into the future that we can't get out of, and our policy-makers deliberately financed it in such a way as to dump the debt onto future generations. As Robert Hormats, the former vice chairman of Goldman Sachs, has pointed out, it is unprecedented in U.S. history that we pay for a war entirely from debt and actually cut taxes repeatedly during wartime (as we did in 2001 and 2003).[6] A consequence of deferring war costs into the future, exacerbated by tax cuts (mostly benefiting the rich), means a reduction in public awareness of those costs. The American public is deprived of the cause and effect of their actions and spared from the knowledge of the financial burdens we are placing on our future selves, making it difficult to demand focus on other priorities. "The budget lights may be flashing red, but they are shielded from our view," said Steven Aftergood in a paper published by Brown University's Watson Institute.[7]

The lesson that America has seemingly forgotten is that sound fiscal policy is connected with national security. As President Eisenhower mentioned in one of the repeated themes of his presidency, he warned Congress that "to amass military power without regard to our economic capacity would be to defend ourselves against one kind of disaster by inviting another."

It's hard to conceptualize $6.4 trillion. How can anyone fathom such a number? And what unit do you use to measure such a cost?

The financial price tag for One World Trade Center, the signature skyscraper at Ground Zero and tallest building in New York City, was $3.9 billion, "making it by far the world's most expensive new office tower," according to the *Wall Street Journal*.[8] However, for the same price as the War on Terror, we could have over 1,500 One World Trade Center buildings—thirty per U.S. state. But rather than conceptualizing the war in terms of things we could have had, perhaps it is best to conceptualize $6.4 trillion in terms of a more basic measurement: the characteristics of the actual, physical dollar notes.

A U.S. bank note is 6.14 inches long.

You could take a $10,000 "brick" of $100 bills—a "rubber-band stack," if you will—and place each brick end to end, lengthwise, and cover the entire 6,917-mile distance from Washington, D.C., to Kabul, Afghanistan—a distance that would span the Atlantic Ocean—across Spain, France, Italy; across the Adriatic Sea; across Montenegro, Kosovo, Macedonia, Bulgaria, Turkey, and the Black Sea; across Armenia, Azerbaijan, Iran, the Caspian Sea; across Turkmenistan and nearly all of Afghanistan—from west to east—to arrive in Kabul.

But that's not all.

You could take this trip more than once. In fact, you could line the nearly seven-thousand-mile route with $10,000 bricks of money roughly nine lengths—more than four round trips or travel around the circumference of the Earth nearly 2.5 times.

Alternatively, you could create a string of single $100 bills lengthwise and take nearly twelve round trips to the moon.[9] Or you could string $10 bills together lengthwise and go from Earth to Mars.[10] Or you could string $1 bills together lengthwise and easily go from Earth to Jupiter.

By contrast, federal funding used to combat climate change in 2014—the last available year published by the U.S. Government Accountability Office (GAO)— broken into $10,000 bricks and strung out lengthwise, would not even cover two loops around Washington, D.C.'s Beltway—a sixty-four-mile ring around the nation's capital.[11] It's a curious thing: when politicians and generals decide it's time to drop bombs, we never talk about costs; but when we are asked to help people, preserve life on this planet, offer health care to our own citizens like the rest of the rich world, create infrastructure fit for America's future, or provide a semi-decent educational system, we are suddenly cost-conscious.[12]

Spending on political violence is not slated to stop.[13] U.S. military spending in 2019, adjusted for inflation, is higher than at any time other than the height of the Iraq War. "The 2019 military budget, approved by an 85-to-10 vote, gives America's armed forces an $82 billion increase from 2017" as it "inches closer to $1 trillion mark," according to the *Washington Post*.[14] Further, spending estimates in the Pentagon's budget indicate that DoD anticipates military operations across the Greater Middle East, "necessitating funding through at least FY2023," according to Brown University's Watson Institute.[15] Roughly 17 percent—or one sixth—of America's $4 trillion federal budget goes to the military, according to the Congressional Budget Office.[16] As a result, the Department of Defense base budget dwarfs other government agencies: Health and Human Services, Transportation, and the Department of Education, just for starters.[17] Military expenditure as a percent of GDP has decreased across the world since 1960 according to the World Bank.[18] And although the United States has followed this trend, to be proportional with the world average, the U.S. would need to slash about one-third of its military expenditure, saving roughly $300 billion per year, which could be reallocated to more important social programs, or returned to taxpayers.

Worse still, to give money to the Department of Defense is to give money to an organization that can't manage money. The DoD has a long and irrefutable history of fiscal impropriety and a demonstrable lack of financial stewardship for taxpayer dollars.

The DoD disastrously failed an audit it had "nearly three decades to prepare for" while simultaneously being the last federal agency to comply with the 1990 law. Making the point stick, the *New York Times* published an article titled "The Pentagon Doesn't Know Where Its Money Goes."[19] In 2016, Reuters stated,

"The Defense Department's Inspector General, in a June report, said the Army made $2.8 trillion in wrongful adjustments to accounting entries in one quarter alone in 2015, and $6.5 trillion for the year. Yet the Army lacked receipts and invoices to support those numbers or simply made them up."[20] The Army couldn't account for 39 UH-60 "Black Hawk" helicopters. This was far better than the Air Force, which identified 478 structures and buildings at 12 installations that were not in its real property system.[21]

And as America struggles with enduring debt from the War on Terror, the military continues to open up new frontiers, creating ever more war.

In January 2019, *Smithsonian* magazine "reveals for the first time that the U.S. is now operating in 40 percent of the world's nations."[22] America is currently conducting direct action, shoot-'em-in-the-face operations in fourteen different countries. We are actively bombing seven countries—that we know of. More violence to justify and legitimize the dollars spent on the defense budget. One of the darkest ironies of Bush's War on Terror is that bankrupting our country was all part of bin Laden's grand strategy. And perhaps what is most frustrating is that it wasn't a secret, but George W. Bush still took the bait.

All that we have mentioned has made it easy for us to provoke and bait this administration. All that we have to do is to send two mujahidin to the furthest point east to raise a piece of cloth on which is written al-Qaida, in order to make the generals race there to cause America to suffer human, economic, and political losses without their achieving for it anything of note other than some benefits for their private companies.

This is in addition to our having experience in using guerrilla warfare and the war of attrition to fight tyrannical superpowers, as we, alongside the mujahidin, bled Russia for 10 years, until it went bankrupt and was forced to withdraw in defeat.
All Praise is due to Allah.

So we are continuing this policy in bleeding America to the point of bankruptcy. Allah willing, and nothing is too great for Allah.

—Osama bin Laden

Our nation—and in a small way I—helped Osama bin Laden achieve more than anything he likely hoped for.

And herein lies a great American tragedy.

America pretends to both goodness and greatness.

9/11—as one of the three times the national territory has been attacked by foreigners—was an affront to greatness.

And so we waged two illegal wars of aggression that, after decades of occupation, killed hundreds of thousands of noncombatants who had nothing to do with it, bankrupted our country, and alienated the world, sending a clear message to all: America is neither good nor great.

OPPORTUNITY COSTS

War spending does not provide the foundations for future growth as well as does other types of investment. A country that borrows to make productive investment—in education, technology, or infrastructure— enhances its future potential: for most countries, the return on these public investments far exceed the cost of capital. Thus, such investments, even when debt financed, strengthen the country's balance sheet and make it more capable of withstanding shocks.

—*Joseph Stiglitz, Nobel Laureate in Economic Sciences*

If we desire to remake America into a country that is not known as "the greatest threat to peace in the world today"—by a large margin, according to leading Western polling agencies (WIN/Gallup)—then we must collectively redress our nation's relationship with the military, military spending, and war.[23] Doing so will be difficult. Confronting the national security leviathan—and America's unquenchable thirst for all things "defense"—will require more than guts and smarts and grit.

I echo the sentiments of former secretary of defense Robert M. Gates, when he said, "This Department's approach to requirements must change . . . Is it a dire threat that by 2020 the United States will have only twenty times more advanced stealth fighters than China? . . . What is required going forward is not more study. Nor do we need more legislation. It is not a great mystery what needs to change. What it takes is the political will and willingness, as Eisenhower possessed, to make hard choices—choices that will displease powerful people both inside the Pentagon and out."[24] But even the secretary of defense—the person you'd imagine would have the power to change such a mind-set—appeared to struggle with making America's defense apparatus "fit for purpose." The "wolf at the door" has never been as big or as bad as the military-industrial complex and some politicians wished us to believe. The time has come to "displease powerful people" because both the direct costs and the opportunity costs—that is, the benefits "that a person could have received, but gave up, to take another course of action"—are too high for us to stand by and watch any longer. Climate change and other issues demand our attention more urgently.

If we, as American citizens, aspire to have a society that benefits the many and not just the few, we will have to distinguish between real and imaginary threats, generate a new list of priorities, and shift resources and focus accordingly.

But before we can change our priorities, we must first change the mind-set that established those priorities. "Being American" now seems less like a free-thinking obligation to dissent, and more like a duty to roll over in the name of lobotomized patriotism.

Of my thirty-four years on this earth, I have spent roughly 25 percent of them living outside America. In discussions with people from the rest of the world, the thoughts presented in this book are almost too obvious to merit discussion, and yet, in my experience, it remains devilishly difficult to have a sober discussion about these same topics with most Americans.

Looking back in time, and looking at America from beyond its borders, it's hard to not see that this resistance is driven in part by the mania, underpinned by fear, that grew out of 9/11. How we spent many times the GDP of Afghanistan, protecting against the alleged threat of Afghanistan; how American politicians and generals promoted policies whereby bombing and shooting Middle Eastern people in their homes was somehow going to engender goodwill and lessen their desire to harm us, in kind.

Fear underpinned this mania. I knew that fear. I felt that fear in my high school chemistry class when I watched the ash-filled aftermath of 9/11. For millennials like myself, 9/11 was one of the defining features of our childhood.

Initially, the fear was unifying. It created a sense of community, where the cost of membership seemed so cheap—only a bumper sticker, a flag on your home, and boundless endorsement of the military. But in the years after, when we felt vulnerable, opportunistic politicians gathered that fear and sharpened it into an instrument to keep us in line. War was an opportunity to advance their party's agenda.

I don't think anyone fully grasped the repercussions and cultural shift that came with shifting to a permanent war footing. Americans became comfortable with the idea of inflicting violence on other people without ever being inconvenienced by knowing what it looks like when that same scale of violence is inflicted on us, in our cities.

We pumped our do-no-wrong military full of growth hormones, inflating its importance and causing it to outgrow its useful role in society.

> *Every gun that is made, every warship launched, every rocket fired, signifies, in the final sense, a theft from those who hunger and are not fed, those who are cold and are not clothed.*
>
> —*President Dwight D. Eisenhower*

The distraction of fear allowed the entrenchment of trends that were already well under way two decades ago: the ever-widening inequality between rich and poor; the shift of social responsibility from the public to the private sector; the decline in spending for education; the willful ignorance of climate change; and the crumbling of our national infrastructure.[25] To get back on track, we not only need to acknowledge that our War on Terror has been profoundly counterproductive; we need to place other values—values that favor the many over the few, that insist on long-term rather than short-term goals—above fear and militarism.

Once we do that, we will be free redraw the blueprint of America and turn our attention to two large and thematic threats: inequality and climate change.

NEW PRIORITIES

Income and Wealth Inequality

> "Belligerency would benefit only the class of people who will be made prosperous . . . who have already made millions and who will make

*millions more . . . We are going to pile up debt that the toiling masses
that shall come many generations after us will have to pay. Unborn
millions will bend their backs in toil in order to pay for the terrible step
we are now about to take."*

—*Senator George W. Norris*
(*Found in* The Price of Liberty, *Robert Hormats*)

One of the biggest and most persistent trends of the last seventy years has been
the ever-widening gulf between the extremely rich and everyone else.

Income inequality isn't about people working eighty hours per week in
demanding, highly skilled white-collar jobs that earn $200,000 per year. It's
about the people making more than ten times that. And the people making
more than ten times that. And the people making more than ten times that.
We are talking about people that have salaries that are base-ten, exponentially
larger.

To draw an anecdote about income inequality in the private sector, top
CEOs receive paychecks that are three hundred times larger than that of their
average worker.[26] This is not how it used to be, when income inequality was less
severe. Fifty years ago, CEOs "averaged twenty times that of the typical worker."[27]
For people who are getting paid larger and larger salaries—ten, one hundred,
one thousand times the median U.S. income—right-leaning politicians have
continued to reduce the top marginal tax rate, further exacerbating not just
income inequality but wealth inequality.

For context, "during the eight years of the Eisenhower presidency, from 1953
to 1961, the top marginal rate was 91 percent. (It was 92 percent the year he came
into office.)"[28] Meanwhile, during the Bush administration—during wartime—
wealthy Americans saw "a sharp drop in their tax burden. The top tax rate—the
income-tax rate on the highest bracket—is now 35 percent, half what it was in
the 1970s."[29]

And middle-income families, well, "middle-income families face a higher rate
than a half-century ago: 28.6 percent in 2014, versus 24.8 percent in 1964."[30]

At this point, wealth inequality in America is so egregious that the three wealthiest people own more wealth than the bottom half of the American people.[31]
Such extreme disparities in wealth equate effectively to the establishment of

nobility without the title. Given America's Gini coefficient (a statistical measure of the distribution of wealth), the United States was dubbed "the Unequal States of America,"[32] according to Allianz's Global Wealth Report.

CNBC reported that "the rich are getting richer and the poor are getting poorer, at least in the United States . . . The top 1 percent of families took home an average of 26.3 times as much income as the bottom 99 percent in 2015, according to a new paper released by the Economic Policy Institute, a non-profit, nonpartisan think tank in Washington, D.C."[33]

It seems perverse to me that the hedge fund manager Steven A. Cohen could net $2.3 billion in 2013 (while the hedge fund that bears his initials, SAC Capital, pled guilty to insider trading), but our country is unwilling to offer an adequate health care system to all of its citizens.[34]

Likewise, the richest country on earth offers some of the most miserly paid leave and unemployment benefits relative to other rich countries (on the basis of paid maternity leave, paid paternity leave, general parental leave, paid holiday allowances, and paid sick leave).[35] All of this impacts the quality of life for ordinary Americans.

My father is eighty years old, and still working full-time (over forty hours per week) to pay the bills. After being hospitalized for two weeks following an emergency surgery, he was afraid that he might be pushing the boundaries of his sick leave. He was worried that his time in the hospital might cause him to be let go from his job. The doctors wouldn't allow him to drive or ride in a car, so, with a PICC line dispensing antibiotics to his heart and a cane in his hand, he subserviently hunched over his computer and got back to work in any way that he could.

I look at other members of my family, stressed as hell, still paying off their student loans in their late thirties and think how much better off their situation would have been had America adopted a tertiary education model in line with the United Kingdom or Australia.

Likewise, my stepmom has been a schoolteacher for decades. Fed up with the discipline issues in public schools, she switched to a private middle school, conceding that the move was worth the reduction of an already paltry teacher's salary. She's in her sixties and still wakes up at four a.m. to avoid rush-hour traffic. Despite having a master's degree and decades of work experience, like many teachers, her stagnant salary hasn't done her any favors. In the United States, teachers earn on average 68 percent of what other university-educated workers make, and U.S. teacher salaries relative to university grad earnings is far below the Organisation for Economic Co-operation and Development (OECD) member-nation average.[36] If her circumstances were different—if my dad couldn't work anymore; if one of her kids were in need—she'd be in the hurt box. In America, it's a vicious irony that education professionals struggle to pay for their own kids' college education.

The truth is, if college were affordable in America—as it is in many of the countries in the rich world—I probably wouldn't have gone to West Point. If America did adequately fund college and I chose a different path, I wouldn't still be wrestling today with the emotions that came from that war.

The Military Got This Right

The military got this right. "I will never leave a fallen comrade." It is directly written into the Soldier's Creed. And yet, when we're talking about a larger unit of Americans—society at large—rather than a platoon or a company, the sentiment is lost. In the military, there is an expectation that no one will be left for dead—such a thing would be considered cowardly and morally repugnant; however, in America, if you expect that no one should be left for dead—you are "Lefty," a "Lib-tard." We celebrate the culture of soldiers providing support to other soldiers; we demonize the culture of Americans providing support to other Americans.

If a struggling soldier is cared for by those who have the capacity to do so, that is "good leadership"; but if a struggling American is cared for by those who have the capacity to do so, that is considered "a handout." The military, the institution that instills the greatest sense of confidence amongst Americans—more than the church, small business, or the police—has the priorities "The mission, the men, and me." And yet, the application of these values to the rest of American society—even just a shade closer—is ridiculed with contempt by the same Republicans who first in-line to slather praise upon the American military.

Servicemen will be the first ones to say they appreciate and value the freedom and development that comes from these far-from-lavish, minimal-threshold pay and benefits, which offer something akin to "a standard issue of dignity." Medical. Dental. More affordable college tuition. Childcare. Access to fitness facilities. Counselling services.

These are the basic services that help our soldiers compete on the battlefield; they are the same basic services that would help American citizens compete at the workplace.

Enacting such big, structural changes, will also require a massive mind-set shift. It will require Americans to treat other Americans like they matter. As if our quality of life and survival depends on the education, training, and health of other Americans—which it does. Here, America's private sector could learn from the military.

In my experience, no General would ever push to increase his or her own salary if it meant cutting benefits to lower-level enlisted. Is it too much to ask private sector executives, who often get paid more than ten times what a general makes, to do the same? Is it too much to ask the beneficiaries of a system that entrenches extreme wealth inequality—those who have more money than they know what to do with—to treat their people—their workers—their countrymen—with dignity? To lead by example? The answer, as modern American politics would suggest, is, "yes—it is too much." But, like military leaders who put themselves above the mission—or above their troops, eventually, they get fired. Our politicians should expect the same.

The story of today's America is one of avoidable suffering. You can't help but think that Americans are ignored by a government that no longer serves us, reminding me of a quote from Pearl S. Buck, author of *The Good Earth*: "The test of a civilization is the way that it cares for its helpless members."[37] How, then, should we think about the current state of America? Facing the challenges we face today, with numerous more, expected and unexpected, on the horizon—with one existential threat, climate change, looming large—collective-action problems will require a "government of the people, by the people, for the people."

The Existential Threat: Climate Change

From the famous image of the "pale blue dot," described in a book by Carl Sagan of the same name, to the seminars made famous by Al Gore in *An Inconvenient Truth*, I learned a long time ago that the earth is a delicate thing.

Perhaps the images of the globe, a bluish apple, with its thin shell of an atmosphere, is so captivating because it is so basic. This thin covering of atmosphere has had just the right ingredients to sustain all of the life on earth—all of the biodiversity, all of the evolution—and we are actively destroying it.

Since the Industrial Revolution, the United States is the world's leading contributor to climate change, emitting more carbon dioxide than the next three countries combined: China, Russia, and Germany.[38] This measure of total emissions (rather than only looking at present-day emissions) is the measure to use when allocating culpability, because gases like carbon dioxide do not dissipate for thousands of years. On the topic of climate change, the United States has demonstrated willful ignorance and active resistance, leaving a soiled legacy for future generations. Our government's response to the climate crisis amounts to environmental *Blitzkrieg* waged against those least capable of defending themselves: other species, the poor, and unborn generations. Although American citizens may not expect perfection from our political leaders, we do expect a level of stewardship greater than complete and utter incompetence. Unfortunately, U.S. policymakers cannot clear this low bar on the urgent topic of climate.

The Climate Change Performance Index, compiled by the Climate Action Network,[39] ranks countries for their actions on climate change, including their climate policies, energy use, and greenhouse gas emissions.[40] Of the sixty countries measured, the United States and Saudi Arabia are fifty-ninth and sixtieth, respectively, on the list.[41] As such, the effects of climate change continue to worsen, leading organizations have become more urgent in their warnings.

We're facing the biggest environmental challenge our species has ever seen. No matter what we're passionate about, something we care about will be affected by climate change.

—*World Wildlife Foundation, "The Effects of Climate Change"*

It makes you wonder: Is there a worse crime? A worse crime than willfully and deliberately undermining organized life on this planet?[42]

Make no mistake—every dollar that America invests in war today is not only a dollar not spent on addressing the direct causes of climate change, but a reinvestment in more and worse wars in the future, caused by climate change.

According to the United Nations High Commissioner for Refugees, "Climate change sows seeds for conflict, but it also makes displacement much worse when it happens."[43] In 2015, the DoD wrote a paper about climate-related security risks, stating that it "recognizes the reality of climate change and the significant risk it poses to U.S. interests globally."[44] The report went on to note that the impacts are already occurring and projected to increase over time. Climate change will "aggravate existing problems—such as poverty, social tensions, environmental degradation, ineffectual leadership, and weak political institutions—that threaten domestic stability in a number of countries."[45] The message that America needs to take away is that *investing in climate change is an investment in national security.* If unity can only be achieved by waging war, then let America have a "war against global warming."

And yet, it's worth pointing out the hypocrisy of the Department of Defense, because although it recognizes the security threats caused by climate change, it is also simultaneously one of the most egregious polluters on earth—dumping more metric tons of CO_2 equivalent into the atmosphere than the U.S. base operations of ExxonMobil and Shell combined.[46] It is said that commanders, as defined by U.S. Army doctrine (Army Regulation 600-20: Army Command Policy), "are responsible for everything their command does or fails to do."[47] Although this phrase is traditionally applied to command-and-control, battlefield-type situations, things change. We must now hold commanders accountable, not only for the servicemen and equipment in their charge, not only for their actions in war, but now also for the waste and pollution they produce on account of the missions they order.

The decision to use military force must be assessed not only against traditional metrics (e.g. likelihood of success, "benefits" of political violence), but also against the inevitable contribution to climate-related risks. A low-value military excursion emitting a lot of CO_2 is a net negative for the planet.

One ancillary benefit of enacting such policies is that once you account for additional externalities of war (paying for wounded civilians on the other side, carbon taxes on military emissions), the real costs of war will be revealed. These costs will not only show how wasteful war is, but taking responsibility for the damage we caused will have the effect of increasing the costs of war, hopefully decreasing the likelihood that we will further entangle ourselves in more low-value conflicts in the future.[48] And once you apply this thinking in practice, new toys like the F-35 fighter jet—the one the American taxpayer just spent $1.5 trillion dollars building—will need to be phased-out and decommissioned. There is an imperative, even for the military, to switch to lower carbon air platforms, namely drones, to decarbonize and drawdown at a rate that averts total environmental collapse.

Decommissioning our fossil fuel military equipment isn't being talked about, but it needs to be.

If a resistant-to-change, fossil fuel-powered military is one of the reasons why this generation fails in its duty to safeguard our planet, then it invites the question, "what is the point of the military, anyway?" Why would the military bother making the world 'safe for democracy' if it is unwilling to make the world safe for life on it? The American military cannot bomb its way out of this one. Nothing but the best of human nature, working together, will be required to heal mother nature.

> *If we're going to win on climate we have to make sure we are counting carbon completely, not exempting different things like military emissions because it is politically inconvenient to count them . . . The atmosphere certainly counts the carbon from the military. Therefore we must as well.*
>
> —*Stephen Kretzmann, director of Oil Change International, quoted in* The Atlantic

So, America is the world's worst polluter. The U.S. military is one of the largest individual polluters on earth. And contribution to climate change is a legitimate security threat that contributes to conflict—the very type we hope to stop.

We have a narrow window to take aggressive and immediate action to achieve deep decarbonization, or climate change will take aggressive action against us.

Past attempts—Kyoto, Paris, and many COPs in between—have not moved the dial. There is more urgency in my generation, and in those who are younger than me.

Whether it is the Green New Deal or some other incarnation of it with a carbon tax, there is a new energy around this issue. And we are beginning to adequately shame politicians and businesses for their resistance.

And in the process of seeing this, the American people have found a new voice. We are putting the out-of-date prejudices and xenophobia of the post-9/11 era farther in the rearview mirror. And this gives me hope for a better future.

This generation demands that climate change be put at the front of the priority list because, as environmentalist rallying cry goes, "There is no Planet B."

Setting a new course for these priorities is our responsibility. As I remember when Al Gore came to address my graduate school class at Oxford, he said something that resonated with me: "Political will is a renewable resource."[49] We must not forget it.

Our Responsibility

Our country is perfectly structured to give us the results we are currently receiving. Those results include: eighteen years of aimless war, systemic racism and sexism, highly profitable companies that pay no federal income taxes, public infrastructure befitting a developing country, winner-takes-all wealth inequality, a political system beholden to corporate money, a healthcare model that overlooks our most vulnerable people, and unforgivable dithering on climate change.

If we do not like these results, if we do not like a power structure designed to serve elites' interests over our own, we must change the forces that guide our nation.

Like the Army doctrine says, until you and I take collective responsibility for everything our nation does—and fails to do—until we truly own it—we should expect more of the same: a power structure designed to serve plutocratic interests over our own.

In a democracy, the people wield the power. Our collective will serves as commander. And as the commander, our orders are executed indirectly, by policymakers, in the form of policy and law. It is imperative, now more than ever, that we adopt a "commander's mind-set."

But adopting a commander's mind-set will include a burden that American citizens are unaccustomed to. We must be responsible for everything our nation does—and fails to do. And as we share the communion of our failures and successes together, as one community, as one world, we will not be driven apart.

The power never left us. We gave it away. We gave it away when we were cowed into fear after 9/11.

We know the truth. The war has been going on long enough. The lies told to us by George W. Bush were debunked long ago and are public knowledge. The Afghanistan Papers revealed that senior U.S. officials knowingly lied about progress long after it was clear that there was none. It does not stop there; we have seen our national war fetish continue in 2020, when President Trump provoked new tensions, assassinating Iran's top general, Qasem Soleimani, a foreign military leader of a country we are not at war with.

It will never stop until we demand that it must. Throughout history, major change comes from the people, up.

If our elected officials do not heed the facts, if they do not heed the will of the people, we must not moan in dejected resignation. No.

Expose their contradictions, and make politicians take responsibility, or hit the bricks.

If your elected representatives do not oppose endless war: fire them.

If your elected representatives do not treat the climate crisis as the leading issue of our generation: fire them.

If your elected representatives use policy to demean others: fire them.

If your elected representatives undermine international law or treaties: fire them.

And if no one steps up: run for office.

There are more Un-Americans than you think—concerned citizens with the power of accurate observation, who recognize America is broken and want to fix it. And once enough get into office, we can reshape what America stands for. We can forge a new vision for the American people, and reclaim a national pride, not ordained by military might, or conflicts, or flag bumper stickers, but by giving every American a standard issue of dignity and contributing to a peaceful, more developed world today, that does not ask us to sacrifice a peaceful, better world tomorrow.

The truth is that, by participating in the War on Terror, I participated in a crime, not a tragedy. A secondary tragedy is that America lacks the courage and conviction to say so.[50]

To stop America's endless wars, we will need Americans to collectively redraw the military's role in society. Doing so is of utmost urgency and importance. America, the leading superpower of the past seventy years, has a responsibility—not only to its own citizens, but to all inhabitants of this planet—to grow our capacity for cooperation, not conflict: to put "planet and people first."

To achieve this, we need way more than hope, or luck. We need you. We need you, the reader, to discuss what this means in action, and get involved. The American Dream depends on it.

And on that day, I'll hoist an American flag with pride—the way I was taught to do in elementary school.

Then I will once again be able to proudly and uncomplicatedly refer to myself as "American."

But this time with eyes wide open.

A NOTE TO VETERANS OF THE "GLOBAL WAR ON TERROR"

If you feel like you may have information about possible war crimes, previously unreported, or have experience with unethical behavior in the military, especially if it involved the death or injury of others, you can reach out directly to me to initiate a conversation:

erik@enedstrom.com

Or you can reach out to a leading newspaper, to provide a tip over a secure server.

For example, the *New York Times*: https://www.nytimes.com/tips

Serving in the military is hard. If you ever feel like you need to speak with someone—don't hesitate. The military provides 24/7 support where you have the opportunity to speak with trained professionals. Your family, friends, and country thank you.

The Veterans Crisis Line can be reached through the following channels:
Website: https://www.veteranscrisisline.net/get-help/hotline
Phone: Call 1-800-273-8255 and Press 1
Text: 838255

ACKNOWLEDGMENTS

This book nearly broke me.

To write this, I have lived inside my brain, with the content you have just read, for a decade. The process of constantly researching the War on Terror and reliving the darkest experiences in my life put me in a bad place, emotionally.

In a way, the publication of this book has been a personal catharsis. To share with you, and put in your hands, the fruit of this decade-long endeavor gives me a feeling of immense happiness and privilege, so let me first say thank you to you, the reader. You "opted in" to hear a tough story, and I hope that across the globe it sparks meaningful conversation about nationalism's shortfalls, the role of the military in society, and the greater challenges—like climate change—to which we should instead be allocating our nation's attention and resources.

Writing this never came easy and within these pages is a separate and more personal story of toil, persistence, and failure, juxtaposed with seemingly small, incremental successes. During the writing of this book I experienced love and heartbreak; triumph and failure; pride and shame; inspiration and aimlessness. But never hopelessness.

I attribute this to having people around me who made the notion of quitting my most ambitious project to date unthinkable.

I'd like to thank Anton Mueller, Morgan Jones, Akshaya Iyer, and Jenna Dutton of Bloomsbury for providing editorial and copy edits to the manuscript, taking it from rough-and-tumble to market-ready.

To my literary agent, Zeynep Sen, thanks for taking a chance with me. You're the best.

My family: Dad, Alanna, Andrea, Dave, and all of the rest of the family, from Boston, Massachusetts, to Gothenburg, Sweden—I love you guys.

To my former soldiers and West Point classmates—thank you for listening with an open mind. Your unconquerable spirit and constant pursuit of "better" has been and always will be inspirational. Fear none of life's hardships and transitions because, as I've witnessed in combat, you can handle it.

To the men of 3rd platoon, Alpha Company, 1-12 Infantry: that was a hell of a year. Words fail to express my sense of gratitude to each of you—for looking out for each other—for being so damn tough—and for making our platoon of "lovable misfits and Marlboro men" an effective team. I love you guys and I feel honored to have served alongside you.

To Oxford University, for being the city of dreaming spires and being the place that allowed me to rewrite the blueprint of my life. To my Oxford MBA and ECM classmates—you're a thousand colors of excellence.

To Afghan interpreters serving U.S. forces, including my own interpreters (Rahmatullah, Fawad, Payman, and Sayed)—thanks for looking out for us. You may even be reading this from Afghanistan. One day, I hope my government will have the decency to issue you the U.S. visa you deserve. It's hard to think of others more deserving of a route to American citizenship.

To every journalist, correspondent, and academic researcher covering these topics—especially those cited in this book—thank you. It takes courage to deploy to a war zone and cover the conflict with unflinching candor. There are many news outlets but a special thanks to the *New York Times*, the *Washington Post*, the *Guardian*, the *Intercept*, Al Jazeera, the *Nation, Democracy Now!*, *Time*, *Boston Globe*, and others. It also takes great resolve to tally the human, social, and financial costs of war for nearly twenty years—a very special thanks to Brown University's Watson Institute for doing so.

To the best people I could ask for, thank you for indulging me, challenging me, and overall, making this book—and life—better than it was: Kate Scott, Chris Keller, Adam Harmon, Michael Aper, Emily Connally, Caryn Davies, Vikraman Selvaraja, Lucy Wark, Sarah Vaughn, Matt Watters, Nat Ware, Jessica Bloom, Kevin Baum, Grant Lubowski, Jon Green, Jon Filbey, and so many more. I appreciate you.

To my friends who gave me a place to live and write: Sven Jungmann, Anders Friden, Lachlan Molesworth, and Olivia Molesworth.

To Noam Chomsky, for being an absolute legend—you've inspired generations of activists. You may not have realized it, but the day you made time to speak with me in your MIT office changed my life.

And sometimes—just sometimes—the fortune cookie is right: "Your persistence will bring the desired results."

NOTES

THREE VISIONS

1. *Terrorism* as defined by the Department of Defense: "The unlawful use of violence or threat of violence, often motivated by religious, political, or other ideological beliefs, to instill fear and coerce governments or societies in pursuit of goals that are usually political ... State actors may use unlawful acts of violence to create effects when lawful conflict between nations does not exist." Joint Staff, "Counterterrorism," Joint Publication 3-26, October 24, 2014: I-5, www.jcs.mil/Portals/36/Documents/Doctrine/pubs/jp3_26.pdf.

2. Joint Economic Committee, "Ten Key Facts about Veterans of the Post-9/11 Era," November 10, 2015, www.jec.senate.gov/public/index.cfm/democrats/2015 /11/ten-key-facts-about-veterans-of-the-post.

3. James Marshall Crotty, "If Massachusetts Were a Country, Its Students Would Rank 9th in the World," *Forbes*, September 29, 2014, www.forbes.com/sites /jamesmarshallcrotty/2014/09/29/if-massachusetts-were-a-country-its-students -would-rank-9th-in-the-world/#2a442c96149b.

4. George Gallup, "Global Results, End of Year Survey," WIN/Gallup International, Gallup International, 2013.

5. "Human Costs," Costs of War, Watson Institute for International and Public Affairs, Brown University, November 2018, https://watson.brown.edu/costsof war/costs/human.

6. Jack Moran, "Murderer Sentenced to Life in Prison," *Register-Guard*, June 3, 2016, www.registerguard.com/article/20160603/NEWS/306039972.

7. "Bush: Don't Wait for Mushroom Cloud," CNN, October 8, 2002, www.edition .cnn.com/2002/ALLPOLITICS/10/07/bush.transcript.

8. This is a reference to the "Ring Poop," a tradition in which Plebes chase Firsties, boxing them in to melodramatically fawn over their newly issued class rings. "Oh, my God, sir/ma'am! What a beautiful ring! What a crass mass of brass and glass! What a bold mold of rolled gold! What a cool jewel you got from your school! See how it sparkles and shines? It must have cost you a fortune! Please, sir/ma'am, may I touch it? May I touch it, please, sir/ma'am?"

9. "Text: President Bush Addresses the Nation," *Washington Post*, September 20, 2001, www.washingtonpost.com/wp-srv/nation/specials/attacked/transcripts/bushaddress_092001.html.

10. "In one bed lay Noor Mohammad, 10, who was a bundle of bandages. He lost his eyes and hands to the bomb that hit his house after Sunday dinner. Hospital director Guloja Shimwari shook his head at the boy's wounds. 'The United States must be thinking he is Osama,' Shimwari said. 'If he is not Osama, then why would they do this?'" Howard Zinn, "The Others," *Nation*, February 11, 2002, www.howardzinn.org/the-others.

11. George W. Bush put his stamp of approval on torture. In particular, waterboarding, one of those approved torture techniques, was a practice for which the United States once punished Japanese war criminals with hanging or lengthy prison sentences. The hypocrisy of mainstreaming a criminal practice that resulted in death is unspeakable. Senator John McCain referenced this in 2007: "I forgot to mention last night that following World War II war crime trials were convened. The Japanese were tried and convicted and hung for war crimes committed against American POWs. Among those charges for which they were convicted was waterboarding." John Frank, "History Supports McCain's Stance on Waterboarding," Politifact, December 18, 2007, www.politifact.com/truth-o-meter/statements/2007/dec/18/john-mccain/history-supports-mccains-stance-on-waterboarding.

12. Secret CIA "black jails" like the infamous "Salt Pit" also operated in Afghanistan, where prisoners from Pakistan, Tanzania, Yemen, Saudi Arabia, and elsewhere were interrogated and tortured. Khaled El-Masri, for example, an innocent German citizen arrested in Macedonia, was transferred to the Salt Pit, then tortured and sodomized for four months. The United States held him for an additional five months after realizing they had mistaken him for another person, then released him at night on a desolate road in Albania without apology or funds to return home. Brendan Fischer and Lisa Graves, "International Law and the War on Terror," Watson Institute for International and Public Affairs, Brown University, 2011, watson.brown.edu/costsofwar/files/cow/imce/papers/2011/International%20Law%20and%20the%20War%20on%20Terror.pdf.

13. The United States conducted an overwhelmingly lethal assault on a Doctors Without Borders (*Médecins sans Frontières*) hospital in Kunduz, killing "at least 42 people, including 24 patients, 14 staff, and 4 caretakers . . . 37 others [were] wounded in the air strike, which destroyed the MSF hospital building and prompted widespread condemnation from human rights groups." "US: Strike on Afghanistan MSF Hospital Not a War Crime," Al Jazeera, April 30, 2016,

www.aljazeera.com/news/2016/04/afghan-msf-hospital-air-strike-war-crime
-160429182003792.html.

14. Chris McGreal, "US Soldiers 'Killed Afghan Civilians for Sport and Collected Fingers as Trophies,'" *Guardian*, September 8, 2010, https://www.theguardian .com/world/2010/sep/09/us-soldiers-afghan-civilians-fingers.

15. Ben Gilbert, "U.S. Military Bulldozes through Kandahar," CBS News, November 10, 2010, https://www.cbsnews.com/news/us-military-bulldozes -through-kandahar.

16. Richard A. Oppel Jr. and Taimoor Shah, "Civilians Killed as U.S. Troops Fire on Afghan Bus," *New York Times*, April 12, 2010, www.nytimes.com/2010/04 /13/world/asia/13afghan.html.

17. "Transcript of President Bush's Speech at the Veterans of Foreign Wars Convention," *New York Times*, August 22, 2007, www.nytimes.com/2007/08/22 /washington/w23policytext.html.

18. In a 2013 speech, Barack Obama indicated that America has been fighting unnecessary wars: "Unless we discipline our thinking, our definitions, our actions, we may be drawn into more wars we don't need to fight." His use of *more wars we don't need to fight* seems to belie his thoughts on the matter. Barack Obama, "Remarks by the President at the National Defense University, May 23, 2013," https://obamawhitehouse.archives.gov/the-press-office/2013/05/23 /remarks-president-national-defense-university.

19. "Text: President Bush Addresses the Nation," *Washington Post*.

AMERICAN BOY

1. Robert Baden-Powell and Elleke Boehmer, *Scouting for Boys: A Handbook for Instruction in Good Citizenship* (Oxford: Oxford University Press, 2005).

2. *Time* magazine reports that cost per flight hour for an F-22A Raptor Fighter is $68,362; assumes a standard football "flyover" requires three aircraft and one hour of flight time. Mark Thompson, "Costly Flight Hours," *Time*, April 2, 2013, www.nation.time.com/2013/04/02/costly-flight-hours.

3. Walter Pincus, "Defense Department Spends $500 Million to Strike Up the Bands," *Washington Post*, September 6, 2010, www.washingtonpost.com/wp-dyn /content/article/2010/09/06/AR2010090603018.html.

4. Ana Livia Coelho, "ESPN Unveils Sponsors for X Games Aspen 2017," ESPN, January 25, 2017, www.espnmediazone.com/us/press-releases/2017/01/espn -unveils-sponsors-x-games-aspen-2017; Jeremy Herb, "National Guard, Senator

Defend Funding for Military NASCAR Sponsorships," *The Hill*, May 23, 2012, thehill.com/policy/defense/229113-national-guard-ind-senator-defend-military -nascar-sponsorships.

5. According to a 2016 Gallup Poll study on military confidence, "Americans continue to place more faith in their military than in any other societal institution, and despite some fluctuations over time, this high level of confidence has not abated. The military maintains this high level of respect even as the public's confidence in many other of society's institutions has declined compared with levels measured a decade ago and further back." Frank Newport, "Americans Continue to Express Highest Confidence in Military," *Gallup*, June 17, 2016, news.gallup.com/poll/192917/americans-continue-express-highest-confidence -military.aspx. Likewise, a 2011 Pew Research study on "The Public and the Military" stated, "At a time when the public's confidence in most key national institutions has sagged, confidence in the military is at or near its highest level in many decades." Pew Research Center, "The Military-Civilian Gap: War and Sacrifice in the Post 9-11 Era," October 5, 2011, http://www.pewresearch.org/wp-content /uploads/sites/3/2011/10/veterans-report.pdf.

6. "A recent innovation, veterans treatment courts are an outgrowth of the drug and mental health specialty or problem-solving court models, which create alternative sentencing and punishment structures emphasizing community-based treatment in lieu of incarceration for offenders whose criminal activity arises out of substance addiction or mental illness . . . These treatment courts are designed to rehabilitate, in non-correctional settings, veterans who commit combat stress-related crimes." Allison E. Jones, "Veterans Treatment Courts: Do Status-Based Problem-Solving Courts Create an Improper Privileged Class of Criminal Defendants?" *Washington University Journal of Law & Policy* 43, no. 307 (2014): 308. Facing five counts of assault with intent to murder and five possible life sentences in the traditional criminal justice system, one former soldier could have this charge dismissed or reduced to a misdemeanor on account of the veterans court program. Erica Good, "Coming Together to Fight for a Troubled Veteran," *New York Times*, July 17, 2011, https://www.nytimes.com/2011/07/18 /us/18vets.html.

7. Phil Klay, "The Warrior at the Mall," *New York Times*, April 4, 2018, https://www .nytimes.com/2018/04/14/opinion/sunday/the-warrior-at-the-mall.html.

8. Research indicates that the military, as an employer, relies on the perception that one can serve a higher purpose. Without this belief, military service may become significantly less attractive:

> *There are two areas, however, in which substantial differences between the military and civilian employment exist: working conditions and the opportunity to serve a higher purpose. An individual might prefer working conditions in the civilian sector to those in the military, where conditions may be onerous or life-threatening. However, that individual is more likely to find a transcendent purpose (e.g., duty to country) by serving in the military rather than being employed in the civilian sector.*

Committee on the Youth Population and Military Recruitment, "Attitudes, Aptitudes, and Aspirations of American Youth: Implications for Military Recruitment," National Research Council of the National Academies, 2003, www.nap.edu/read/10478/chapter/2.

9. "Division 1: Deployment Allowance," ADF Pay and Conditions, Australian Government Department of Defence, accessed April 27, 2019, http://www .defence.gov.au/PayAndConditions/ADF/Chapter-17/Part-7/Div-1.asp.

10. Rana Forooha, "The US College Debt Bubble Is Becoming Dangerous," *Financial Times*, April 9, 2017, www.ft.com/content/a272ee4c-1b83-11e7-bcac-6d03d067f81f.

11. 107th Congress, 2001.

12. Matthew F. Rech, "Recruitment, Counter-Recruitment and Critical Military Studies," *Global Discourse* 4, no. 2–3 (April 16, 2014): 244–62, https://doi.org /10.1080/23269995.2014.909243.

13. Name, date of birth, gender, mailing address, e-mail address, race and ethnicity, telephone number, high school name, graduation date, GPA, college intent, military interest, field of study, and the ASVAB test score. New York Civil Liberties Union: Nava, 2010.

14. The JAMRS database, subcontracted by Equifax (which was breached in a 2017 cyberattack, compromising the personal data of 143 million Americans), holds the personal details of over 30 million minors and young adults for the purpose of military recruitment. As the *New York Times* described the cyberattack, "This is about as bad as it gets," and "on a scale of 1 to 10 in terms of risk to consumers, this is a 10." Tara Siegel Bernard et al., "Equifax Says Cyberattack May Have Affected 143 Million in the U.S.," *New York Times*, September 7, 2017, www .nytimes.com/2017/09/07/business/equifax-cyberattack.html.

15. Richard S. Carvalho et al., "Department of Defense: Youth Poll Wave 19—June 2010," Arlington, VA: Fors Marsh Group, Defense Human Resource Activity, December 2010, https://jamrs.defense.gov/Portals/20/Documents /Youth_Poll_15.pdf.

16. The Royal Children's Hospital Melbourne, "Bedwetting," *Kids Health Info* (blog), March 2018, https://www.rch.org.au/kidsinfo/fact_sheets/Bedwetting.

17. Army Educational Outreach Program, 2017.

18. The United Nations Convention on the Rights of the Child—a near unanimously accepted human rights instrument—has been ratified by every UN member except one: the United States. Many of the provisions would be in direct conflict with the state's severe treatment of juveniles in the prison system, but there is one optional protocol that is problematic for America as it pertains to its predatory military recruitment tactics: "Persons who have not attained the age of 18 years are not compulsorily recruited into their armed forces." "11. b) Optional Protocol to the Convention on the Rights of the Child on the Involvement of Children in Armed Conflict," United Nations, Treaty Series, vol. 2173, February 12, 2002, treaties.un.org/doc/Publication/MTDSG/Volume%20I /Chapter%20IV/IV-11-b.en.pdf. The Convention also ensures safeguards for children subjected to voluntary recruitment. According to the *American Journal of Public Health*, "The United States would be out of compliance with this protocol because our federal government currently mandates that military recruiters have full access to the nation's public high schools for purposes of aggressively recruiting youngsters." In this respect, as it pertains to our reluctance to ratifying a widely uncontentious set of Rights for Children, America is truly exceptional. Amy Hagopian and Kathy Barker, "Should We End Military Recruiting in High Schools as a Matter of Child Protection and Public Health?" *American Journal of Public Health* 101, no. 1 (2011): 19–23.

19. Committee on the Youth Population and Military Recruitment, "Attitudes, Aptitudes, and Aspirations."

20. The ability to re-form people's minds, especially minds as curious and pliable as children's, is a marketing dream. "If marketing has one goal, it's to reach consumers at the moments that most influence their decisions." With near-mandatory exposure to the military in school, the military is added to the career consideration set of nearly all American children, almost without exception (David Court et al., "The Consumer Decision Journey," *McKinsey Quarterly*, June 2009, www.mckinsey.com/business-functions/marketing-and-sales/our -insights/the-consumer-decision-journey). The military is one career option that everyone seemingly knows about.

21. "DoD Reported Annual Allotments for Military Service Component Advertising Programs in 2017" is estimated to be $574.9 million. United Sates Government Accountability Office, "DOD Advertising: Better Coordination, Performance

Measurement, and Oversight Needed to Help Meet Recruitment Goals," GAO-16-396, May 2016, www.gao.gov/assets/680/677062.pdf.

22. Recruiters are trained using the *School Recruiting Program Handbook*, which is used to "assist recruiters in penetrating their school market" to "obtain the maximum number of quality enlistments." United States Army Recruiting Command, *School Recruiting Program Handbook*, USAREC Pamphlet 350-13, www.grassrootspeace.org/army_recruiter_hdbk.pdf.

23. Ibid.

24. Ibid.

25. Avoiding discussions about risk—or misrepresenting it altogether—was not just my experience; academic research in Texas indicated that "86% of respondents [prospective military recruits in high school] said military service was never portrayed to them as dangerous." Adam McGlynn and Jessica Lavariega Monforti, "The Poverty Draft? Exploring the Role of Socioeconomic Status in U.S. Military Recruitment of Hispanic Students," prepared for presentation at the American Political Science Association Annual Meeting, Washington, D.C., September 2–5, 2010, www.researchgate.net/publication/228212120_The _Poverty_Draft_Exploring_the_Role_of_Socioeconomic_Status_in_US _Military_Recruitment_of_Hispanic_Students.

26. Recruiters certainly don't want to talk about the more dire aspects: "The wars have caused mental and emotional health problems in 31 percent of vets—more than 800,000 of them." Rajiv Chandrasekaran, "After the Wars: A Legacy of Pain and Pride," *Washington Post*, March 29, 2014, www.washingtonpost.com /sf/national/2014/03/29/a-legacy-of-pride-and-pain. In one of the largest surveys available on post-9/11 soldiers, "40 percent of veterans polled had considered suicide at least once after they joined the military," and roughly twenty veterans commit suicide daily—a staggering figure. Kime, Patricia, "More Post-9/11 Veterans Have Considered Suicide, Survey Says," *Military Times*, May 24, 2016, www.militarytimes.com/veterans/2016/05/24/more-post-9-11-veterans-have -considered-suicide-survey-says.

27. Fourteen years past R-Day (Reception Day) for the West Point Class of 2007, my classmates and I still get drunk and talk about the same stories. Leave a few Old Grads in a room for twenty minutes and listen to them reminisce: West Point pranks like hiding alarm clocks set to go off hourly throughout the night; sharing misery in the form of starvation and sleep deprivation at Ranger School; war stories of being hit by a suicide bomber during deployment; eulogizing the friends killed in combat. We all go back to being kids—if those are things that

normal kids do. At each discrete step of the way, you measure your options, and may think that your actions make sense, until they don't any longer—and you're stuck. At this moment, the bubble pops, and you realize that the noble ideals that you were sold on the day you signed up aren't lived up to in practice.

With these considerations, I'd recommend future generations to take stock of their dreams; if it doesn't look like things are adding up, ask in a Socratic way if there isn't something else they could do with their lives. And if they don't know, reassure them that it's okay. Just don't get involved in something you can't take back when you do realize what you want, because it's highly unlikely that you, in a few years, will want the same things as you, now.

I want to tell servicemen that places exist where everyone will accept you as you are, and that finding a place that actually cares about your interests and thoughts isn't "weakness," a "crutch," or a "handout." There are easier, less demeaning ways to pay for college.

28. Marc Larocque, "See Where Brockton Ranks on List of Most Dangerous U.S. Cities," *Enterprise News*, January 9, 2017, www.enterprisenews.com/news /20170109/see-where-brockton-ranks-on-list-of-most-dangerous-us-cities.

29. Milton Academy, "Quick Facts," https://www.milton.edu/about/quick-facts.

30. John Pilger described the first Gulf War in the *Guardian*: "Ten years ago, when 200,000 Iraqis died during and immediately after the slaughter known as the Gulf war, the scale of this massacre was never allowed to enter public consciousness in the west. Many were buried alive at night by armoured American snowploughs and murdered while retreating." "Afghanistan," *Guardian*, October 3, 2001, www.theguardian.com/world/2001/oct/04/afghanistan.terrorism7.

31. In addition to lacking what are often considered standard modern amenities, much of Afghanistan, especially during the initial U.S. bombing campaign of 2001, suffered from food scarcity. The *Guardian* reported, "United Nations human rights commissioner Mary Robinson has called for a pause in the U.S.-led bombing of Afghanistan to allow food aid into the country and prevent a 'Rwanda-style' humanitarian disaster." Staff and agencies, "UN Commissioner Warns of Afghan Starvation Threat," *Guardian*, October 14, 2001, www .theguardian.com/world/2001/oct/14/afghanistan.terrorism3. Another article from the *Guardian* reported, "According to the United Nations, 7.5 million people face starvation in Afghanistan, because of the severe food shortages and the onset of winter." Anthony Browne, "Can We Stop the Starvation?" *Guardian*, October 20, 2001, www.theguardian.com/world/2001/oct/21/terro rism.afghanistan.

32. "Afghanis" are the domestic currency of the country of Afghanistan. "Afghans" are the people of Afghanistan.

33. It's unclear if being stoned to death by your own people is better or worse than being bombed to death by foreigners; I didn't know it at the time, but in October 2002, ten months after 9/11, "more than 5,000 civilians have been bombed to death in stricken Afghanistan, the latest a wedding party of 40 people, mostly women and children." John Pilger, "The Great Charade," *Guardian*, July 13, 2002, https://www.theguardian.com/world/2002/jul/14/usa.terrorism.

34. In 1999, *Foreign Affairs* magazine ran an article detailing the extent of damage caused by economic sanctions, referring to them as "economic warfare." These sanctions disproportionately impacted and killed the most vulnerable people in Iraq. The article went on to report, "Economic sanctions may well have been a necessary cause of the deaths of more people in Iraq than have been slain by all so-called weapons of mass destruction throughout history. It is interesting that this loss of human life has failed to make a great impression in the United States . . . Yet the massive death toll among Iraqi civilians has stirred little public protest, and hardly any notice." John Mueller and Karl Mueller, "Sanctions of Mass Destruction," *Foreign Affairs*, May/June 1999, www.foreignaffairs.com /articles/iraq/1999-05-01/sanctions-mass-destruction. The *New York Times*, reporting on the medical effects of sanctions on Iraq, referenced a 1995 *Lancet* study stating, "As many as 576,000 Iraqi children may have died since the end of the Persian Gulf war because of economic sanctions." The *Lancet* study concluded, " 'These findings illustrate a strong association between economic sanctions and increase in child mortality and malnutrition rates.' " Barbara Crossette, "Iraq Sanctions Kill Children, U.N. Reports," *New York Times*, December 1, 1995, www.nytimes.com/1995/12/01/world/iraq-sanctions-kill -children-un-reports.html.

35. In January 2003, roughly six months before I reported to West Point on R-Day, the *New York Times* reported on the pope's articulated opposition to America's pending invasion of Iraq. "Pope John Paul II today expressed his strongest opposition yet to a potential war in Iraq, describing it as a 'defeat for humanity' and urging world leaders to try to resolve disputes with Iraq through diplomatic means. 'No to war!' the pope said during his annual address." Frank Bruni, "Threats and Responses: The Vatican; Pope Voices Opposition, His Stron-gest, to Iraq War," *New York Times*, January 14, 2003, www.nytimes.com/2003/01 /14/world/threats-responses-vatican-pope-voices-opposition-his-strongest-iraq -war.html.

36. Embarrassingly, after sixteen years of war, many senior American lawmakers don't even know where our troops are deployed to commit political violence. " 'I didn't know there was 1,000 troops in Niger,' said Senator Lindsey Graham, R-South Carolina." Daniella Diaz, "Key Senators Say They Didn't Know the US Had Troops in Niger," CNN Politics, October 23, 2017, https://www.cnn.com /2017/10/23/politics/niger-troops-lawmakers/index.html; Dana Milbank and Claudia Deane, "Hussein Link to 9/11 Lingers in Many Minds," *Washington Post*, September 6, 2003, www.washingtonpost.com/archive/politics/2003/09 /06/hussein-link-to-911-lingers-in-many-minds/7cd31079-21d1-42cf-8651-b67e 9335ofde.

37. Bijal P. Trivedi, "Survey Reveals Geographic Illiteracy," *National Geographic*, November 20, 2002, news.nationalgeographic.com/news/2002/11/geography -survey-illiteracy.

38. I'm embarrassed to admit it, but at that age, when I committed to West Point, I didn't know much of anything. Things I did not know at that time: none of the nineteen hijackers on 9/11 were Iraqi or Afghan citizens, and neither the governments of Iraq nor Afghanistan supplied the funds for 9/11. Nor did Iraq's autocratic ruler have nuclear or other weapons of mass destruction, nor was he in any way involved with Al Qaeda. Instead, as revealed in the leaked Downing Street memo, President Bush "wanted to remove Saddam, through military action ... The intelligence and facts were being fixed around the policy." Bush had "made up his mind to take military action ... but the [legal] case was thin" (Don Van Natta Jr., "Bush Was Set on Path to War, British Memo Says," *New York Times*, March 27, 2006, www.nytimes.com/2006/03/27/world/europe/bush-was-set-on -path-towar-british-memo-says.html). Meanwhile, Bush and his top officials continued to publicly push fraudulent evidence indicating that Iraq was "reconstituting its nuclear weapons program" (Wolf Blitzer, "Did the Bush Administration Exaggerate the Threat from Iraq?" CNN, July 8, 2003, www.cnn.com /2003/ALLPOLITICS/07/08/wbr.iraq.claims). This claim would be explicitly contradicted by the U.S. intelligence community's prewar National Intelligence Estimate, which stated that Saddam Hussein's regime "did not have 'sufficient material' to manufacture nuclear weapons and that 'the information we have on Iraqi nuclear personnel does not appear consistent with a coherent effort to reconstitute a nuclear weapons program'" (Jason Leopold, "The CIA Just Declassified the Document That Supposedly Justified the Iraq Invasion," *Vice*, March 19, 2015, news.vice.com/en_us/article/9kve3z/the-cia-just-declassified-the -document-that-supposedly-justified-the-iraq-invasion). The very justification

for Bush's invasion and occupation of that country, in other words, was built upon lies. When I arrived at West Point, I didn't even know that the Iraq War breached the UN Charter. Months later I was deaf to the news when the Iraq War was declared "illegal" by Kofi Annan, the United Nations secretary-general (Ewen MacAskill and Julian Borger, "Iraq Was Illegal and Breached UN Charter, Says Annan," *Guardian*, September 15, 2004, www.theguardian.com /world/2004/sep/16/iraq.iraq). None of the instructors at West Point, in any official capacity, would condemn the Iraq War as "illegal"—maybe "ill-conceived" or a "blunder" but never illegal. Most held the position that a *military invasion* was actually a *humanitarian intervention*, therefore permissible, morally and legally. Unfortunately, as it pertains to international law, this argument, taken to its full extent, seems to lead us to one of two logical conclusions: (1) The UN made a mistake and doesn't know how to interpret its own charter—highly unlikely; or, (2) international law doesn't matter. In effect, the most serious transgressions of international law don't count so long as it is the United States who is responsible for the transgressions. To say that the Iraq War was legal—the prevailing view taught in the military—is to say our president, our country, is above the law. In this way, it is easy to join the military apparatus and play a small part in a great tragedy without even knowing about it.

WEST POINT

1. *Squirter* is military jargon for people escaping from an objective or target.
2. Behind the scenes, the dead are referred to as "bug splats." Michael Hastings, "The Rise of the Killer Drones: How America Goes to War in Secret," *Rolling Stone*, April 16, 2012, www.rollingstone.com/politics/politics-news/the-rise-of -the-killer-drones-how-america-goes-to-war-in-secret-231297.
3. There were some exceptions. One of my classmates, Charlie Eadie, a Marshall scholar, was busted selling anabolic steroids to an undercover cop in Columbus, Georgia. He did this while serving as a U.S. Army captain. Thomas E. Ricks, "A Good Army Officer Goes Bad? Or Slides Back to His Old Ways? Either Way, It's Sad," *Foreign Policy*, June 21, 2012, foreignpolicy.com/2012/06/21/a-good -army-officer-goes-bad-or-slides-back-to-his-old-ways-either-way-its-sad.
4. See Yuval Noah Harari in *Sapiens: A Brief History of Humankind* (New York: HarperCollins, 2015):

> *Until the eighteenth century, religions considered death and its aftermath central to the meaning of life. Beginning in the eighteenth century,*

religions and ideologies such as liberalism, socialism and feminism lost all interest in the afterlife. What, exactly, happens to a Communist after he or she dies? What happens to a capitalist? What happens to a feminist? It is pointless to look for the answer in the writings of Marx, Adam Smith or Simone de Beauvoir. The only modern ideology that still awards death a central role is nationalism. In its more poetic and desperate moments, nationalism promises that whoever dies for the nation will forever live in its collective memory. Yet this promise is so fuzzy that even most nationalists do not really know what to make of it.

5. Associated Press, "Fort Lewis Army Captain Pleads Guilty to Stealing $690,000," *Seattle Times*, December 7, 2009, www.seattletimes.com/seattle -news/fort-lewis-army-captain-pleads-guilty-to-stealing-690000.

6. Kim Murphy, "Army Officer Who Oversaw Iraq Cash Is Accused of Theft," *Chicago Tribune*, April 13, 2009, www.chicagotribune.com/news/ct-xpm-2009 -04-13-0904130030-story.html.

7. There are differing theories and frameworks defining social psychological conditioning. Lieutenant Colonel Dave Grossman, author of *On Killing*, suggests that recruit training commonly involves four types of conditioning: brutalization, classical conditioning, operant conditioning, and role modeling. It's hard to present sanctimonious judgments about which, if any, in a wishy-washy liberal-arts view of the world, is actually "right" or "wrong." One such framework, however, seemed to resonate with me. It captured my lived experience. However, the intended use of this framework wasn't for conventional military indoctrination, but rather indoctrination of violent extremist groups.

There seems to be a spooky similarity between the way in which members of the military are conditioned. Both in terms of deindividuation and demonizing of the enemy.

Interestingly, his abstract summarizes that these groups "use cult-like conditioning techniques to convert normal individuals into remorseless killers . . . Resources should focus on eradicating . . . training camps where the conditioning takes place, rather than on trying to find terrorists after they have already been conditioned."

Taken out of the context of traditional "terrorists"—fragmented, informal, violent, religious groups—and applied to "state terrorism" we arrive at some uncomfortable considerations. Sure, killing for the state has been considered a traditionally accepted standard of conduct, but does it make it less bad?

What does this mean for places like West Point if the United States is responsible for state terrorism? Does it, mean that during wars of aggression it is a training camp for state terrorism? Dave Grossman, *On Killing: The Psychological Cost of Learning to Kill in War and Society* (New York: Open Road Media), 2014.

The Five Phases of Social Psychological Conditioning
Phase 1—Depluralization: stripping away all other group member identities
Phase 2—Self-deindividuation: stripping away each member's personal identity
Phase 3—Other-deindividuation: stripping away the personal identities of enemies
Phase 4—Dehumanization: identifying enemies as subhuman or nonhuman
Phase 5—Demonization: identifying enemies as evil

Phases 1 and 2 address indoctrination of individual members of the group. Phases 3, 4, and 5 address the treatment of the "enemies." Anthony Stahelski, "Terrorists are Made, Not Born: Creating Terrorists Using Social Psychological Conditioning," originally published in the *Online Journal of Homeland Security*, March 2004; republished in *International Cultic Studies Review* 4 (1), 2005: 30–40.

8. The United States Military Academy website also refers to West Pointers being the "best and brightest" on their "Academic Pillar" page: https://westpoint.edu /academic_pillar.

9. Eric Hoffer, *The True Believer: Thoughts on the Nature of Mass Moments* (New York: Harper Perennial Modern Classics, 2010).

10. Sports, plus extra or remedial training, plus physical education classes like swimming, gymnastics, and boxing.

11. Cadet lore: for giggles, cadets would polish the horse's balls a brilliant gold, which contrasted with the oxidized green metal.

12. Here are a few examples of required, verbatim recitation. "How is the Cow?": "She walks, she talks, she's full of chalk, the lacteal fluid extracted from the female of the bovine species is highly prolific to the nth degree"; "The Definition of Leather": "If the fresh skin of an animal, cleaned and divested of all hair, fat, and other extraneous matter, be immersed in a dilute solution of tannic acid, a chemical combination ensues; the gelatinous tissue of the skin is converted into an inputrescible substance, impervious to and insoluble in water; this is leather." I can safely say that none of this rote memorization served me elsewhere in life.

13. "Spooky father figure" refers to a stand-up comedy routine from George Carlin.

14. The Pennsylvania Athletic Club, located in Philadelphia. Instead of taking summer leave, I spent it training for the next crew season. Penn AC boasts a number of Olympic medalists amongst its members.

15. From C. A. J. Coady, *Morality and Political Violence* (Cambridge University Press, 2007):

> *Given the appalling record of states in the unjustified employment of lethal force to devastate populations, economies, and cultures over the centuries, I am unimpressed by any attempt to put a conceptual or moral gulf between the resort to such force (or, as I would prefer to say, violence) for political purposes by state agencies and its political employment by nonstate actors. The tendency to talk of the state as using "force" and of terrorists or revolutionaries as using "violence" embodies an attempt to bring initial opprobrium upon the non-state actors (via the negative connotation of "violence") and to give an a priori mantle of respectability to the state actors. When the qualification "political" is added only to the activities of the nonstate agents and withheld from the state's operations, even where the means employed are identical or similar in kind, this can suggest that the purposes of state violence are somehow above politics and presumptively acceptable, at least when employed by "our" state. But we should not smuggle into the terms of our discussion some bias in favour of states when they employ morally contestable means. Indeed, give the power of states, their deployment of the sword is more likely to wreak morally objectionable damage, at least in terms of scale, than anything nonstate agents can achieve. These facts can be concealed by the anodyne expression "force," which is one reason why I prefer to use the term "violence."*

16. Joe Quinn, "The Real Lesson of Sept. 11," *New York Times*, September 10, 2018, www.nytimes.com/2018/09/10/opinion/911-lessons-veteran.html.

17. President Barack Obama said in 2014, "America must move off a permanent war footing." Matt Spetalnick, "Obama Urges Guantanamo Closure This Year, Shift from 'Permanent War Footing,'" Reuters, January 28, 2014, www.reuters.com/article/us-usa-obama-speech-foreignpolicy/obama-urges-guantanamo-closure-this-year-shift-from-permanent-war-footing-idUSBREA0S06J20140129.

18. Dave Philipps, "At West Point, Annual Pillow Fight Becomes Weaponized," *New York Times*, September 4, 2015, www.nytimes.com/2015/09/05/us/at-west-point-annual-pillow-fight-becomes-weaponized.html.

19. By and large, female cadets were safe from these types of birthday parties.

20. The most-hated upperclassmen got the most preparation. For some birthday parties, Plebes would take milk from the mess hall, days in advance, and leave it next to their heater so it would curdle and go horrendously sour. This would be then used to defile the senior cadet.

21. As a vestige from the Cold War, all of the green pop-up targets at American military rifle ranges are affectionately named "Ivan."

22. "Others will debate the controversial issues, national and international, which divide men's minds . . . These great national problems are not for your professional participation or military solution. Your guidepost stands out like a tenfold beacon in the night: Duty, Honor, Country." General Douglas MacArthur's farewell speech given to the Corps of Cadets at West Point, May 12, 1962.

23. I'm not taking jabs—many of the military instructors I had were great role models; clever and hard-working, they were likely among the highest-ranking cadets at West Point in their day. However, you can't skirt objective truth: these specific military instructors are not academics and would not possess the minimum experience to teach at many civilian universities.

24. Ben Stocking, "Agent Orange Still Haunts Vietnam, US," *Washington Post*, June 14, 2007, www.washingtonpost.com/wp-dyn/content/article/2007/06/14/AR2007061401077.html.

25. Jason von Meding, "Agent Orange, Exposed: How U.S. Chemical Warfare in Vietnam Unleashed a Slow-Moving Disaster," *Conversation*, October 3, 2017, theconversation.com/agent-orange-exposed-how-u-s-chemical-warfare-in-vietnam-unleashed-a-slow-moving-disaster-84572.

26. "President Obama described Laos as the most heavily bombed nation in history. Eight bombs a minute were dropped on average during the Vietnam war between 1964 and 1973—more than the amount used during the whole of World War Two." "Laos: Barack Obama Regrets 'Biggest Bombing in History,'" BBC News, September 7, 2016, https://www.bbc.com/news/world-asia-37286520.

27. Stephen L. Carter, "Destroying a Quote's History in Order to Save It," *Bloomberg*, February 9, 2018, https://www.bloomberg.com/opinion/articles/2018-02-09/destroying-a-quote-s-history-in-order-to-save-it.

28. Environmental destruction of crops and livestock—exactly what the U.S. military did with Agent Orange in campaigns such as "Operation Ranch Hand"—are explicitly cited in U.S. military doctrine as common tactics, techniques, and procedures employed by terrorist groups. "Terrorists employ a variety of tactics,

techniques, and procedures—some small scale, some large scale—to produce fear in their intended audience . . . Their targets may be . . . agricultural (livestock, crops) . . . Their goal is not just to win favor for their causes, but to erode the confidence, capability, and legitimacy of the government or societies they wish to coerce. The most common TTP employed by terrorist groups are . . . environmental destruction." *Antiterrorism*, Joint Publication 3-07.2, November 24, 2010, www.bits.de/NRANEU/others/jp-doctrine/JP3_07.2(10).pdf. "We owe no debt for mass slaughter and for leaving three countries in ruins, no debt to the millions of maimed and orphaned, to the peasants who still die today from exploding ordnance left from the U.S. assault. Rather, our moral debt results only from the fact that we did not win." Edward S. Herman and Noam Chomsky, *Manufacturing Consent: The Political Economy of the Mass Media* (New York: Knopf Doubleday, 2011), 240.

29. Coady, *Morality and Political Violence.*

30. The way in which West Point treats America's political violence is in itself a brazen violation of its very own honor code, which instructs that "a cadet will not lie, cheat, steal, or tolerate those who do."

31. Sally Quinn, "What Ben Bradlee Would Think of Donald Trump," *Politico*, July 13, 2018, www.politico.com/magazine/story/2018/07/13/trump-ben-bradlee -truth-219005.

32. Ray Dalio, *Principles: Life and Work* (New York: Simon & Schuster, 2017).

33. One can depart the academy of one's own accord in the first two years; thereafter, you will be obligated to serve at least five years on active duty. Failure to graduate from West Point can result in serving your service obligation as a Specialist (E-4): "Upon graduation, you will be commissioned as a second lieutenant in the Army and serve for five years on active duty (if you choose to depart the Army after five years, you will be required to serve three years in the Inactive Ready Reserve [IRR])." "Your Career After West Point," United States West Point Military Academy, https://westpoint.edu/admissions/careers.

34. Retention at the Academy is a fascinating case study. The irony is that the Plebes and Yuks have more real power than the Cows and Firsties: the two underclasses have the freedom to quit and leave, giving them some level of bargaining power— like a worker's union—to make their conditions better; however, they rarely exercise these rights. Meanwhile, the upperclassmen are legally bound under threat of severe UCMJ punishment to stay in the military for a minimum of five years after graduation (plus the two until they graduate) and have lost all bargaining power ("Least Happy Students 2016," *The Princeton Review*, https://www.princetonreview.com/college-rankings?rankings=least-happy-stu

dents). In some sort of perverse role reversal, the tormenting upperclassmen are in the cage, believing they are free and better off, and the tormented underclassmen are on the outside, but tragically, they have been trained not to see; they are raised like docile circus elephants who have accepted their role as a stage prop when they have the ultimate power to walk away and take the entire circus show with them. All they need to do is leave while they still can.

35. This particular saying has its own acronym at West Point: IHTFP. You can see it, or its counterpart BOHICA, "Bend Over, Here It Comes Again" scrawled in dark locations around the academy. Other sayings included "West Point: the best second-rate education you could get." Rebellion came in many forms.

36. But don't get me wrong: West Point cadets, as a group, are *not* going to win the "Suffering Olympics." Groups of people the world over have experienced far greater privations. The millions of people displaced by America's wars in Iraq and Afghanistan, for example, are clearly worse off. They are in a completely different league.

37. Sexual oppression occurred digitally too. The challenges were numerous: the firewall blocked all of the main porn sites; you had to keep your door open every morning; you always lived with one if not two other dudes in the same room. It seemed perverse that I could simulate killing men with a silenced sniper rifle in Germany, doing summer training with the Special Forces, but couldn't hope to see some computer boobs. You couldn't even masturbate in peace.

38. "Five-beer serenade" refers to the passengers. We made sure to keep a designated driver.

39. McRaney, *You Can Beat Your Brain.*

40. Andrew J. Bacevich, *America's War for the Greater Middle East: A Military History* (New York: Random House, 2017).

41. Joshua Partlow and Lonnae O'Neal Parker, "A Sad Milestone at West Point," *Chicago Tribune*, September 8, 2006, https://www.chicagotribune.com/news/ct -xpm-2006-09-28-0609280138-story.html.

42. I heard this phrase used by my friend Sam. It has stuck with me.

43. U.S. Army, "The 75th Ranger Regiment," https://www.army.mil/ranger.

44. Michael de Yoanna and Mark Benjamin, "'Kill Yourself. Save Us the Paperwork,'" *Salon*, February 10, 2009, www.salon.com/2009/02/10/coming_home_two.

45. Ibid.

46. Not long before this, another soldier, Specialist Marko, was charged with raping and murdering a nineteen-year-old developmentally disabled woman he had met online. Specialist Marko admitted to the police that he took his victim "to the mountains overlooking Colorado Springs, blindfolded and raped her, then slit

her throat." This was done because he believed he was an "alien dinosaur-like creature, and that he would transform from his human form into his Black Raptor form on his 21st birthday." Dan Frosch and Lizette Alvarez. "Mental State of Soldier Questioned," *New York Times*, November 20, 2008, https://www .nytimes.com/2008/11/21/us/21army.html.

47. Robert H. Scales, *Yellow Smoke: The Future of Land Warfare for America's Military* (Lanham: Rowman & Littlefield Publishers, 2002).

48. Richard A. Oppel Jr., "Veterans Watch as Gains Their Friends Died for Are Erased by Insurgents," *New York Times*, June 13, 2014, www.nytimes.com/2014 /06/14/us/us-veterans-watch-gains-made-with-blood-erased-by-insurgents-in -iraq.html.

FIRST CONTACT

1. A single-handed curved sword of the Pashtun people.

2. Platoon leader, platoon sergeant, radio-telephone operator, forward observer, FO RTO, and medic.

3. Charles A. Henning, "U.S. Military Stop Loss Program: Key Questions and Answers," Congressional Research Service, April 7, 2010, www.dtic.mil/dtic/tr /fulltext/u2/a520802.pdf.

4. Cora Currier, "How the U.S. Paid for Death and Damage in Afghanistan," *Intercept*, February 27, 2015, https://theintercept.com/2015/02/27/payments -civilians-afghanistan.

ANNUS HORRIBILIS

1. Norah Niland, "Democratic Aspirations and Destabilizing Outcomes in Afghanistan," Watson Institute for International and Public Affairs, Brown University, October 15, 2014, watson.brown.edu/costsofwar/files/cow/imce /papers/2014/COW%20Niland%2061615.pdf.

2. "The Economist Intelligence Unit's Democracy Index," infographics.economist .com/2018/DemocracyIndex.

3. World Justice Project, "WJP Rule of Law Index 2017–2018," worldjusticeproject .org/our-work/wjp-rule-law-index/wjp-rule-law-index-2017%E2%80%932018.

4. United Nations Development Programme, "The 2018 Multidimensional Poverty Index (MPI)," Human Development Reports, hdr.undp.org/en/2018-MPI.

5. Noah Shachtman, "No Jail Time for Army Contractor in Revenge Killing," *Wired*, May 8, 2009, www.wired.com/2009/05/no-jail-time-in-human-terrain-slaying.

6. The U.S. Manual on Detainee Operations states:

> *As a subset of military operations, detainee operations must comply with the law of war during all armed conflicts . . . Common Article 3 to the Geneva Conventions of 1949, as construed and applied by U.S. law, establishes minimum standards for the humane treatment of all persons detained by the United States, coalition, and allied forces. Common Article 3 prohibits at any time and in any place: "violence to life and person, in particular murder of all kinds, . . . [and] the carrying out of executions without previous judgment pronounced by a regularly constituted court, affording all the judicial guarantees which are recognized as indispensable by civilized peoples."*

International Committee of the Red Cross, "Practice Relating to Rule 89. Violence to Life," Customary IHL, IHL Database, https://ihl-databases.icrc.org/customary-ihl/eng/docs/v2_rul_rule89.

7. "Malalai of Maiwand, the Pride of Afghans," *Pashtun Times*, July 27, 2016, thepashtuntimes.com/malalai-of-maiwand-the-pride-of-afghans.

8. Barry Neild, "Is Afghanistan Really a 'Graveyard of Empires'?" CNN, December 7, 2009, edition.cnn.com/2009/WORLD/asiapcf/12/07/afghanistan.graveyard/index.html.

9. Yochi J. Dreazen and Peter Spiegel, "General Seeks Shift in Afghan Strategy," *Wall Street Journal*, September 1, 2009, www.wsj.com/articles/SB125171718622772181.

10. Peter Graff, "July Equals Deadliest Month of Afghan War," Reuters, July 15, 2009, www.reuters.com/article/us-afghanistan/july-equals-deadliest-month-of-afghan-war-idUSISL51965120090715.

11. "August Is Deadliest Month for U.S. Military in Afghanistan," CNN, August 28, 2009, edition.cnn.com/2009/WORLD/asiapcf/08/28/afghanistan.us.troop.deaths/index.html.

12. Jonathan Adams, "Deadliest Month yet for NATO in Afghanistan," *Christian Science Monitor*, June 29, 2010, www.csmonitor.com/World/terrorism-security/2010/0629/Deadliest-month-yet-for-NATO-in-Afghanistan.

13. Central Statistics Organization (2010), 32, cso.gov.af/Content/files/%D8%B3%D8%A7%D9%84%D9%86%D8%A7%D9%85%D9%87%20%D8%A7%D8%AD%D8%B5%D8%A7%D8%A6%DB%8C%D9%88%DB%8C/2010-11/population%20.pdf.

14. Nick Schifrin and Matt McGarry, "Battle for Kandahar, Heart of Afghanistan's Taliban Country," ABC News, May 24, 2011, abcnews.go.com/International/Afghanistan/battle-kandahar-heart-taliban-country/story?id=10729732.

15. Ben Farmer with 101st Airborne Division in Zhari, "Troops Call It the Heart of Darkness, the Spiritual Home of the Taliban," *Telegraph*, July 2, 2010, https://www.telegraph.co.uk/news/worldnews/asia/afghanistan/7868176/Troops-call-it-the-Heart-of-Darkness-the-spiritual-home-of-the-Taliban.html.

16. Linda Bilmes, "The Financial Legacy of Iraq and Afghanistan: How Wartime Spending Decisions Will Constrain Future National Security Budgets," March 2013, research.hks.harvard.edu/publications/workingpapers/citation.aspx?PubId=8956; David Francis, "Each Injured US Soldier Will End Up Costing $2 Million On Average," *Business Insider*, May 15, 2013, www.businessinsider.com/it-will-cost-2-million-for-each-injured-us-soldier-from-iraq-and-afghanistan-2013-5/. According to the *Los Angeles Times*, MRAPs exhibit such high operating costs that the U.S. military decided to chop up as many as approximately two thousand of the $1 million vehicles for scrap to avoid paying the $250,000 to $450,000 of costs required to ship and rebuild them to standard in the United States. David Zucchino, "From MRAP to Scrap: U.S. Military Chops Up $1-Million Vehicles," *Los Angeles Times*, December 27, 2013, articles.latimes.com/2013/dec/27/world/la-fg-afghanistan-armor-20131227.

17. Lawrence Freedman, *The Future of War* (New York: Public Affairs, 2017).

18. Ben Brody, "Afghanistan: A Tale of Two Districts," PRI, July 12, 2011, www.pri.org/stories/2011-07-12/afghanistan-tale-two-districts.

19. Ibid.

20. Colonel Dale C. Eikmeier, "A Logical Method for Center-of-Gravity-Analysis," *Military Review*, September–October 2007, www.armyupress.army.mil/Portals/7/military-review/Archives/English/MilitaryReview_20071031_art009.pdf.

21. Anthony H. Cordesman, "Shape, Clear, Hold, and Build: The Uncertain Lessons of the Afghan and Iraq Wars," Center for Strategic & International Studies, August 17, 2009, www.csis.org/analysis/shape-clear-hold-and-build-0.

22. Encyclopædia Britannica, "Countervalue Targeting," https://www.britannica.com/topic/countervalue-targeting.

23. In Karl A. Slaikeu, "Winning the War in Afghanistan: An Oil Spot Plus Strategy for Coalition Forces":

> *The oil spot (OS) COIN strategy draws on the analogy of a cheese cloth representing a country. Drops of oil, one at a time and over time, eventually cover the entire cloth. The process begins with establishing a 100% secure perimeter, accomplished by CF in the first instance, and then transferred to local military in a particular village or other area of operation, and then, within this safe environment, launching stability initiatives, including services, governance and development. With one OS functioning and*

> *under the protection of local army and police, CF partners with the Afghan Security Forces (AFS) to launch other OS villages. The advantages of this approach lie in the discrete gains that can be protected (as in shape, clear, hold, and build [FM 3.24]), and most important, each oil spot is a visible manifestation of the desired end state for the entire war. Any friend, foe, or fence sitter can see what CF is up to by looking at security protected and services rendered within the oil spot village/town/city.*

Small Wars Journal, May 18, 2009: 3–4, smallwarsjournal.com/blog/journal /docs-temp/227-slaikeu.pdf.

24. John Solomon and Buck Sexton, "Trump Slams Bush for 'Worst Single Mistake' in U.S. History," *The Hill*, September 19, 2019, thehill.com/hilltv/rising/407398 -trump-slams-bush-for-worst-single-mistake-in-us-history.

25. Joe Klein, "Afghanistan: A Tale of Soldiers and a School," *Time*, April 15, 2010, content.time.com/time/magazine/article/0,9171,1982319,00.html.

26. Laura A. Zimmerman et al., "Training Methods to Build Human Terrain Mapping Skills," *Research Report 1933*, U.S. Army Research Institute for the Behavioral and Social Sciences, October 2010, www.dtic.mil/dtic/tr/fulltext/u2 /a532276.pdf.

27. Ibid.

28. Whitney Kassel, "The Army Needs Anthropologists," *Foreign Policy*, July 28, 2015, foreignpolicy.com/2015/07/28/the-army-needs-anthropologists-iraq -afghanistan-human-terrain.

29. Karin Brulliard, "Local Strongman Is U.S. Troops' Most Reliable Friend in Kandahar," *Washington Post*, July 29, 2010, http://www.washingtonpost.com /wp-dyn/content/article/2010/07/28/AR2010072806147_2.html.

30. Klein, "Afghanistan: A Tale of Soldiers and a School."

31. Nathan Hodge, "U.S.'s Afghan Headache: $400-a-Gallon Gasoline," *Wall Street Journal*, https://www.wsj.com/articles/SB1000142405297020490380457 7080613427403928.

32. F-16C-$22,514 per hour; F-22- $68,362 per hour; HH60-G-$24,475 per hour Mark Thompson, "Costly Flight Hours," *Time*, April 2, 2013, www.nation.time .com/2013/04/02/costly-flight-hours.

33. Pete Blaber, *The Mission, the Men, and Me: Lessons From a Former Delta Force Commander* (Dutton Caliber, 2010).

34. Zucchino, "From MRAP to Scrap: U.S. Military Chops Up $1-Million Vehicles."

35. "For every one of the 866,181 soldiers officially counted injured casualties in Iraq and Afghanistan, the government is expected to spend some $2 million

in long-term medical cost" or killed during the build phase—it's a multi-million-dollar nightmare (Francis, "Each Injured US Soldier Will End Up Costing $2 Million on Average"; Bilmes, "The Financial Legacy of Iraq and Afghanistan").

36. Business Air directory of used Gulfstream IV Jets for sale: http://www
.businessair.com/jet/gulfstream/iv

37. "Twelve U.S. Soldiers Face Trial After Afghan Civilians 'Were Killed for Sport and Their Fingers Collected as Trophies,'" *Daily Mail*, September 10, 2010, https://www.dailymail.co.uk/travel/travel_news/article-1310540/Twelve-US -soldiers-face-trial-Afghan-civilians-killed-sport—whistle-blower-originally -ignored.html.

FRIEND OR FOE

1. Dexter Filkins, "Convoy Guards in Afghanistan Face an Inquiry," *New York Times*, June 6, 2010, https://www.nytimes.com/2010/06/07/world/asia/07 convoys.html.

2. Cat Astronaut, "'We're Making Real Progress,' Say Last 17 Commanders in Afghanistan," Duffel Blog, February 27, 2017, https://www.duffelblog.com/2017 /02/were-making-real-progress-say-last-17-commanders-in-afghanistan.

3. Mark Wise, "Wounded Soldiers Race to the South Pole," *New York Times*, May 15, 2013, atwar.blogs.nytimes.com/2013/05/15/wounded-soldiers-race-to-the -south-pole.

4. Mark Boal, "The Kill Team: How U.S. Soldiers in Afghanistan Murdered Innocent Civilians," *Rolling Stone*, March 28, 2011, https://www.rollingstone.com /politics/politics-news/the-kill-team-how-u-s-soldiers-in-afghanistan-murdered -innocent-civilians-169793.

5. Rod Nordland, "U.S. Military Faults Leaders in Attack on Base," *New York Times*, February 5, 2010, www.nytimes.com/2010/02/06/world/asia/06afghan.html.

6. C. J. Chivers, "Vantage Point: Restraint After Dark," *New York Times*, March 2, 2011, atwar.blogs.nytimes.com/2011/03/02/vantage-point-restraint-after-dark.

7. "U.S. Troops Battle Both Taliban and Their Own Rules," *Washington Times*, November 16, 2009, www.washingtontimes.com/news/2009/nov/16/us-troops -battle-taliban-afghan-rules.

KILL

1. Joe Klein, "Afghanistan: A Tale of Soldiers and a School," *Time*, April 15, 2010, http://content.time.com/time/magazine/article/0,9171,1982319,00.html.

2.   Green Beans is a chain of coffee shops that are in themselves a meme. It is known to soldiers as an icon of the Fobbit.

3.   Richard A. Oppel Jr. and Taimoor Shah, "Civilians Killed as U.S. Troops Fire on Afghan Bus," *New York Times*, April 12, 2010, https://www.nytimes.com /2010/04/13/world/asia/13afghan.html.

4.   Richard A. Oppel Jr., "Tighter Rules Fail to Stem Deaths of Innocent Afghans at Checkpoints," *New York Times*, March 26, 2010, www.nytimes.com/2010/03 /27/world/asia/27afghan.html.

5.   Oppel and Shah, "Civilians Killed as U.S. Troops Fire on Afghan Bus."

6.   I have chosen the masculine pronoun because the overwhelming majority of interpreters I interacted with were men. I certainly acknowledge the risks that female interpreters in Iraq and Afghanistan also face.

7.   Oppel and Shah, "Civilians Killed as U.S. Troops Fire on Afghan Bus."

8.   Ibid.

9.   Joseph J. Collins, "Afghanistan: Winning a Three Block War," *Journal of Conflict Studies* 24, no. 2, 2004.

10.   Lawrence Freedman, *The Future of War: A History* (New York: PublicAffairs, 2017).

11.   Oppel and Shah, "Civilians Killed as U.S. Troops Fire on Afghan Bus."

12.   Oppel, "Tighter Rules Fail to Stem Deaths of Innocent Afghans."

13.   Richard A. Oppel Jr. and Taimoor Shah, "A Killing Further Erodes Afghan Faith in Leaders," *New York Times*, April 20, 2010, www.nytimes.com/2010/04 /21/world/asia/21afghan.html.

14.   Brad Simpson, "East Timor Truth Commission Finds U.S. 'Political and Military Support Were Fundamental to the Indonesian Invasion and Occupation,'" National Security Archive, January 24, 2006, nsarchive2.gwu.edu/NSAEBB /NSAEBB176/index.htm.

15.   "Politically, the weakness of the argument has always been that those who choose the lesser evil forget very quickly that they chose evil," in Hannah Arendt, "Personal Responsibility Under Dictatorship."

THE AWAKENING

1.   Oxford Dictionaries define "rogue state" as "breaking international law and posing a threat to the security of other nations." America's Terror Wars have violated elementary norms of international law, making it a rogue state.

2.   A slogan dumped by the U.S. Navy.

3.   CIF team; a premier, direct shoot-'em-in-the-face unit for hostage rescue, etc.

4.   Michael Zenko and Jennifer Wilson, "Scary Fact: America Dropped 26,171 Bombs in 7 Countries in 2016," *National Interest*, January 6, 2017,

nationalinterest.org/blog/the-buzz/scary-fact-america-dropped-26171-bombs-7
-countries-2016-18961.

5. Rajiv Chandrasekaran, "After the Wars: A Legacy of Pain and Pride," *Washington Post*, March 29, 2014, www.washingtonpost.com/sf/national/2014/03/29
/a-legacy-of-pride-and-pain.

6. Where is the movie scene where the soldier can't get out of the MRAP armored truck during a firefight because his stupid seat belt is caught on his MBITR radio? Where is the moment where there aren't enough body bags? Where is the moment where the gunner has food poisoning from unhygienic food and is vomiting off the side of the truck and shitting into a plastic MRE bag because the convoy won't stop?

7. The closest analogue in American history to project on their situation might be the American Revolution, although the British had far greater claim to be in the United States in the 1700s than the United States has claim to be in the Middle East in the 2000s.

WHAT HAS BEEN LOST?

1. "'Deaths of Despair': An American Epidemic," *Chicago Tribune*, June 15, 2018, www.chicagotribune.com/news/opinion/editorials/ct-edit-suicide-opioids
-despair-20180615-story.html.

2. The resolution stated, "The President is authorized to use all necessary and appropriate force against those nations, organizations, or persons he determines planned, authorized, committed, or aided the terrorist attacks that occurred on September 11, 2001, or harbored such organizations or persons." 107th Congress Public Law 40, www.govinfo.gov/content/pkg/PLAW-107publ40/html/PLAW
-107publ40.htm.

3. Glenn Greenwald, "Barbara Lee's Lone Vote on Sept. 14, 2001, Was as Prescient as It Was Brave and Heroic," *Intercept*, September 11, 2016, theintercept.com
/2016/09/11/barbara-lees-lone-vote-on-sept-14-2001-was-as-prescient-as-it-was
-brave-and-heroic.

4. Conor Friedersdorf, "Angry Letters to the One Member of Congress Who Voted Against the War on Terror," *Atlantic*, September 14, 2014, www.the
atlantic.com/politics/archive/2014/09/the-vindication-of-barbara-lee
/380084.

5. "Bush Rejects Taliban Offer to Hand Bin Laden Over," *Guardian*, October 14, 2001, www.theguardian.com/world/2001/oct/14/afghanistan.terrorism5.

6. Geoffrey Robertson, *Crimes Against Humanity: The Struggle for Global Justice, Revised and Updated Edition* (New York: New Press, 2007).

7. Ibid.

8. John Pilger, "John Pilger: Why Are Wars Not Being Reported Honestly?" *Guardian*, December 10, 2010, www.theguardian.com/media/2010/dec/10/war-media-propaganda-iraq-lies.

9. "In the days following 9/11, Donald Rumsfeld and his deputy, Paul Wolfowitz, attempted to include Iraq in the war on terror. When the established agencies came up empty-handed, and were unable to link Iraq and al-Qaida, the OSP [Office of Special Plans] was given the task of looking more carefully . . . [The Office of Special Plans was] a shadow agency of Pentagon analysts staffed mainly by ideological amateurs" set up by Rumsfeld to second-guess and circumvent the opinions of established intelligence and military agencies. The actions of the OSP were reported to be a "complete mystery" to the DIA and the Pentagon. One senior officer said, "No one from the military staff heard, saw or discussed anything with them."

    According a senior official in the state department's intelligence bureau, the OSP "surveyed data and picked out what they liked . . . The whole thing was bizarre. The secretary of defence had this huge defence intelligence agency, and he went around it." Cheney pressed on the CIA to demand a more "forward-leaning" interpretation of the threat posed by Saddam. The *Guardian* reported that Cheney's involvement "put pressure on CIA officials to come up with the appropriate results." Julian Borger, "The Spies Who Pushed for War," *Guardian*, July 17, 2003, https://www.theguardian.com/world/2003/jul/17/iraq.usa.

10. Ibid.; Lawrence Wilkerson, "I Helped Sell the False Choice of War Once. It's Happening Again," *New York Times*, February 5, 2018, www.nytimes.com/2018/02/05/opinion/trump-iran-war.html.

11. Paul Harris, "How Private Firms Have Cashed in on the Climate of Fear since 9/11," *Guardian*, September 5, 2011, www.theguardian.com/world/2011/sep/05/private-firms-fear-9-11.

12. Micah Zenko, "Terrorism Is Booming Almost Everywhere but in the United States," *Foreign Policy*, June 19, 2015, foreignpolicy.com/2015/06/19/terrorism-is-booming-almost-everywhere-but-in-the-united-states-state-department-report.

13. "The Taliban Now Hold More Ground in Afghanistan Than at Any Point Since 2001," *Military Times*, June 16, 2016, https://www.militarytimes.com/2016/06/16/the-taliban-now-hold-more-ground-in-afghanistan-than-at-any-point-since-2001.

14. Reuters, "US Airport Screenings Fail to Detect Mock Weapons in 95% of Tests," *Guardian*, June 2, 2015, www.theguardian.com/us-news/2015/jun/02/us-airport-security-raised-after-fake-weapons-missed-by-screenings.

15. Ken Silverstein, "The Stolen War," *New Republic*, August 22, 2016, newrepublic.com/article/135682/stolen-war.

16. Patrick Cockburn, "Patrick Cockburn: The Death of the American Dream in Afghanistan," *Independent*, February 5, 2012, www.independent.co.uk/voices/commentators/patrick-cockburn-the-death-of-the-american-dream-in-afghanistan-6422973.html.

17. Patrick Cockburn, *The Age of Jihad: Islamic State and the Great War for the Middle East* (New York: Verso Books, 2016).

18. "If it were my call I would not discontinue those programs," he told Fox Business. "I'd have them active and ready to go . . . And I'd go back and study them and learn." Henry Fernandez, "US Should Revive Enhanced Interrogation Techniques: Dick Cheney," Fox Business, May 10, 2019, www.foxbusiness.com/politics/us-should-revive-enhanced-interrogation-techniques-dick-cheney.

19. "That's the first time I've ever signed a waterboard," said Cheney. "Cheney told Fox News that interrogation techniques like waterboarding should still be in place because 'it worked.'" Robert Rorke, "Waterboard Signed by Dick Cheney Pops Up on eBay—Then Mysteriously Disappears," *New York Post*, July 23, 2018, nypost.com/2018/07/23/waterboard-signed-by-dick-cheney-pops-up-on-ebay-then-mysteriously-disappears.

20. In an article for the *Guardian*, George Monbiot wrote:

    "Mere words cannot match the depths of your sorrow, nor can they heal your wounded hearts . . . These tragedies must end. And to tend them, we must change." Every parent can connect with what Barack Obama said about the 2012 murder of twenty children in Newtown, Connecticut. There can scarcely be a person on earth with access to the media who is untouched by the grief of the people of that town. It must follow that what applies to the children murdered there by a deranged young man also applies to the children murdered in Pakistan by a somber American president.

    "In the US, Mass Child Killings Are Tragedies. In Pakistan, Mere Bug Splats," *Guardian*, December 17, 2012, www.theguardian.com/commentisfree/2012/dec/17/us-killings-tragedies-pakistan-bug-splats.

21. Physicians for Social Responsibility, *Body Count: Casualty Figures after 10 Years of the "War on Terror": Iraq, Afghanistan, Pakistan*, March 2015, www.psr.org/wp-content/uploads/2018/05/body-count.pdf.

22. "Civilians Killed & Wounded," Watson Institute, Brown University, watson .brown.edu/costsofwar/costs/human/civilians; Neta C. Crawford, "Human Cost of the Post-9/11 Wars: Lethality and the Need for Transparency," Watson Institute, Brown University, November 2018, watson.brown.edu/costsofwar/files/cow /imce/papers/2018/Human%20Costs%2C%20Nov%208%202018%20CoW.pdf.

23. The indirect death toll—the people who die because of the negative effects of war, for example, on public health infrastructure and as a consequence of displacement and malnutrition, is difficult to estimate. The Geneva Declaration Secretariat, which closely examined data from armed conflicts occurring in the period of 2004–2007, suggests that "a reasonable average estimate would be a ratio of four indirect deaths to one direct death in contemporary conflicts." If we use this ratio, the ongoing war in Afghanistan is perhaps responsible for as many as an additional 360,000 indirect deaths. Geneva Declaration Secretariat, "Geneva Declaration: Global Burden of Armed Violence," September 2008, www.refworld.org/pdfid/494a455d2.pdf.

24. Afghanistan & Pakistan (Oct. 2001–Oct. 2018) and Iraq (March 2003– Oct. 2018). Crawford, "Human Cost of the Post-9/11 Wars."

25. "US & Allied Killed," Watson Institute, Brown University, watson.brown.edu /costsofwar/costs/human/military/killed.

26. "September 11 Terror Attacks Fast Facts," CNN, September 2, 2018, www.cnn .com/2013/07/27/us/september-11-anniversary-fast-facts/index.html.

27. "Costs of War," Watson Institute, Brown University, watson.brown.edu /costsofwar.

28. Crawford, "Human Cost of the Post-9-11 Wars."

29. "Civilians Killed & Wounded."

30. "US & Allied Killed."

31. Neta C. Crawford, "United States Budgetary Costs of Post-9/11 Wars Through FY2018: A Summary of the $5.6 Trillion in Costs for the US Wars in Iraq, Syria, Afghanistan, and Pakistan, and Post-9/11 Veterans Care and Homeland Security," Costs of War, Watson Institute, Brown University, November 2017, watson .brown.edu/costsofwar/files/cow/imce/papers/2017/Costs%20of%20U.S.%20 Post-9_11%20NC%20Crawford%20FINAL%20.pdf.

32. Ibid.

33. Rich Morin, "Section 2: Injured Post-9/11 Veterans," Social & Demographic Trends, Pew Research Center, November 8, 2011, www.pewsocialtrends.org/2011 /11/08/section-2-injured-post-911-veterans.

34. Niall McCarthy, "2.77 Million Service Members Have Served On 5.4 Million Deployments Since 9/11 [Infographic]," Forbes, March 20, 2018, www.forbes

.com/sites/niallmccarthy/2018/03/20/2-77-million-service-members-have
-served-on-5-4-million-deployments-since-911-infographic/#4961260750db.

35. Rajiv Chandrasekaran, "After the Wars: A Legacy of Pain and Pride," *Washington Post*, March 24, 2014, www.washingtonpost.com/sf/national/2014/03/29/a -legacy-of-pride-and-pain/.

36. Ibid.

37. "VA National Suicide Data Report, 2005–2016," Office of Mental Health and Suicide Prevention, September 2018, https://www.mentalhealth.va.gov/docs /data-sheets/OMHSP_National_Suicide_Data_Report_2005-2016_508.pdf; Nikki Wentling, "VA Reveals Its Veteran Suicide Statistic Included Active-Duty Troops," *Stars and Stripes*, June 20, 2018, www.stripes.com/news/us/va-reveals -its-veteran-suicide-statistic-included-active-duty-troops-1.533992.

38. Erik Goepner, "War State, Trauma State: Why Afghanistan Remains Stuck in Conflict," Cato Institute, June 19, 2018, www.cato.org/publications/policy -analysis/war-state-trauma-state-why-afghanistan-remains-stuck-conflict #endnote-045.

39. Ibid.

40. Neta C. Crawford, "War-Related Death, Injury, and Displacement in Afghanistan and Pakistan 2001–2014," Costs of War, Watson Institute, Brown University, May 22, 2015, watson.brown.edu/costsofwar/files/cow/imce/papers/2015 /War%20Related%20Casualties%20Afghanistan%20and%20Pakistan%202001 -2014%20FIN.pdf. In 2009, the Afghan Ministry of Public Health cited statistics that 66 percent of Afghans suffer mental health problems (ibid.).

41. "In all, 349 service members took their own lives in 2012, while a lesser number, 295, died in combat." Ed Pilkington, "US Military Struggling to Stop Suicide Epidemic Among Young War Veterans," *Guardian*, February 1, 2013, www.the guardian.com/world/2013/feb/01/us-military-suicide-epidemic-veteran.

42. Ibid.

43. Jack Moran, "Murderer Sentenced to Life in Prison," *Register-Guard*, June 3, 2016, www.registerguard.com/rg/news/local/34433962-75/murderer-of-eugene -man-gets-life-in-prison.html.csp.

44. Ibid.

45. Lance Benzel, "Soldier Testifies That Army Buddy Picked Victim, Ordered Killing," *Colorado Springs Gazette*, May 12, 2011, gazette.com/soldier-testifies -that-army-buddy-picked-victim-ordered-killing/article/118039.

46. Priscilla Alvarez, "'How Much More Merit Do You Need Than Saving American Lives?'" *Atlantic*, July 25, 2018, www.theatlantic.com/politics/archive/2018 /07/trump-immigration-crackdown-visas/565949.

47. Dianna Cahn, "Special Visas Dwindle for Afghan, Iraqi Interpreters," *Stars and Stripes*, April 26, 2018, www.stripes.com/news/us/special-visas-dwindle-for -afghan-iraqi-interpreters-1.524194.

48. Matthew La Corte, "Our Immigration System Is Killing Our Allies," Foundation for Economic Education, August 4, 2015, fee.org/articles/our-immigration -system-is-killing-our-allies.

49. Will Denn, "No One Left Behind," *Kennedy School Review*, July 4, 2014, ksr .hkspublications.org/2014/07/04/no-one-left-behind.

50. Ibid.

51. Sgt. Jorden Weir, "Until Dawn: The Battle of Boz Qandahari," U.S. Central Command, February 6, 2017, www.centcom.mil/MEDIA/NEWS-ARTICLES /News-Article-View/Article/1071685/until-dawn-the-battle-of-boz-qandahari.

52. Shereena Qazi, "US Forces Admit Killing 33 Civilians in Taliban Clash," Al Jazeera, January 12, 2017, www.aljazeera.com/news/2017/01/military-admits-33 -civilians-killed-taliban-clash-170112081032540.html.

53. Mujib Mashal, "Kunduz Attack in November Killed 33 Civilians, U.S. Military Says," *New York Times*, January 12, 2017, www.nytimes.com/2017/01/12/world /asia/kunduz-attack-afghanistan-civilian-deaths.html.

54. Qazi, "US Forces Admit Killing 33 Civilians in Taliban Clash."

55. Michael Hastings, "The Runaway General; The Profile that Brought Down McChrystal," June 22, 2010, http://www.rollingstone.com/politics/news/the -runaway-general-20100622.

56. Grégoire Chamayou, *Drone Theory* (New York: Penguin Random House, 2015).

57. "LT. Tyler Edward Parten USA (KIA)," www.west-point.org/users/usma2007 /63805.

58. Yuval Noah Harari, *Homo Deus: A Brief History of Tomorrow* (New York: Random House, 2016).

COSTS, OPPORTUNITY COSTS, AND OPPORTUNITIES

1. Steve Clemons, "The Geopolitical Therapist," *Atlantic*, August 26, 2016, www .theatlantic.com/international/archive/2016/08/joe-biden-interview/497633.

2. Yuval Noah Harari, Homo Deus: A Brief History of Tomorrow (New York: Random House, 2016).

3. Micah Zenko, "Americans Are as Likely to Be Killed by Their Own Furniture as by Terrorism," *Atlantic*, June 6, 2016, www.theatlantic.com/international /archive/2012/06/americans-are-as-likely-to-be-killed-by-their-own-furniture-as -by-terrorism/258156.

4. "Costs of War," Watson Institute, Brown University; Jack Moore, "The Cost of War for the U.S. Taxpayer Since 9/11 Is Actually Three Times the Pentagon's Estimate," *Newsweek,* November 18, 2017, www.newsweek.com/how-many -trillions-war-has-cost-us-taxpayer-911-attacks-705041.

5. Neta C. Crawford, "United States Budgetary Costs of the Post-9/11 Wars Through FY2019: $5.9 Trillion Spent and Obligated," Watson Institute of International and Public Affairs, Brown University, November 14, 2018, watson .brown.edu/costsofwar/files/cow/imce/papers/2018/Crawford_Costs%20of%20 War%20Estimates%20Through%20FY2019.pdf.

6. Robert Hormats, *The Price of Liberty* (New York: Holt Paperbacks, 2008); Linda Bilmes, "The Financial Legacy of Iraq and Afghanistan: How Wartime Spending Decisions Will Constrain Future National Security Budgets," March 2013, research .hks.harvard.edu/publications/workingpapers/citation.aspx?PubId=8956.

7. Steven Aftergood, "The Costs of War: Obstacles to Public Understanding," Watson Institute of International and Public Affairs, Brown University, November 14, 2018, https://watson.brown.edu/costsofwar/files/cow/imce /papers/2018/Costs%20of%20War%20-%20Aftergood%20paper_FINAL.pdf.

8. Alan Taylor, "From Cornerstone to Skyscraper: One World Trade Center," *Atlantic,* September 11, 2018, www.theatlantic.com/photo/2018/09/from -cornerstone-to-skyscraper-one-world-trade-center/569932; Eliot Brown, "Tower Rises, and So Does Its Price Tag," *Wall Street Journal,* January 30, 2012, www .wsj.com/articles/SB10001424052970203920204577191371172049652.

9. NASA Space Place, Space.com, "How Far Away Is the Moon?" spaceplace.nasa .gov/moon-distance/en.

10. Nola Taylor Redd, "How Long Does It Take to Get to Mars?" *Space,* November 14, 2017, www.space.com/24701-how-long-does-it-take-to-get-to-mars.html.

11. "Federal funding for climate change research, technology, international assistance, and adaptation has increased from $2.4 billion in 1993 to $11.6 billion in 2014." "Climate Change Funding and Management," U.S. Government Accountability Office, www.gao.gov/key_issues/climate_change_funding _management/issue_summary. According to the Wikipedia entry for Interstate 495 (Capital Beltway), "(I-495) is a 64-mile (103 km) Interstate Highway that surrounds Washington, D.C., the capital of the United States of America, and its inner suburbs in adjacent Maryland and Virginia." $10,000 stacks of money (6.14 inches long), placed lengthwise over this sixty-four-mile distance, would be worth roughly $6.6 billion. Therefore, two loops is greater than the approximately $11.6 billion of federal funding spent on climate change in 2014.

12. Although slightly more broad, this paragraph was inspired by Andrew Bacevich, West Point graduate, Vietnam veteran, author, and professor at Boston University, who said, "You know, we live in a country where if you want to go bomb somebody, there's remarkably little discussion about how much it might cost, even though the costs almost inevitably end up being orders of magnitude larger than anybody projected at the outcome. But when you have a discussion about whether or not we can assist people who are suffering, then suddenly we come very, you know, cost-conscious." "Prof. Bacevich on Iraq, ISIS, and More," Boston University, June 28, 2014, www.bu.edu/pardeeschool/2014/06/28 /bacevich-on-iraq-isis-and-more.

13. As an aside, it's worth considering the costs required to maintain the nation's nuclear weapons arsenal. For the pleasure of maintaining a chance to plunge the world into internecine nuclear warfare, Trump's plan to remake and strengthen the nuclear arsenal will require $1.2 trillion according to a report from the Congressional Budget Office. Consider that in any given year there is a chance, however small it may be, that there will be a nuclear war of "fire and fury like the world has never seen." It's not hard to imagine a scenario where one nuclear-armed dimwit threatens another, and soon it all spirals out of control, precipitating a chain of events that leads to the destruction of organized life on this planet. For as long as nuclear weapons exist, so does this threat. And if there is always this probability, our fate is sealed. All it takes is to extrapolate out far enough into the future.

Mathematically, if the chance that armed conflict spirals out of control into a fire-and-brimstone, earth-shattering, nuclear holocaust is less than 1 percent, but the value associated with this probability is infinitely bad, then every instance of political violence becomes stupid and illogical. Any unlikely event multiplied by an infinitely bad outcome is still infinitely bad. Alternatively, we could just freeze and dismantle all nuclear weapons globally and empower an international order that puts sufficient pressure on countries that dare rattle the saber. But in today's America, the notion of de-weaponizing, de-threatening, and decreasing military funding seems not so much unlikely as preposterous.

William J. Broad and David E. Sanger, "Trump Plans for Nuclear Arsenal Require $1.2 Trillion, More than 20 Percent Higher than Earlier Figures," *New York Times*, October 31, 2017, www.nytimes.com/2017/10/31/us/politics /trump-nuclear-weapons-arsenal-congressional-budget.html; Peter Baker and Chloe Sang-Hun, "Trump Threatens 'Fire and Fury' Against North Korea if

It Endangers US," *New York Times*, August 8, 2017, www.nytimes.com/2017/08/08/world/asia/north-korea-un-sanctions-nuclear-missile-united-nations.html.

14. Jeff Stein, "US Military Budget Inches Closer to $1 Trillion Mark as Concerns over Federal Deficit Grow," *Washington Post*, June 19, 2018, www.washingtonpost.com/news/wonk/wp/2018/06/19/u-s-military-budget-inches-closer-to-1-trillion-mark-as-concerns-over-federal-deficit-grow/.

15. Crawford, "United States Budgetary Costs of the Post-9/11 Wars Through FY2019."

16. "Defense and National Security," Congressional Budget Office, www.cbo.gov/topics/defense-and-national-security.

17. "Discretionary Spending in 2017: An Infographic," Congressional Budget Office, March 5, 2018, www.cbo.gov/publication/53626.

18. "Military Expenditure," World Bank, n.d., data.worldbank.org/indicator/ms.mil.xpnd.gd.zs.

19. Editorial Board, "The Pentagon Doesn't Know Where Its Money Goes," *New York Times*, December 1, 2018, www.nytimes.com/2018/12/01/opinion/sunday/pentagon-spending-audit-failed.html.

20. Scot J. Paltrow, "U.S. Army Fudged Its Accounts by Trillions of Dollars, Auditor Finds," Reuters, August 19, 2016, www.reuters.com/article/us-usa-audit-army/u-s-army-fudged-its-accounts-by-trillions-of-dollars-auditor-finds-idUSKCN10U1IG.

21. Jim Garamone, "DoD Owes Taxpayers Full Accounting of Assets, Comptroller Tells House," U.S. Department of Defense, January 10, 2018, dod.defense.gov/News/Article/Article/1412459/dod-owes-taxpayers-full-accounting-of-assets-comptroller-tells-house.

22. Stephanie Savell, "This Map Shows Where in the World the U.S. Military Is Combatting Terrorism," *Smithsonian Magazine*, January 2019, www.smithsonianmag.com/history/map-shows-places-world-where-us-military-operates-180970997.

23. The United States was the overwhelming choice (24 percent of respondents) for the country that represents the greatest threat to peace in the world today. This was followed by Pakistan (8 percent); China (6 percent); and North Korea, Israel, and Iran (5 percent). Respondents in Russia (54 percent), China (49 percent), and Bosnia (49 percent) were the most fearful of the United States as a threat. "Happy New Year? The World's Getting Slowly More Cheerful," BBC News, December 30, 2013, www.bbc.com/news/world-25496299.

24. "Secretary of Defense Speech," U.S. Department of Defense, May 8. 2010, archive.defense.gov/speeches/speech.aspx?speechid=1467.

25. The American Society of Civil Engineers' Report Card gave America's infrastructure a grade of "D+" again ("Making the Grade," 2017 Infrastructure Report Card, n.d., www.infrastructurereportcard.org/making-the-grade). The *Wall Street Journal* cited the report, stating, "Getting roads, bridges and other structures to a safe, functioning level would cost $4.59 trillion over the next decade." Cameron McWhirter, "U.S. Infrastructure Gets 'D+' Grade from Civil Engineers," *Wall Street Journal*, March 9, 2017, www.wsj.com/articles/u-s-infrastructure-gets-d-grade-from-civil-engineers-1489069827. However eye-watering this number, had we not had the War on Terror, we could have covered all of these costs with enough left over to wipe out all U.S. credit card debt.

26. Paul Hodgson, "Top CEOs Make More Than 300 Times the Average Worker," *Fortune*, June 22, 2015, fortune.com/2015/06/22/ceo-vs-worker-pay.

27. Robert B. Reich, *Saving Capitalism: For the Many, Not the Few* (New York: Alfred K. Knopf, 2015).

28. Joshua Gillin, "Income Tax Rates Were 90 Percent Under Eisenhower, Sanders Says," Politifact, November 15, 2015, www.politifact.com/truth-o-meter/statements/2015/nov/15/bernie-s/income-tax-rates-were-90-percent-under-eisenhower-.

29. Paul Krugman, "The Tax-Cut Con," *New York Times*, September 14, 2003.

30. David Leonhardt, "A Tax Plan to Turbocharge Inequality, in 3 Charts." *New York Times*, December 17, 2017, www.nytimes.com/2017/12/17/opinion/taxes-inequality-charts.html.

31. Tom Kertscher, "Bernie Sanders: Bill Gates, Jeff Bezos, Warren Buffett Have More Wealth than Bottom Half of U.S." Politifact, July 19, 2018, www.politifact.com/wisconsin/statements/2018/jul/19/bernie-sanders/bernie-sanders-bill-gates-jeff-bezos-warren-buffet.

32. In a report studying fifty-five countries, "Allianz calculated each country's wealth Gini coefficient—a measure of inequality in which 0 is perfect equality and 100 would mean perfect inequality, or one person owning all the wealth. It found that the U.S. had the most wealth inequality, with a score of 80.56, showing the most concentration of overall wealth in the hands of the proportionately fewest people." Erik Sherman, "America Is the Richest, and Most Unequal, Country," *Fortune*, September 30, 2015, fortune.com/2015/09/30/america-wealth-inequality.

33. Carmen Reinicke, "US Income Inequality Continues to Grow," CNBC Markets, July 19, 2018, www.cnbc.com/2018/07/19/income-inequality-continues-to-grow-in-the-united-states.html.

34. Agustino Fontevecchia, "Steve Cohen Personally Made $2.3B in 2013 Despite Having to Shut Down SAC Capital," *Forbes*, March 13, 2014, www.forbes.com

/sites/afontevecchia/2014/03/13/steve-cohen-personally-made-2-3b-in-2013
-despite-having-to-shut-down-sac-capital/#469b56232c2a.

35. Lydia Dishman, "How U.S. Employee Benefits Compare to Europe's," *Fast
Company,* February 17, 2016, www.fastcompany.com/3056830/how-the-us
-employee-benefits-compare-to-europe.

36. Dominic Rushe, "The US Spends More on Education Than Other Countries.
Why Is It Falling Behind?" *Guardian,* September 7, 2018, www.theguardian
.com/us-news/2018/sep/07/us-education-spending-finland-south-korea.

37. Pearl S. Buck, *My Several Worlds* (London: Methuen, 1954), 337.

38. Duncan Clark, "Which Nations Are Most Responsible for Climate Change?"
Guardian, April 21, 2001, www.theguardian.com/environment/2011/apr/21
/countries-responsible-climate-change.

39. The Climate Change Performance Index 2019, New Climate Institute,
December 10, 2018, newclimate.org/2018/12/10/the-climate-change-performance
-index-2019.

40. Ben Doherty, "Australia Only Nation to Join US at Pro-Coal Event at COP24
Climate Talks," *Guardian,* December 10, 2018, www.theguardian.com
/environment/2018/dec/11/australia-only-nation-to-join-us-at-pro-coal-event-at
-cop24-climate-talks.

41. According to the Climate Change Performance Index,

> *The United States fall by three positions to 59th place, ranking low or very
> low for the index categories GHG Emissions, Renewable Energy and Energy
> Use. This continues the downwards trend after the country's withdrawal
> from the Paris Agreement. The refusal of President Trump to acknowledge
> climate change being human-caused, and his dismantling of regulation
> designed to reduce carbon emissions, result in the United States also being
> rated very low for its national and international climate policy perfor-
> mance. However, national experts continue to highlight positive signals at
> the subnational level, with cities and states pushing for ambitious climate
> action such as with the US Climate Alliance. The Democrats, after winning
> the majority in the House of Representatives, have pledged to place climate
> policy on the political agenda. But this hasn't yielded tangible results yet.*

Results 2019, newclimate.org/wp-content/uploads/2018/12/CCPI-2019-Results
.pdf.

42. Seventeen of the eighteen warmest years on record have occurred since 2001
(climate.nasa.gov). According to the UN, we have a dozen years to limit

catastrophic effects of climate change (Jonathan Watts, "We Have 12 Years to Limit Climate Change Catastrophe, Warns UN," October 8, 2018, www .theguardian.com/environment/2018/oct/08/global-warming-must-not-exceed -15c-warns -landmark-un-report). Urgent changes are needed to cut risk of extreme heat, drought, floods, and poverty, according to the Intergovernmental Panel on Climate Change. The World Health Organization warns that the resulting climate change brings "a range of risks to health, from deaths in extreme high temperatures to changing patterns of infectious diseases" ("10 Facts on Climate Change and Health," World Health Organization, n.d., www .who.int/features/factfiles/climate_change/facts/en).

Humanity has wiped out 60 percent of animal populations since 1970 (Damian Carrington, *Guardian*, October 29, 2018, www.theguardian.com /environment/2018/oct/30/humanity-wiped-out-animals-since-1970-major -report-finds); 50 percent of the remaining species will be facing extinction by the end of the century (Robin McKee, *Guardian*, February 25, 2017, www.the guardian.com/environment/2017/feb/25/half-all-species-extinct-end-century -vatican-conference).

As of 2019, NASA recorded atmospheric CO_2 at 410 parts per million (ppm)—the "highest in 650,000 years" (climate.nasa.gov). The last time CO_2 levels were this high, *Homo sapiens* didn't exist.

43. "Frequently Asked Questions on Climate Change and Disaster Displacement," November 6, 2015, UNHCR, www.unhcr.org/uk/news/latest/2016/11/581f 52dc4/frequently-asked-questions-climate-change-disaster-displacement.html.

44. "National Security Implications of Climate-Related Risks and a Changing Climate," July 23, 2015, archive.defense.gov/pubs/150724-congressional-report -on-national-implications-of-climate-change.pdf.

45. Ibid.

46. "The U.S. Military is by some accounts the largest single consumer of petroleum in the world. In 2011, the Department of Defense releases, at minimum, 56.6 million metric tons of CO_2 equivalent into the atmosphere, more than the U.S. base operations of ExxonMobil and Shell combined." Naomi Klein, *This Changes Everything: Capitalism vs. The Climate* (New York: Simon & Schuster, 2015).

47. Army Command Policy, Army Regulation 600–20, June 7, 2006, www.nrc.gov /docs/ML0807/ML080790409.pdf.

48. For military leadership, their environmental footprint must be measured and tracked as a key performance indicator. Failure to drastically reduce emissions should result in firings and passed-over promotions for military leadership, else

contribute further to the climate-related global instability such military leaders purportedly aim to stop.

49. Mike Cummings "Gore to Kerry: 'Political Will Is a Renewable Resource,'" *YaleNews*, October 27, 2017, news.yale.edu/2017/10/27/gore-kerry-political-will -renewable-resource.

50. Edward S. Herman and Noam Chomsky, *Manufacturing Consent: The Political Economy of the Mass Media* (New York: Penguin Random House, 2002).

A NOTE ON THE AUTHOR

Erik Edstrom graduated from West Point in 2007. He was an infantry officer, Army Ranger, and Bronze Star Medal recipient who deployed as a lieutenant to Afghanistan and served as the Honor Guard's Presidential Escort Platoon Leader during the Obama administration. After his military service he received a dual degree (MBA/MSc) from Oxford University and worked in Australia as a management consultant at both Boston Consulting Group (BCG) and McKinsey & Company. He lives in Greater Boston.